T0313244

MARX'S CRITIQUE OF POLITICAL ECONOMY

Intellectual Sources and Evolution
Volume I: 1844 to 1860

Allen Oakley

Department of Economics,
University of Newcastle, Australia

Routledge & Kegan Paul
London, Boston, Melbourne and Henley

In memoriam
Janice Oakley (née Harsley)
20.VII.1943 to 13.I.1969

Contents

Preface

This is the first of two volumes in which I undertake an analysis of the intellectual sources and evolution of Marx's critique of political economy prior to his main work of the *Capital* manuscripts. The period treated in this volume of the study, from 1844 to 1860, takes us from Marx's first studies of political economy to the detailed critical investigations of the *Grundrisse* manuscripts and their presentation in the *Contribution to the Critique of Political Economy*. The second volume deals with Marx's massive critical exposé of antecedent political economy in the 'Theories of surplus value' manuscripts, written during 1862–3.

In writing this study, I worked on the premise that a deeper understanding of the evolution of the critico-theoretical core of Marx's work than is presently available is needed if we are fully to appreciate his contributions to intellectual history. This evolution, I argue, is best understood through a textual-exegetical analysis of Marx's pre-*Capital* writings, paying particular attention to his critical use of the received body of thought with which he worked in his 'intellectual laboratory'. Such an approach to the study of Marx's critical theory facilitates a more complete comprehension of its origins and *raison d'être*, aspects not readily apparent from a reading of *Capital*. I argue that Marx relied very heavily on the political economy that he studied in formulating his critical paradigm of capitalism as a contradiction-ridden and crisis-prone social and economic system. At the same time, though, he went to great lengths in order to differentiate and distance his critical theory from the work of his antecedents.

To write about Marx in the context of the multiple dimensions of contemporary controversy over his work is to be tempted to strive to resolve *all* the issues and to transcend *all* the previous interpretations. There is also the probability that some readers expect this to be achieved. I would thus like to emphasise that my study sets out to do much less than this. What I have concentrated upon is the provision of a clear and open analytical exposition of the contents of Marx's texts that are pertinent to a comprehension of the intellectual influences on him and the consequent evolution of the critico-theoretical core of his work. My intention is to clarify Marx's own view of what hē was trying to achieve through his critique of political economy. As my objective is expositional, polemic (where I could not resist it) has been relegated to the footnotes.

The consequence of my approach will inevitably be that for some readers I will have written the wrong book, while for others I will have written only part of a book. My response in anticipation must be that I do not consider my study, in spite of its length, to be definitive (if such a term has any relevance in intellectual history). If my interpretations generate dissent and further research and debate, I will be very pleased.

The study began as a doctoral thesis project in the Department of Economics of the University of Adelaide, South Australia. Since then the work has been substantially expanded and revised.

In preparing the material for this study, I have received most support and encouragement from Geoffrey Harcourt who supervised the project in its doctoral thesis stage. Others who have made helpful comments on various parts of the research are Jon Cohen, Peter Groenewegen, Samuel Hollander, David Laibman, the late Ronald Meek and Anwar Shaikh. None of these scholars is in any way responsible for the interpretations that appear in this study. Indeed, most of them would dispute, in one way or another, the views that I present.

My warmest thanks are due also to my wife, Renate, who so ably assisted me with the tasks of editing and typing the manuscript as well as with some translations and the preparation of the index.

Allen Oakley
Newcastle, Australia

Acknowledgments

The following works are subject to copyright and extracts from them have been quoted with the permission of the publishers:

Karl Marx, *Grundrisse: Foundations of the Critique of Political Economy (Rough Draft)*, translated with a Foreword by Martin Nicolaus (Allen Lane, 1973). Translation and Foreword © Martin Nicolaus, 1973. Reprinted by permission of Penguin Books Ltd and Random House, Inc.;

Karl Marx and Friedrich Engels, *Collected Works*, volumes 1, 3, 4, 5, 6, 9 and 10 (Lawrence & Wishart, 1975–8), © Progress Publishers, Moscow. Reprinted by permission of Lawrence & Wishart Ltd.

Abbreviations used in citations

The following abbreviations are used for works frequently cited in the text. More details about the editions of these works are given in the Bibliography.

CCPE   Marx, *A Contribution to the Critique of Political Economy*.

CHPR   Marx, *Critique of Hegel's Philosophy of Right*.

CW   Marx and Engels, *Collected Works*.

G   Marx, *Grundrisse: Foundations of the Critique of Political Economy*.

G(EV)   Marx, *Grundrisse der Kritik der politischen Ökonomie* (Europäische Verlagsanstalt).

GI   Marx, *The German Ideology* (in CW, 5).

HF   Marx, *The Holy Family* (in CW, 4).

K(PE)   Marx, *Capital: A Critique of Political Economy* (Penguin edition), Volume I.

MEGA   Marx and Engels, *Historische-kritische Gesamtausgabe*, Section I.

MESW   Marx and Engels, *Selected Works*, Part 1.

MEW   Marx and Engels, *Werke*.

PP   Marx, *The Poverty of Philosophy*.

TF   Marx, 'Theses on Feurbach' (in CW, 5).

TSV   Marx, *Theories of Surplus Value*, Parts I to III.

Notes

1 The section of the Marx–Engels *Gesamtausgabe* referred to in the text comprises several volumes. A citation such as *MEGA*,I/3,410 refers to page 410 in Section I, Volume 3 of the work.

2 In other multi-volume works, the abbreviated form is followed by a volume number and a page number, e.g. *MEW*,31,534 refers to page 534 in Volume 31 of the Marx–Engels *Werke*.

3 In the passages quoted from these works, any emphasis is Marx's unless otherwise stated.

Introduction

In developing his critique of political economy, Marx was influenced to varying degrees by particular political economists and other antecedent intellectuals. For Marx, political economy represented the formal intellectual manifestation of the socially and politically dominant vision of early nineteenth century capitalism. He found this vision to be distorted and misleading and he sought to expose the *essential*, as distinct from the *apparent*, structure and nature of capitalism as a *human* social and economic system. That is, Marx's concern was with the ability and capacity of the system to deliver the material and non-material requirements of *human* fulfilment to the *totality* of the members of society. On these criteria, capitalism had failed except in its *aggregate* physical capacity to produce material things.

Marx's *modus operandi* was to expose, through the application of his critical method, the limitations of antecedent political economy both with respect to its method and its analytical substance. In part, the results of this critique comprised an alternative *critical* understanding of how capitalism worked and how it generated the complex of social and economic effects that were so apparent to any observer. There was, then, a distinct *critical filiation* between Marx and his antecedents. But, as I will emphasise, Marx began from a quite different vision of what was to be explained and why. He thus pursued a quite different *telos*.[1]

My analysis gives particular emphasis to those of Marx's writings in which the various dimensions of his evolving critique of

1

political economy are most in evidence. The period to be covered in detail in the present volume of this study begins in early 1844 when Marx first read the main works of political economy. The evolution of his critique is then traced during the years until 1860.

In the process of its evolution, Marx's critical theory involved a complex mixture of continuity and discontinuity because of its organic and dialectical nature. The shift of emphases within the elements of continuity are only able to be perceived through a careful study of the *totality* of his critico-theoretical writings. No reading of *Capital* in isolation and out of its bibliographical context is able to provide an adequate appreciation of the *raison d'être*, methodology and analytical substance of Marx's critique of political economy.[2]

In the intellectual pursuit of his *telos*, Marx devised and continually revised the terms of the problematic[3] that he considered would most appropriately serve his purposes. Both the *telos* and the problematic underwent an evolution involving shifts of emphasis and change of content. At the very roots of Marx's critical theory, then, as well as in its methodology and substance, there are elements of continuity and discontinuity to be sorted out.

The question of the 'scientific' definitude of his critical theory troubled Marx very much. He agonised over the analytical scope required for his critique to be 'complete'. In bibliographical terms, the problem contributed to Marx's life-long indecision with respect to the appropriate 'plan' for his critical theory and his consequent failure to 'finish' *Capital*.[4] It was the question of where to 'start' and where to 'end' his analyses which plagued the methodological and substantive development of his critique.

The issue of analytical sufficiency, of 'scientificity', is most appropriately considered as comprising two dimensions for Marx. Firstly, one of his objectives in formulating the critical theory was to provide an analysis of capitalism that fully accounted for the observed phenomena of the system that involved human material conditions. While he considered the phenomena of exploitation and oppression, inequitable distribution of income and wealth, poverty in all its dimensions, alienating working conditions and frequent crises to be obvious, the formal analyses of capitalism to be found in political economy gave virtually no attention to these issues and their human ramifications. Political economy was sterile when assessed against its capacity to *explain* these things. Marx's critique centred upon correcting this astounding intellectual lacuna. In this sense, to the extent that his critical theory left any phenomenon unaccounted for by reasoned analysis, it remained incomplete and could not be considered to be wholly 'scientific'.

Secondly, by virtue of his *telos*, the ultimate 'test' of Marx's critical theory was to be its *practical effectiveness* in generating a widespread proletarian self-consciousness that would induce and facilitate the revolutionary transcendence (*Aufhebung*[5]) of capitalism and the subsequent emergence of a truly human, free socialist–communist society. Marx's '*complete*' critical theory never faced this 'test' simply because he never thought that it was ready to do so. Moreover, the parts so 'tested' through publication as *A Contribution to the Critique of Political Economy* of 1859 (CCPE) and as *Capital*, Volume I, of 1867 (K(PE),I), made very little immediate impact on the proletariat or anyone else at the time. Marx was left with little incentive to go on with the critical project under this second view of its 'scientific' viability and efficacy.

SOME INTELLECTUAL ORIGINS OF MARX'S CRITIQUE OF POLITICAL ECONOMY

From their very beginning, Marx's writings indicated a concern for *critically* comprehending the nature and determinants of human existence.[6] His philosophical background and observations of social reality led him to develop an anthropological-materialist ontology in which the *socially dependent individual* is the central figure. At university, his philosophical studies provided the first guidelines for his endeavour to understand the human situation and its historical progress. He read the works of many Greek philosophers and, among others, those of Kant, Fichte and Hegel. Both Kant and Fichte made *man* central to an understanding of history. Man was interpreted to be an active and creative being who applies autonomous, practical reason in a process of *self*-determination. Man *is* what he *does*. His existence is something that he creates for himself and Fichte viewed this activity as taking place in a *social* setting. Later, Marx was to bring forward these ideas as the basis for his *humanist-materialist* interpretation of history.

Hegel preserved the dominant theme of philosophy as the analysis of man in history, but he replaced the humanism of Kant and

Fichte with a rational idealism which gave autonomy to transcendental *Reason* in the form of an *Absolute Spirit*. In Hegel's interpretation, man moved from being the *subject* of history to being the mere *predicate* of an omnipotent supreme *Being*. The real became rational and the rational became real.[7]

Marx never fully embraced this Hegelian ontology. He indicated his rejection of it in his doctoral thesis, 'Difference between the Democritean and Epicurean philosophy of nature', written over the period from 1839 to 1841 (CW,1,25ff.).[8] In this work, Marx defended the autonomy of the human spirit espoused by Epicurus against the Democritean view of a deterministic existence for man. This defence reinforced the influence of French Enlightenment liberalism that he experienced during his high school days in Trier, a Rhineland city once under French rule. Even under the dominance of Prussia, the spirit of human freedom remained a central theme in the intellectual life of Trier. Marx's father and a family friend with whom the young Marx had a lot of contact, the Baron von Westphalen, were both active in the liberal 'underground' of the city.

Marx became involved in the anti-Hegelian discussions and writings of the left 'Young Hegelians' while at university in Berlin.[9] It was especially the writings of Ludwig Feuerbach that appealed to Marx and he adopted the materialist view of man's place in history from this source. But, in spite of his joining in the critical polemic against Hegel's ontology and idealist reading of history, Marx was profoundly influenced by his dialectical method. Marx retained the notion that history should be viewed as a dialectical process of becoming that is driven by the resolution of contradictions. It was to be these philosophical influences that were to be developed into the methodological core of Marx's critique of political economy, *historical materialism*.

During his teenage years in Trier, Marx also came into contact with the possibility of social and economic change as a means to improve the human situation. The Baron von Westphalen especially had drawn the young Marx's attention to the ideas of the French utopian socialists Fourier and Saint-Simon. It was during his period as a journalist and editor in 1842 and 1843 that Marx recognised the *need* to strive for human emancipation from all forms of domination. His observations of the social, economic and political realities of Germany during these years made him aware that man lived under a range of oppressions that curtailed freedom and the realisation of a truly human existence. It was in this context that Marx's life as a social critic really began to take shape.

In a series of articles for the *Rheinische Zeitung*, and in some other pieces written during this period, Marx gave expression to his misgivings about the world in which man finds himself.[10] He argued at length about the *human* ramifications of censorship of the press and the tendential nature of law making through the machinations of the state's political apparatus. In each case, the state was found to defy the demands of a human society by restricting freedom and mediating in the service of narrow class interests. Eventually, the Prussian government found this sort of attack intolerable and the *Rheinische Zeitung* was closed down in early 1843.

Marx took this opportunity to retire to his study once more. In an endeavour to comprehend the situation of human irrationality and lack of freedom he had observed, he undertook a critical reading of the dominant political philosophy of the period that he found in Hegel's *Philosophy of Right* (1821). In his writings on this theme, the development of Marx's critical acuity made rapid advances.[11]

Several subsequently important themes emerged in this critique. Firstly, Marx adopted Feuerbach's methodological inversion of Hegel's view of the determination of historical progress. In his *Essence of Christianity* (1841), Feuerbach argued that God is the idealised, metaphysical predicate of a *subject man's* thought. This represented an inversion of religious orthodoxy as reflected in Hegel's speculative idealism where God as the *Absolute Spirit* appeared as the dominant subject and man the dependent predicate. Feuerbach's critique indicated that man can release himself from religious domination by a self-conscious appreciation of his existential primacy. In a later work, 'Provisional theses for the reform of philosophy' (early 1843), Feuerbach applied this inversion to Hegel's speculative philosophy itself. The finite being, man, became the *operational subject* of life and history. Man's potentialities are *human* and are therefore not the realisation of some infinite transcendental Spirit. Thus Feuerbach charged Hegel with mysticism in ascribing to the Spirit that which really belongs to man as a conscious, reasoning and free being.

This inversion represented a profound shift in the approach to the interpretation of the situation of man in the world. The determinants of his *being* were now immediately *human*, including his material needs and their satisfaction. This satisfaction proceeded by means of a *real* interaction with nature in the vital ontological process of *labour*. Through labour, man creates and expresses himself. Hegel had given prominence to labour in his philosophical system, but in a purely *ideal* sense separated from the realities of its socio-political situation. By contrast, for Marx it was the form and situation of man's labour that were the primary factors affecting the nature of man's existence. In the *material* dimensions of life were to be found the keys to the comprehension of its *totality*.

Feuerbach recognised this, but his materialism remained a naturalism unaffected by the socio-political realities of man's actual historical situation. As Marx noted in a letter to Arnold Ruge dated 13 March 1843,

Feuerbach's aphorisms seem to me incorrect only in one respect, that he refers too much to nature and too little to politics. That, however is the only alliance [i.e. with politics] by which present day philosophy can become truth. (*CW*,1,400)

Feuerbach had failed to give due emphasis to the social and political dimensions of man's being. The man–nature interaction was, for Marx, necessarily mediated by *society*. This belief was to be perpetuated in the method of social-humanist materialism that he developed and in the critique of political economy that embodied the method.

A second important theme to emerge in Marx's critique of Hegel's political philosophy was the concept of the *proletariat* as a universal class and the mediation in the revolutionary transcendence of capitalism. Marx was aware of the idea of a *universal class* as one whose collective interest is that of society as a whole through Hegel's espousal of the bureaucracy in this role.[12] Marx's rejection of this group as having demonstrated a less than universal *self*-interest led him to consider alternatives. It was evident to him that a *class revolution*, such as the French Revolution of 1789, would not achieve the goal of a truly human society unless the class concerned could bring *all* men under its auspices. The proletariat was in this regard an operational 'bottom-line' to which all men could gravitate to form a classless society. The currency of this concept of the proletariat in Parisian socialist circles confirmed the idea for Marx after his arrival in the city in October 1843 and it appeared in his article 'Critique of Hegel's philosophy of right: introduction' early in 1844 (*CHPR*,131ff.).

In his critique of Hegel's political philosophy, Marx also had his attention drawn to the formal organisation and operations of man's pursuit of his material interests. The dictates of burgeoning capitalism were such that this pursuit was posited by Hegel as essentially an individualistic activity – or at best a narrow class activity – which comprised what he referred to as *civil society*. In this context, Marx also would have noted that political economy had a crucial role in interpreting the nature of civil society, for Hegel referred to it in this context in the *Philosophy of Right*.[13] Very soon, political economy was to come very much to the fore in Marx's social critique and remain there for the rest of his life.

At this point, it is pertinent to quote at length Marx's own 1859 recollections of this early 1840s period in which he set out his objectives and achievements:

Although I studied jurisprudence, I pursued it as a subject subordinated to philosophy and history. In the year 1842–43, as editor of the *Rheinische Zeitung*, I first found myself in the embarrassing position of having to discuss what is known as material interests. The deliberations of the Rhenish *Landtag* [Parliament] on forest thefts and the division of landed property; the official polemic . . . about the condition of the Moselle peasantry, and finally the debates on free trade and protective tariffs caused me in the first instance to turn my attention to economic questions . . . [On the closure of the *Rheinische Zeitung*] I eagerly grasped the opportunity to withdraw from the public stage to my study.

The first work which I undertook to dispel the doubts assailing me was a critical re-examination of the Hegelian philosophy of law [*Recht*] . . . My inquiry led me to the conclusion that neither legal relations nor political forms could be comprehended whether by themselves or on the basis of a so-called general development of the human mind, but that on the contrary they originate in the material conditions of life, the totality of which Hegel, following the example of English and French thinkers of the eighteenth century, embraces within the term 'civil society' [*bürgerliche Gesellschaft*]; that the anatomy of this civil society, however, has to be sought in political economy. (*CCPE*, 19–20)

This passage was written after Marx's first major attempt to set out the totality of his critique of political economy in the *Grundrisse* manuscripts of 1857–8 (see *G*). The points that he emphasised as being of significance in his intellectual development during the early 1840s are the ones that I have discussed above.

Throughout the writings that I have considered so briefly above, Marx emphasised the use of *critique* as a theoretical weapon by means of which a self-conscious awareness of oppression is generated as the inducement for social action. For Marx, *theory and practical action were a unity* and this situation of theory pervaded all of his writings. The application of this theoretical weapon took Marx through a sequence of philosophical criticisms in which the objects were, in turn, religion, society, politics and political economy. He was concerned especially with what each reflected about the state of the human condition. He argued that *philosophy* is the intellectual spirit of an age and an integral part of the world itself.[14] Philosophy is the key to a critique of reality in its various dimensions. Thus Marx wrote in 1843 that:

It is above all the task of philosophy, which is in the service of history, to unmask human self-alienation in its secular forms, once its sacred form has been unmasked. Thus, the critique of heaven is transformed into the critique of the earth, the critique of religion into the critique of law [*Recht*], the critique of theology into the critique of politics. (*CHPR*,132)

This transition from the critique of *metaphysical* dimensions to the critique of *real* dimensions was very soon to be followed by the emergence of an appreciation that the essential nature of the real had to be sought in its material dimension, that is, through political economy.

For Marx, then, the task of philosophy was to generate doubts about the necessity and permanency of contemporary human reality and an awareness of the need and potential for change. In this, it provides an assessment of reality and arraigns it before the rational, that is, the *is* before the *ought*. No retreat into historical necessity could protect reality against critique, irrespective of whether the necessity was argued in empiricist or idealist terms. Marx viewed the *ought* as the result of the dialectical development of the *is*. Rational critical theory had an integral role to play in this development in that it would provide the means to ensure the realisation of the immanent process, viz. a self-conscious and informed proletariat that appreciates the role of human action in the process of social change. The 'sufficiency' of the critical theory may then be assessed by its effectiveness in this role.

It is evident that for Marx, critical theory and practical action were *necessarily* a unity. He expressed this notion clearly in the following important passage written in 1843:

> The weapon of criticism certainly cannot replace the criticism of weapons; material force must be overthrown by material force; but theory, too, becomes a material force once it seizes the masses. Theory is capable of seizing the masses once it demonstrates *ad hominem*, and it demonstrates *ad hominem* once it becomes radical. To be radical is to grasp matters at the root. But for man the root is man himself. . . . The critique of religion ends in the doctrine that man is the supreme being for man; thus it ends with the categorical imperative to overthrow all conditions in which man is a debased, enslaved, neglected, contemptible being. . . . (*CHPR*,137)

Thus, in Marx's view, the role of his critical theory was to 'seize' the mass of the people, the proletariat, through the provision of a conscious understanding of the source of *their* adverse human-material situation in the presence of such obvious material wealth. The purpose of theory was thus to expose the necessity for action in the pursuit of *human freedom and well-being*. As Marx reasoned it, 'The head of . . . emancipation is philosophy, its heart is the proletariat', and he went on, 'Just as philosophy finds its material weapons in the proletariat, so the proletariat finds its spiritual weapons in philosophy . . .' (*CHPR*,142). Marx's 'philosophy' was to comprise the critique of political economy and an analysis of the development of this critique is my objective in the present study.

MARX'S BIBLIOGRAPHY IN THE CRITIQUE OF POLITICAL ECONOMY, 1844 TO 1860[15]

Paris, 1844–5

It was probably late in 1843 that the young Friedrich Engels submitted his article 'Outlines of a critique of political economy' to the *Deutsch-französische Jahrbücher* for publication (*CW*,3,418ff.). As one of the editors, Marx would have read the piece and Engels's passionate critique of man's material situation under capitalism is the most likely intellectual catalyst that drew Marx towards a study of political economy.

Marx's first known studies in political economy were recorded in a series of nine notebooks written early in 1844 in Paris (*MEGA*,I/3,410ff. and 447ff.). The notebooks contained three different elements recording the progress of his reading. Marx was a patient scholar and his research always centred around verbatim, or near verbatim, excerpts copied, sometimes at great length from the books that he read. The subsequent notes then included one or both of the following: firstly, a critical commentary on the text that he had transcribed; and secondly, some independent, intuitive development of the ideas on which he had commented. It is important to recognise that this sort of methodology continued throughout Marx's life as the basis of his evolving critique of political economy.

The Paris Notebooks contained excerpts and comments pertaining to the work of seventeen writers, including Adam Smith, Jean-Baptiste Say, David Ricardo and James Mill. Marx's critical comments and independent ideas were quite fragmentary at this stage, as would be expected, with one important exception. In notebook IV of the series, while reading and noting James Mill's *Elements of Political Economy* (1821), Marx wrote in two pieces his first sustained critical analysis of the human ramifications of exchange and production under capitalism. The *style* of the pieces was, to some extent, similar to that of Engels's article, although less polemical, but the *scope* of Marx's ideas was not constrained by what he had read in that article (*CW*,3,211ff.).

Having filled nine notebooks, Marx began drafting a set of manuscripts in which he planned to collate and clarify what he had learnt and apply it to a rigorous critique of capitalism as a human social and economic system. These manuscripts have become known as *The Economic and Philosophic Manuscripts of 1844* or the *Paris Manuscripts* (CW,3,229ff.). Unfortunately, they have not been preserved in their entirety. The *contents* of what remains, parts of it left unfinished by Marx, are outlined below.

Preface

First Manuscript
Wages of labour
Profit of capital
1   Capital
2   The profit of capital
3   The rule of capital over labour and the motives of the capitalist
4   The accumulation of capitals and the competition among the capitalists.
Rent of land
Estranged labour
(broken off unfinished after twenty-seven large manuscript pages)

Second Manuscript
Antithesis of capital and labour. Landed property and capital.
(only the last four of forty-three manuscript pages have been preserved)

Third Manuscript
Private property and labour. Political economy as a product of the movement of private property
Private property and communism
Human requirements and division of labour under the Rule of private property
The power of money
The critique of the Hegelian dialectic and philosophy as a whole
(Forty-one manuscript pages, apparently a completed first draft)

The Preface cited above is of particular bibliographical interest. Marx wrote it towards the end of the third manuscript and it contained his *first plan* for his future work in critical theory (CW,3,231). This was to be the first element in the complex set of projections and changes that were to characterise his bibliography in the critique of political economy. It is apparent from the Preface that Marx's initial intention was to undertake an extensive critique of theory. One work would not be enough and his project included 'a series of distinct, independent pamphlets' followed by a systematic, total critique in two stages: firstly, 'a special work' bringing together the arguments of the pamphlets on 'the state, law, ethics, civil life, etc.' and political economy and secondly, a critique focusing on the extant treatment of the material by speculative (Hegelian) philosophy. The *Paris Manuscripts* were to concentrate on the political economy of capitalism independently of issues of politics, law, ethics, etc.

The work on the manuscripts ceased in August 1844 when Marx was visited by Engels and the two decided to collaborate on a work of philosophical polemic directed against the idealist philosophy and political theory of the remaining pseudo-radical 'Young Hegelians' led by Bruno Bauer. Both Marx and Engels were concerned to push ahead with the development of the humanist-materialist philosophy adumbrated by Feuerbach. To this end, *The Holy Family, or Critique of Critical Criticism. Against Bruno Bauer and Company*, published in February 1845 (CW,4,5ff.), sought to discredit the *socially* empty theories of the 'Young Hegelians'.

During the last months of 1844, Marx continued to work on his massive critical project and formulated a plan for his pamphlet on the politics of the modern state (CW,6,666). Early in 1845, he arranged with the Darmstadt publisher Karl Leske a contract for the publication of the first two 'pamphlets' in the form of a two-volume work to be entitled *Critique of Politics and Political Economy*. Presumably, the work would have combined the reworked *Paris Manuscripts* and an elaboration of the plan for politics just referred to, but it was never completed and Leske cancelled the contract early in 1847.

Brussels, 1845–8

Having been expelled from Paris by government order, Marx moved to Brussels in February 1845. He continued his research into political economy and economic history and made use of a trip to Manchester in July and August of 1846 to read some additional sources. These studies were recorded in a series of twelve notebooks from 1845 and 1846 (outlined in *MEGA*,I/6,597ff.). Among the many authors from whose works Marx took excerpts were Babbage, Bray, Buret, McCulloch, J.S. Mill, Owen, Quesnay, Senior, Sismondi, Thompson, Tooke and Ure.

Also, in March 1845, Marx drafted out a critical review of Friedrich List's 1841 book *The National System of Political Economy*, First Volume (CW,4,265ff.). The manuscripts of the review remained unfinished and unpublished in Marx's lifetime.

During April of the same year Marx continued to pursue the self-clarification of his methodological premises. This resulted in the drafting of his eleven aphoristic, but highly significant, 'Theses on Feuerbach' (CW,5,3ff.). In these pieces, Marx reiterated his view that critical theory, based upon humanist-materialist reason, should form an integral part of the process of revolutionary social change if such change were to be effective.

Marx continued this methodological self-clarification process in November of 1845 when he joined Engels in drafting out their massive manuscript entitled *The German Ideology. Critique of Modern German Philosophy According to its Representatives Feuerbach, B. Bauer and Stirner, and of German Socialism According to its Various Prophets* (CW,5,19ff.). In Chapter 1 of this work, unpublished in the authors' lifetimes, is to be found the first coherent outline of the methodological centrepiece of Marx's critique of political economy, *historical materialism*. The work on this manuscript was abandoned in the latter half of 1846.

In December 1846 Marx read with great dissatisfaction the latest work of Pierre-Joseph Proudhon, *System of Economic Contradictions or the Philosophy of Poverty*. This work cut across Marx's intentions for his own critique of political economy and he set out immediately to discredit both the method and substance of Proudhon's analyses. The result was the polemical book *The Poverty of Philosophy: Answer to the Philosophy of Poverty by M. Proudhon* which Marx had published in July 1847 (CW,6,105ff.).

Early in 1847 Marx joined the newly formed Communist League and became its main theoretician. In this role, he was required to prepare his critical ideas on the nature of capitalism for dissemination to the workers and the public generally. This involved him in a series of propagandist writings and activities during 1847 and 1848.

The first opportunity for Marx to give his critique publicity came

13

in September 1847 at the International Congress of Economists held in Brussels. Marx, Engels and other members of the Communist League attended and Marx prepared a speech on the theme of free trade and protectionism for the conference. But, after his comrade Georg Weerth had presented his attack on free trade for its detrimental effects on the working class, the organisers would not allow Marx to speak. Marx summarised his speech as a press release (CW,6,279ff.), but no Belgian newspaper would print it. Engels reported on the Congress in the English Chartist weekly *The Northern Star* on 9 October 1847 and included a summary of Marx's ill-fated speech (CW,6,282ff.). It was not until the Democratic Association of Brussels meeting on 9 January 1848 that Marx was able to present his ideas on free trade in person. This version of his speech was published as a pamphlet in French a few weeks later (CW,6,450ff.) and translated into German later in the year.

Marx and Engels attended the second Congress of the Communist League in London during November and December of 1847. During the year Engels had prepared in catechism form two pieces in which he set out the beliefs and objectives of the members of the League. These two pieces were the 'Draft of a communist confession of faith' (CW,6,96ff.) and its elaboration the *Principles of Communism* (CW,6,341ff.). Engels and Marx were subsequently charged with the writing of the manifesto for the League and the *Manifesto of the Communist Party* (CW,6,477ff.) was published in London in February 1848. In the contents of the work set out below, the two authors explained the dialectical materialist view of history and the dynamics of the human situation within it. The immanent contradictions of the capitalist system were argued to ensure its transcendence (*Aufhebung*) through proletarian revolution.

Manifesto of the Communist Party

    I Bourgeois and proletarians
   II Proletarians and communists
  III Socialist and communist literature
  IV Position of the communists in relation to the various existing opposition parties

The German Workers' Association of Brussels called upon Marx to give a series of lectures on the critique of political economy during December of 1847. The contents of these lectures can be gleaned from two sources. One is a manuscript entitled 'Wages' ('*Arbeitslohn*') (*CW*,6,415ff.), and the other is an incomplete series of articles published in the *Neue Rheinische Zeitung* during April 1849 under the title 'Wage-labour and capital' (*CW*,9,197ff.). The relationship between these two sources and the lectures themselves is not clear. A reading of the '*Arbeitslohn*' manuscript suggests that it was a set of notes prepared during the period in which the lectures were given. Marx referred at the beginning of the manuscript to what had been 'explained already' (*CW*,6,415). This can reasonably be taken to refer to the *lectures* already given, for so much of the manuscript material is treated again in 'Wage-labour and capital'. One or two points are made more explicit in the former piece, and it also contains some points not covered in 'Wage-labour and capital', most especially the effects of worker combinations. Moreover, it may only be *assumed* that 'Wage-labour and capital' is a record of the lectures in Brussels for there is no extant documentation of them. The contents of this latter piece are summarised below.

'Wage-labour and capital'[16]

The nature of wages
Determination of the price of commodities
Determination of wages
The nature and growth of capital
Relation of wage-labour to capital
General law of the determination of the rise and fall of wages and
    profits
The diametrically opposed interests of wage-labour and capital
The effect of the growth of productive capital on wages
The effects of capitalist competition on the various classes

Marx had an opportunity to present his critical ideas publicly again when he attended the First Workers' Association meeting in Vienna on 2 September 1848. A report of his speech on this occasion was carried by the democratic newspaper *Die Constitution* on 5 September (*CW*,7,573).

The revolutions of 1848 had an immediate effect on Marx's life in Brussels. The Belgian government took steps to remove all politically active émigrés from the country and Marx was on the move again as a political undesirable. After brief stays in Paris and Cologne he found his way to London which from late 1849 was to be his home for the rest of his life.

London, 1849 and beyond

When, in 1859, Marx reflected on the late 1840s and his move to London, it was evident to him that the move had been an intellectually fortuitous one. The key factors in this assessment were his access to the 'enormous amount of material relating to the history of political economy assembled in the British Museum'; the fact that London was 'a convenient vantage point for the observation of bourgeois society'; and the fact that England had reached a 'new stage of development' which he ascribed to the discovery of gold in California and Australia (*CCPE*,22–3). Thus it was that Marx was now well placed to observe the most advanced of all capitalist societies that was beginning to feel the effects of sustained 'boom' conditions in the late 1840s. Moreover this advanced state of development of capitalism had brought with it the formulation of some relatively sophisticated analyses of the system. These analyses, political economy, were, to Marx's mind, the *valid* intellectual reflections of the dominant view of the nature of nineteenth century capitalism.

The effect of this new situation on Marx's intellectual development was that it 'induced . . . [him] to start again from the very beginning and to work carefully through the new material' (*CCPE*,23). The quantity and variety of the material relating to political economy now available to him, though, also caused him to widen the scope of his studies, and the fact that his 'studies led partly of their own accord to apparently quite remote subjects' (*CCPE*,23) slowed down the development of his critical theory.

Three articles that Marx wrote for the *Neue Rheinische Zeitung, Politisch–ökonomische Revue* during 1850 are of interest in tracing the evolution of Marx's critique of political economy. These articles comprised critical reviews of current events in England and Europe and included the prediction that an economic and consequent political crisis would follow from the 'boom' conditions of the late 1840s (*CW*,10,257ff.,338ff.,490ff.).

In June of 1850, Marx obtained a reader's ticket for the British Museum Library. From September 1850 to May 1854, he compiled twenty-eight notebooks of excerpts and commentaries on a wide range of subjects that he thought pertinent to his critical theory or to his other writings. His initial focus was largely on political economy, but his attention ever broadened over the period. The notebooks eventually encompassed all of the following topics, *inter alia*: commodities, money, capital, wage labour, landed property, international trade, history of technology and inventions, credit, population problems, economic history, history of morals, literature, the world market, the colonial system and events leading up to the Crimean War (*G(EV)*,768, editor's note).

Unfortunately, it is not possible to provide details of these studies for the notebooks have not been published in full. Evidently, Marx's most intensive year of study in the library was 1851. During this year, he filled some fourteen notebooks in following out the pattern of studies set out below.[17]

> *January* theory of rent (Ricardo, *et al.*), money and currency circulation (Bailey, Carey, *et al.*)
> *February–March* money and currency (Gray, Smith, Torrens, Hume, Locke, *et al.*)
> *April–May* money (Torrens, *et al.*), Ricardo's theories of political economy, land fertility
> *May* wages (Carey), population problem (Malthus)
> *June* theory of value and wealth (Torrens, Carey, Malthus)
> *July* labour problems (Owen, Hodgskin, *et al.*) factory system, agriculture and agricultural chemistry
> *August* population and agriculture, colonisation and slavery, Roman political economy
> *September–October* banking, agronomy, history of technology

The only details of these studies that have been published are from notebooks IV and VIII of the series where Marx dealt at some length with Ricardo's *Principles of Political Economy and Taxation*, third edition (1821). These notebooks date from November–December 1850 and April 1851 respectively. His study of Ricardo's book was quite detailed and covered virtually all of the topics to be found in the *Principles* (*G(EV)*,765ff.). But, it is to be emphasised that this work was more of a process of education for Marx than a critique. Much of his study consisted of writing out large excerpts or paraphrasing passages from the *Principles*. Marx's own comments were sometimes lengthy and appear to have been mainly for the purpose of self-clarification. At times, though, he did begin to question some of the analyses, most especially with respect to the theory of rent and the *origin* of the economic surplus, and to propose alternative approaches to the problems dealt with. In all, Marx must have emerged from this lengthy study of the *Principles* with a substantial grasp of the orthodox theory of political economy as it was presented by Ricardo.

In a separate notebook, evidently not numbered in the main series and dated 1851 by Engels, Marx wrote out a subject index for Ricardo's *Principles* along with a brief comment relating Ricardo's analysis of taxes to social classes (*G(EV)*,783ff.). The significance of this notebook goes beyond these pieces because the editors record that it also contains the *end* of the manuscript to which Marx gave the cryptic title 'The completed monetary system' ('*Das vollendete Geldsystem*') (*G(EV)*,782). The contents and date of composition of this manuscript are not able to be established from extant evidence. The bibliography of the period also remains unclear with respect to another unpublished manuscript evidently entitled 'The monetary system; credit; crises' and dating from 1854–5.[18]

It is indeed unfortunate that these and most of the other manuscript materials written by Marx during the period 1850 to 1856 remain unpublished. This situation leaves a considerable void in the material needed for a complete analysis of the evolution of his critical theory of capitalism.

In his endeavours to have his critico-theoretical work published, the early 1850s again appear to have been a period of frustration for Marx. He now referred to the work he intended to publish as simply the 'Economics' and throughout his most intensive year of study, 1851, his correspondence revealed a consistent sanguinity about the completion of the project. A potential publisher proved difficult to find in spite of the efforts by Marx's friends. On the basis of extant evidence, though, the ultimate tentative arrangement to have the work published was quite premature. It reflected more the confidence of Marx's friends in his work than the realities of the progress that he had made on it. As has already been suggested above, in 1851 Marx's studies were intensive, but they were also *extensive* and really involved little beyond basic preparatory research.

It emerged from Marx's correspondence of 1851 that his critique would be presented in a *three-volume* format dealing with the 'critique of political economy', 'socialists' and 'history of political economy' (see the letters Lassalle to Marx, 12 May 1851[19] and Marx to Engels, 24 November 1851, *MEW*,27,370). But, in spite of Marx's claims to the contrary, there is no evidence that he made any effective progress in drafting the first two of these works. That he *was* at least working on the critical history of political economy is indicated by his offer to the Leipzig publisher Heinrich Brockhaus of two articles, one dealing with the state of British political parties and one dealing with 'The modern literature of political economy in England from 1830 to 1852' (Marx to Brockhaus, 19 August 1852, *MEW*,28,546). This offer was refused and no drafts of these articles are extant.

Marx did not return to his critique of political economy with any serious purpose for about four years. Occasionally he would return to his interest in issues of political economy, but mostly in the context of his reporting for newspapers. He wrote a large number of reports on British and European political and economic affairs for the *New York Daily Tribune* and the *Neue Oder-Zeitung* during this period (see *CW*, Volumes 11 to 14). He recalled in 1859 (*CCPE*,23) that the imperative at the time was to earn an adequate living through journalism. This contributed to the curtailment of his theoretical studies and led him to concerns with 'practical detail, which, strictly speaking, lie outside of the sphere of political economy'.

This intimate contact with current issues was to be of some significance in the next stage of Marx's intellectual evolution. He continued to believe in the impending doom of capitalist society through immanently generated crises and consequent social revolution. This belief, founded in the late 1840s and early 1850s, was to come to the fore again in 1857 and stimulate him to return to work on his critical theory.

THE *GRUNDRISSE* AND ITS RESULTS, 1857–60

Since his 1850 studies of economic fluctuations in England, Marx had been observing the statistics. On many occasions he detected signs of the onset of a crisis but his prognoses were each time unrealised. It was in 1857 that the evidence of an imminent crisis became so overwhelming that it induced him to renew his efforts to complete his critique of political economy.[20] His objective was to provide a sound theoretical basis upon which the social revolution that would *necessarily* ensue as a consequence of a severe economic depression could proceed. Such was the degree of pressure that Marx felt himself to be under that in less than a year, from August 1857 to about June 1858, he wrote a prodigious manuscript of some 800 printed pages. Rough drafted though it was, with many digressions, the *Grundrisse* (G) represented Marx's first large-scale attempt to set down his independent critical thought in political economy. The sophistication and novelty of the analyses reached well beyond that which he achieved in any known earlier writing. However, the significance of the work must be kept in perspective. Profound though his advances may have been, much room for development remained.

The *Grundrisse* manuscripts comprised seven main notebooks together with an 'Introduction' found in a separate notebook marked 'M'. The 'Introduction' was methodological and the remainder was divided into two 'chapters', the 'Chapter on money' and the far longer 'Chapter on capital'.

In the manuscripts, Marx wrote down several plans for his future work on the critique of political economy and these were amplified in his letters and later manuscripts. From these plans it is possible to trace the developing conception that Marx held of the scope and method of his critique.

The first of these plans was written down as part of the 'Introduction' to the *Grundrisse* during September 1857 (G,108). The format of this plan followed on from Marx's discussions of methodology in which he advocated 'ascending' in abstract analysis from the simplest, ahistorical categories of political economy through to those appropriate to the more complex and compound analysis of bourgeois reality, both in the national and international setting. Five topic headings were included and these reflected this procedure. They may be summarised thus: (1) simple, ahistorical categories which are common to the understanding of any economic system presented in the abstract; (2) bourgeois categories of political economy; (3) the bourgeois state; (4) international political economy; (5) the world market and crises.

When Marx began writing the 'Chapter on money', and indeed throughout the *Grundrisse* and after, he found it appropriate to consider only the categories of capitalism. He deleted the first of the above topic headings from the second of his plans (G,227). A new 'first section' was substituted in which 'exchange value, money, prices' were to be dealt with on the presupposition that commodities had already been produced. These most apparent and superficial categories of political economy were only a starting point and Marx revised the second topic of the plan to blend with the first. He wrote, 'But by itself, it [the exchange–circulation process] points beyond itself towards the economic relations which are posited *as relations of production*. The internal structure of production therefore forms the second section' (G,227). This approach very much reflected the framework within which Marx worked in the *Grundrisse* and can be traced even in *Capital*. The 'third', 'fourth' and 'final' sections of this second plan followed closely those proposed in the first plan.

In the 'Chapter on capital', Marx wrote down two further plans before the end of 1857 (G,264 and 275). These were similar to each other but departed to some extent from those just outlined. The *operational* categories exchange–circulation and production were now moved out of prominence to be replaced by those categories basic to the *appearances* of bourgeois class division and income distribution, viz. Capital, Landed Property and Wage Labour.

Marx had already given notice, even before the *first* of the above plans was written down, that he considered *capital* to be the most important operational and structural category with which he would have to deal. He wrote that 'capital is the all-dominating economic power of bourgeois society. It must form the starting-point as well as the finishing-point ...' (G,107). After writing some of the 'Chapter on capital', it must have become clear to him that to give capital the major emphasis and to follow this with an examination of landed property and wage labour would be the most appropriate structural framework for the critique of political economy.

In these plans, it was the dominant category *capital* which received most attention. The projected section on this topic was outlined at some length. While there were differences in the details of expression of the *capital* plans, the main topics included were money capital, capital in general, capital in its particular forms (circulating capital and fixed capital at this stage), capital and profit (no surplus value concept as yet), interest, competition of capitals, accumulation of capital, share capital and credit.

The third plan comprised six sections in all. Three of these have been mentioned, viz. Capital, Landed Property and Wage Labour. The rest were similar to those of the earlier plans, the State, the State Externally, and World Market and Crises. Little elaboration of the projected contents of these latter sections was ever provided by Marx.

As Marx developed his theory of capital, some revision of the above 'Capital' framework was to prove necessary. This was required especially in order to separate the theory of surplus value from the phenomenal forms of non-labour income, profit and interest, and to separate the dichotomy constant capital–variable capital, appropriate for production analysis, from circulating capital–fixed capital, appropriate for the analysis of post-production circulation. In addition, some treatment of wage labour and crises was undertaken in the 'Capital' discussions.

Three letters of 1858 gave more details of the plans for Marx's 'Economics'. He wrote to Lassalle on 22 February (*MEW,29,550f.*) and presented a two-part outline of the project. Firstly, and much along the lines of the project proposed in 1851, he posited three separate *works* to be written: (1) a critique of economic categories or the system of bourgeois economy critically presented; (2) a critique and history of political economy and socialism; (3) a short historical sketch of the development of economic relations and categories. Now while the *Grundrisse* contained material that could be related to each of these works, the emphasis was very clearly upon the first.

The second outline which Marx described to Lassalle provided more details of the first work. It was to comprise six 'Books' respectively covering the sections of the third *Grundrisse* plan. Beyond informing Lassalle that Book I, 'Capital', would include 'several introductory chapters', Marx gave no other details of the 'books'. Further information on 'Capital' was provided in another letter to Lassalle on 11 March (*MEW,29,554*). It was to contain sections on the production process of capital, the circulation process of capital, and their unity in the analysis of capital, interest and profit.

It was in a letter to Engels of 2 April 1858 that the nature of the previously mentioned 'introductory chapters' was revealed (*MEW*,29,312ff.). What had been missing from the plans posited after the second one in the *Grundrisse* was any explicit mention of the topics dealt with in the 'Chapter on money' of that work. Now the 'first section' of the second plan re-emerged and Book I, 'Capital', was to comprise the following structure:

A   Capital in general
    (I) Value
    (II) Money
    (III) Capital
B   Competition
C   Credit
D   Share capital

Marx keyed the *Grundrisse* materials to this format in two indexes written in notebook 'M' in June 1858 (*G(EV)*,855ff.). The emphasis, though, was on Part A above with Book I 'Capital' comprised of three 'chapters': 'I. Value', 'II. Money', and 'III. Capital in general', much as had been suggested to Engels. The 'third chapter' was to be divided into two of the sections mentioned to Lassalle, '(1) Production process of capital', and '(2) Circulation process of capital'. The third section on the unity of these two was not mentioned in the present context.

Lassalle had found a publisher for this first book of the Critique and Marx agreed to have it ready by May 1858. This was not to be and Marx could only finish the first two chapters. These were published as *A Contribution to the Critique of Political Economy* in June 1859 (*CCPE*). Marx undertook to prepare the 'third chapter' as a second volume as soon as possible.

In a notebook dating from February or March 1859, Marx had set out in some detail the projected contents of the 'third chapter' keying each topic to the *Grundrisse* material (*G(EV)*,969ff.). The three-part treatment of 'Capital' adumbrated to Lassalle in March 1858 emerged again. The parts were to be the production process of capital, the circulation process of capital and the relationship between capital and profit. A fourth part called 'Miscellaneous' was appended for the considerable amount of *Grundrisse* material left over. The ultimate destination of these topics evidently remained uncertain.

Marx's endeavours to get the 'third chapter' to the publisher during 1859 were not successful. Moreover, there is no extant manuscript evidence to indicate how he did progress, if at all. From early in 1860 until August 1861 Marx gave virtually no attention to his critique of political economy. He returned to the project with renewed enthusiasm once again, as in 1857, late in 1861 and the period 1861–3 was especially productive. This period is the subject of Volume II of the present study.

Part I
Philosophical critique, capitalism and political economy

CHAPTER 1

Marx discovers political economy

INTRODUCTION

Marx moved from Kreuznach to Paris in October 1843 with one of his intentions being to collaborate with Arnold Ruge in editing the *Deutsch-französische Jahrbücher*. In Kreuznach Marx had been working on his critical reading of Hegel's book *The Philosophy of Right* (1821) and the critique of political philosophy continued to preoccupy him in Paris. From his study manuscripts (*CHPR*,3ff. and *CW*,3,3ff.), he prepared two articles for the *Jahrbücher* on the theory and practice of human emancipation from oppressions. These were entitled 'On the Jewish question' (*CW*,3,146ff.) and 'Contribution to the critique of Hegel's philosophy of right: introduction' (*CHPR*,129ff. and *CW*,3,175ff.) and they appeared in the one and only edition of the journal in February 1844.

In the present context, though, it is Engels's contribution to the *Jahrbücher* that claims our attention. The 'Outlines of a critique of political economy' (*CW*,3,418ff.) gave Marx his first explicit insights into the nature of capitalism and stimulated his interest in political economy as *the* source of a critical comprehension of the contemporary human situation. This stimulus was catalytic in the sense that Marx's reading of Engels's piece did not define or limit the scope of his own studies. He did make some reading notes on the article (*CW*,3,375f.), but these were brief and sketchy and Marx did not express any recognition of the details of Engels's critical arguments and insights. However, Marx's appreciation of the article was soon to be heightened by his own reading of the works of political economy. This is evident from the fact that soon after beginning his independent studies, Marx was able to write a similar sustained and passionate critical essay on the human ramifications of capitalism.

During early 1844, Marx made rapid progress in his study of political economy. Most of his reading was of French language translations of English works, but some original French and German sources were included. He recorded his studies in the series of nine Paris notebooks, most of which have been preserved although not all the notes have been published (*MEGA*,I/3,410ff. and 447ff.).

The study records from this period comprise a series of excerpts from the works with some comments by Marx setting out his reactions to the argument he was reading. Only one of the commentaries was substantial enough to contain any sustained argument formulated by Marx himself. He wrote this substantial comment in the context of taking excerpts from James Mill's *Elements of Political Economy* (1821) and the resulting critical essay carries the editorial title 'Comments on James Mill' (*MEGA*,I/3,530ff. and *CW*,3,211ff.). Its content, though, ranged across many topics not considered in the parts of the *Elements* that he was reading. The rest of the comments in the notebooks were fragmentary and rough-drafted in a mixture of French and German, but certain key ideas can be discerned in them. Of the sixteen other authors that Marx read and noted, his most thorough study was of Adam Smith's *Wealth of Nations* (1776), Jean-Baptiste Say's *Traité d' économie politique* (third edition, 1817), and David Ricardo's *Principles of Political Economy and Taxation* (second edition, 1819). He also took substantial excerpts from the lesser-known works of Friedrich List, Eugène Buret and Pierre le Pesant de Boisguillebert, although the notes on the former two have not been reprinted.

Beyond this, Marx abandoned the notebook format and began work on what we know as the *Paris Manuscripts* (*CW*,3,229ff.). This work comprised a reorganised and deeper investigation and extension of some of the ideas set out in the notebooks, especially those in the 'Comments on James Mill'. Most of the writers whose works Marx studied and excerpted in the notebooks were not referred to in the *Paris Manuscripts* where he almost exclusively used Adam Smith's *Wealth of Nations* as *the* source of the political economy of capitalism. In addition to this, he found support for his critical view of capitalism in the lesser-known works of Wilhelm Schulz-Bodmer and Constantin Pecqueur together with Eugène Buret's book that he had previously studied and noted. In the *Paris Manuscripts* themselves, there are two stages in the early evolution of Marx's social and economic critique. He began with an exposition of the image of capitalism that he found in political economy – especially in the *Wealth of Nations*. He structured this exposition around the basic class categories of income distribution, viz. wages of labour, profit of capital and rent of land, with an emphasis upon the role and situation of *labour* and *private property* in the system. This statement of the 'facts' of capitalism, for Marx did accept the image presented by Adam Smith as a faithful abstract replica of the reality of capitalism as it was comprehended at the time, was followed by Marx's own critical exposé of the nature of the system. He adopted a humanistic viewpoint for his critique, and through a detailed consideration of the adverse situation of labour under capitalism, which he linked to the dominance of private property, he concluded that the transcendence (*Aufhebung*) of private property is a necessary step towards man's emancipation from oppression and man's full human realisation through free labour.

Some of the key ideas in these 1844 manuscripts were reiterated by Marx in two immediately subsequent pieces of writing. In a part of the philosophical polemic *The Holy Family, or Critique of Critical Criticism* (Chapter 4, Part 4), he considered the critical ideas of Pierre-Joseph Proudhon on private property in the book *Qu'est-ce que la propriété?* (second edition, 1841) (CW,4,23ff.). At this stage, he praised Proudhon's critique as far as it went, but noted its limitations. Then, in a draft of a critical review of Friedrich List's book *Das nationale System der politischen Oekonomie, Erster Band* (1841), Marx had another opportunity to restate his critical, humanistic interpretation of capitalism while condemning List's distortions of the system to suit his own bourgeois ends (CW,4,265ff.). Each of these pieces must have helped Marx to clarify his ideas on the critique of political economy and capitalism as they were further developed during 1845–6 through another extensive reading of the available literature. During this period, Marx filled twelve notebooks with excerpts from and comments on the works of fifty-four writers (*MEGA*,I/6,597ff. outlines these studies).

Marx's first studies of political economy and the nature of capitalism are considered in this chapter and the next. The present chapter deals with Engels's article and Marx's 'Comments on James Mill'. Then, in Chapter 2, the *Paris Manuscripts* and the subsequent pieces referred to are discussed.

ENGELS'S 'OUTLINES OF A CRITIQUE OF POLITICAL ECONOMY'

Marx's notes on Engels's 'Outlines of a critique of political economy' open with the idea that *trade* is a consequence of *private property*, an idea taken directly from the article (CW,3,422) – indeed, all of the notes comprised summary assertions of Engels's arguments. In considering the capitalist economy at the level of exchange and circulation, Engels did not question the nature of the production process itself. The social division of labour was thus not recognised as the *origin* of the exchange–circulation phenomenon, although he was clearly aware that private property had a determining role to play in the process. He noted that the development of formalised trade based on private property was reflected in the development of political economy and the tone of his critique was set in the following opening passage:

Political economy came into being as a natural result of the expansion of trade, and with its appearance elementary, unscientific huckstering was replaced by *a developed system of licensed fraud, an entire science of enrichment.*
This political economy or science of enrichment born of the merchants' mutual envy and greed, bears on its brow the mark of the most detestable selfishness. (CW,3,418, emphasis added)

At first, in the earliest mercantilist period of organised trading, the selfish and competitive nature of the process was quite obvious:

The mercantile system still had a certain artless Catholic candour and did not in the least conceal the immoral nature of trade. We have seen how it openly paraded its mean avarice. . . . Public opinion had not yet become humanised. Why, therefore, conceal things which resulted from the inhuman, hostile nature of trade itself? (*CW*,3,422)

The 'humanisation' of the eighteenth century and reactions against mercantilism Engels saw as having led to the endeavour to present trade as a process of equity and harmony. This, he argued, began the obscurantism of political economy with respect to the essentially conflict-ridden and sub-human nature of life under capitalism. Adam Smith may have been '*the economic Luther*' (*CW*,3,422) in his rejection of the constraints of mercantilism in favour of the spirit of free trade, but his *human* interpretation of such trade was false and misleading (*CW*,3,422–3). Engels referred to the 'sham humanity of the modern economists [that] hides a barbarism of which their predecessors knew nothing' (*CW*,3,421). The true basis for exchange at all levels would always be competition and self-interest, although as Engels pointed out, the so-called 'free' trade of modern capitalism is based on a 'hidden' monopoly that is more dominant and restrictive than the mercantilist formalities, viz. *the rule of private property* (*CW*,3,421). And yet, 'It did not occur to economics to question the *validity of private property*' (*CW*,3,419), an institution which is responsible for the worst facets of capitalism in Engels's view:

The premises [of 'freedom' and private property] begot and reared the factory system and modern slavery, which yields nothing in humanity and cruelty to ancient slavery. Modern economics – the system of free trade based on Adam Smith's *Wealth of Nations* – reveals itself to be that same hypocrisy, inconsistency and immorality which now confront free humanity in every sphere. (*CW*,3,420)

Thus Engels wanted to expose private property's role as a socio-legal instrument of oppression, an objective which Marx, too, was to set himself in his Paris writings.

The category *value* also caught Marx's attention in Engels's article. It was presented as being an immediate consequence of the compulsion to trade under the rule of private property, but its origin in the production system based on the social division of labour was not made clear. In Marx's summary of his reading of

Engels's treatment of value, he did note the distinction drawn by Engels between two 'determining features' of 'abstract real value' evident in political economy, viz. *utility* and *cost of production* (*CW*,3,375). It is evident that Marx sensed the more essential status and logical priority of production costs in value determination, although adequate utility, implying demand, remained a necessary condition for the production decision to be rendered viable in the exchange process through the *realisation* of real value. He went on to note also that Engels had distinguished the existence of an *exchange* value, or *price*, that emerged as a consequence of the distortion of the cost of production-based real value by the exercise of monopoly power in the market (*CW*,3,375).

Engels's own arguments concerning capitalist value determination were more elaborate and critical than revealed in Marx's notes. For Engels, the immediate focus of his critique was the self-interest pursued by traders in the exchange process. He interpreted the cost of production concept of real value as an attempt by political economists to render the value form *objective* and free from association with the subjective evils of 'huckstering'. Such an abstract value form had no effective meaning in a world where the ultimate determinant of realisable value in the exchange process is utility and the maximisation of self-interest (*CW*,3,425–6). It was Engels's conclusion that:

The difference between real value and exchange-value is based on a fact – namely, that the value of a thing differs from the so-called equivalent given for it in trade; i.e., that this equivalent is not an equivalent. This so-called equivalent is the *price* of the thing, and if the economist were honest, he would employ this term for 'value' in exchange'. But he has still to keep up some sort of pretence that price is somehow bound up with value, lest the immorality of trade become too obvious. (*CW*,3,427)

Under the demands of competition, participants in the world of exchange are forced to become *speculators*, each out to take selfish advantage of market situations at the expense of others. Against this self-seeking behaviour as the basis for economic society, Engels set the humanistic ideal of a co-ordinated relation of production to consumption needs as developed in the works of the English socialists and of Fourier (*CW*,3,435).

In the treatment of value considered above, there is no mention of the role of *labour*. There was no attempt by Engels to formalise value in embodied-labour terms. He did make the point that labour is the 'main factor in production, the "source of wealth" ' (CW,3,431) but it was not linked directly to value formation except through the wages of labour considered as a cost of production alongside the profit of capital and the rent of land. The predominant influence of Adam Smith is noticeable here. Engels went on, though, to develop the labour–wealth–cost of production link in two ways, both of which would later be taken up by Marx. Firstly, Engels argued that the capital–labour distinction that political economy made is effectively false because capital is stored-up past labour. This gives the value of capital an embodied-labour status to which Engels did not refer explicitly. Instead, he noted that this left production with only two categories of input, viz. *man* and his *labour* and *nature* in the form of land; the subjective and the objective respectively (CW,3,427–8). Secondly, Engels also expressed the concern that in spite of labour being crucial in wealth creation, it 'comes off badly with the economist' (CW,3,431). Here Marx read the following piece in which Engels argued the rudiments of the adverse situation of labour under capitalism and its link to private property as it affected income distribution:

Just as capital has already been separated from labour, so labour is now in turn split for a second time: the product of labour confronts labour as wages, is separated from it, and is in its turn as usual determined by competition – there being . . . no firm standard determining labour's share in production. *If we do away with private property, this unnatural separation also disappears. Labour becomes its own reward* . . . (CW,3,431, emphasis added)

Thus man's situation is determined through his labour being rewarded only by a wage which *he produces* and yet over which he has no control. The control of private property over distribution is dominant and the abolition of this mediation in the production process would allow a direct control by man over the reward *for* his labour and the reward *from* his labour.

Monopolisation and value are related, Engels also argued, and this is most evident in the valuation of land and the determination of its rent return. He rejected Ricardo's theory of differential rent as the *sole* explanation because it left out of account the effects of *competition* – ironically based on the monopolisation of land – in the face of scarcity. It is private property in land that is ultimately the condition for rent to be paid *as a form of income*. Without the monopolisation of land, the return from land and land valuation become simply reflections of the differential productivities of land worked by equal quantities of labour (CW,3,429–30).

The problem of income distribution was considered further by Engels using the basic classical framework of classes, viz. workers, capitalists and landowners. This pattern of distribution is consequent upon the separation of labour, capital and land as factors of production with access to shares in what is produced. The separation to which Engels gave most attention is that between capital and labour, an imposed separation based on the existence of private property which gave the owners the right to appropriate the total product of labour and thus an income for themselves in the form of profit. Engels summarised the situation this way:

the economist separates capital from labour, and yet clings to the division without giving any other recognition to their unity than by his definition of capital as 'stored-up labour'. The split between capital and labour resulting from private property is nothing but the inner dichotomy of labour corresponding to this divided condition and arising out of it. And after this separation is accomplished, capital is divided once more into the original capital and profit – the increment of capital, which it receives in the process of production . . . (CW,3,430)

Clearly, Engels found the *origin* of profit to be in production, more particularly in what labour adds to the original capital advanced, but he did not go on to analyse this important insight any further. His concern was with income distribution as a process that involves the resolution of a socio-economic conflict over shares in the produced output, a resolution for which there exists no objective standard. Instead, 'it is an entirely alien and . . . fortuitous standard that decides – competition, the cunning right of the stronger' (CW,3,431). The consequence for the worker is that his power disadvantage relative to private property forces him to accept the minimum return for his labour that the capitalist will pay him, 'whilst the largest part of the products is shared between capital and landed property' (CW,3,441). Once again, though, the adverse human ramifications of this system of distribution could be overcome by the abolition of its necessary condition, viz. *private property* (CW,3,431).

One further aspect of the production system based on capital which Engels considered, but which Marx did not refer to in his notes, was the *inherent instability* of such a system. The dominance of competition between capitals leads to production decisions which are not geared to effective demand. The political economists had no qualms about this as a problem at the *aggregate* level, for they retreated to the harmony of 'Say's law'. But, in spite of this *theoretical* harmony, it was Engels's experience that the system is characterised by a more or less continuous imbalance of supply and demand, both in individual sectors of production and in the aggregate. This imbalance appears as constant price fluctuations and quantity adjustments in production (CW,3,433). Engels saw *any* overproduction to be an unhealthy state for an economic system to be in and projected that it would have profound long-term consequences for capitalism. He summarised his *impressions*, unsupported by any formal analysis, in the following passage where Marx's yet to be formulated view of overproduction crises is so clearly foreshadowed:

as long as you continue to produce in the present unconscious, thoughtless manner, at the mercy of chance – for just so long trade crises will remain; and each successive crisis is bound to become more universal and therefore worse than the preceding one; is bound to impoverish a larger body of small capitalists, and to augment in increasing proportion the numbers of the class who live by labour alone, thus considerably enlarging the mass of labour to be employed (the major problem of our economists) and finally causing a social revolution such as has never been dreamt of in the philosophy of the economists. (CW,3,434)

It was Engels's view that competitive capital accumulation would bring about a centralisation of the ownership of capital as overproduction causes the failure of small-scale businesses and their assets and operations are taken over by the owners of large-scale capital (CW,3,440–1). One effect of this would be to exacerbate the struggle between the workers for the available jobs as the failed capitalists join the ranks of the proletariat. In the overall competitive struggle that characterises capitalism, the degree of neglect of the *human* side of man's life is thus further increased because of the imperative demands of material survival:

The struggle of capital against capital, of labour against labour, of land against land, drives production to a fever-pitch at which production turns all natural and rational relations upside-down . . . No one at all who enters into the struggle of competition can weather it without the utmost exertion of his energy, without renouncing every truly human purpose. (CW,3,435)

Considerations of this sort led Engels to *assert* that the fate of capitalism must be to experience a social-revolutionary reaction against its dehumanising effects on the majority of people. The proximate objective of such a revolution would be to abolish private property, the most essential condition of the system. Reformist measures could not have the desired impact because the effects of capitalism's contradictions are immanently generated such that:

All the laws, all the dividing of landed property, all the possible splitting-up of capital, are of no avail: this result must and will come, unless it is anticipated by a total transformation of social conditions, a fusion of opposed interests, an abolition of private property. (CW,3,441)

This idea of social revolution to abolish private property and humanise economic society is a theme that Marx was to take up and develop much further in his critique of capitalism and political economy.

POLITICAL ECONOMY AND CAPITALISM

I have selected for consideration here two sets of comments that Marx wrote during his first studies of political economy in early 1844. They indicate clearly the critical priorities that he was to carry forward into his future critique of political economy.

The first of the two pieces, the comments on Ricardo's *Principles*, do not comprise a single coherent argument, but they are more substantial and more revealing than those on Say and Smith, for example, to whose work Marx devoted equally thorough attention. The excerpts from and comments on these three writers take up the bulk of notebooks I to IV in the Paris series. The other commentary to be considered here is the more coherent and substantial 'Comments on James Mill' which, as already indicated, were not really *on* Mill at all. Rather, the piece represents Marx's first sustained endeavour to organise his critical thought on capitalism as the system was portrayed in the works that he had been reading. Both of the sets of comments considered here were written in notebook IV of the series.

Marx had available to him a French translation of Ricardo's *Principles* in its *second* edition. His excerpts and comments cover eighteen pages in the reprinted version (*MEGA*,I/3,493ff.) They deal with material from the whole book and include about fifteen brief comments and three larger comments spread throughout the notes. Some of Marx's argument is difficult to understand, but the importance of the pieces is that they indicate the sort of themes that attracted his attention and brought some critical reaction in these early days of the critique of political economy.

In the comments on the *Principles*, Marx's general concern was to elicit the implications of capitalism for the situation of the working proletariat. Several of his comments emphasised the process of distribution which, with its form determined by the existence of capital as private property in the means of production, disadvantaged the workers in spite of their contribution to production. Indeed, as Marx read it, the workers did not really matter very much at all in the arguments of political economy beyond their *functional* existence and survival.

Marx noted that the existence of capital with its private property rights over what is produced led to commodity *costs* which were greater than their *worth*. The reason for this he saw as the ability of capital to attract a 'tribute' (*MEGA*,I/3,494). Capital demands and holds a 'plus' beyond the *necessary production costs* of reproducing the means of production, servicing the land and maintaining the labour. From this 'plus' is to be drawn the non-labour incomes of profit, interest and rent (*MEGA*,I/3,501). Marx dissociated the existence of the 'plus' from any *contribution* to production by capital or land. Rather, he argued that the actual outcome of the distribution process in terms of wages, profit and rent is the result of a process of competition based on traditional patterns of income and the exercise of monopoly power (*MEGA*,I/3,501). This argument did not make the *origin* of the 'plus' very clear, but it is evident that the orthodox 'trinitarian' formula of distribution was already rejected by Marx in favour of some *subjective* view of the process.

A broader view of the situation of the worker was taken when Marx commented on the nature of the *role* of labour in capitalist production. He saw the *purpose* of work to be purely the provision of the material means of subsistence. Other dimensions of life are not relevant (*MEGA*,I/3,504). Thus it was the peak of the infamy of political economy to make the distinction between gross and net revenue for this facilitates an emphasis on the latter and the consequent analytical disappearance of any concern for the material well-being of the worker as an object of study. The outcome of the capitalist processes is assessed only by the size of the surplus (*Überschuss*) generated. Indeed, this focus entails and encourages the view that the costs of production *per se*, including labour, should be minimised in a quantitative sense.

However, as Marx argued, the implications of the analysis were *qualitative* as well. Minimising the cost of labour effectively turns it into just another material input. Human life has no relevance beyond its 'machine' dimension and no outlay on labour should go beyond maintaining man as an efficient 'working machine' (*MEGA*,I/3,514). Considerations of humanity could not be the province of political economy with its concern for a category that has no direct relevance for the well-being of the workers (*MEGA*,I/3,515). The welfare of the whole nation is identified with net revenue generation, even though it is the source of income for only the small minority of people who own property! Through 'an artificial fiction [*Fiktion*] of political economy', the nation is understood as 'the *sum of the capitalists*' and national and private property interests are thus conflated (*MEGA*,I/3,517).

Marx's reading of the problems of capital accumulation considered by Ricardo did not result in very lucid comments. The main points that he wanted to make are evident, although the argument surrounding them remained impressionistic and casual. Firstly, he found Ricardo's theory of the falling rate of profits less than adequate because it failed to take account of the limited opportunities for the *application* of the accumulating capital in the various branches of production. Such competition for placement, he thought, must lower the required rate of return on capital. In this respect, he found Adam Smith's approach to the issue to be a more intuitively appropriate basis for analysing this fundamental puzzle besetting the process of capital accumulation. Secondly, Marx argued that the *dynamic* implications of 'Say's law' drawn by Ricardo were counterfactual. It was simply not in accordance with the evidence to suggest that all accumulated capital could find some placement. Demand required to validate production is not necessarily generated by the production itself and Marx cited bankruptcies and periodic crises of trade as indicative of the lack of any such automatic correction to overproduction (*MEGA*,I/3,511). Thirdly, Marx rejected the idea that capital accumulation would be favourable to the workers. His rejection was based on the empirical *assertion* that there exists an excess supply of labour in all industrial nations. The consequence of this is that any increase in demand for labour could be met from the unemployed proletariat without competitive wage increases. The falling rate of profits associated with capital accumulation has no necessary wage-rise implications (*MEGA*,I/3,511).

One further point from Marx's reading of the *Principles* is of ongoing importance. Even at this early stage, he recognised in Ricardo's writing a penchant for frank expressions of the nature of capitalism independently of any implications that his revelations might have for particular interest groups. He referred to this as Ricardo's 'cynicism' ('*Zynismus*') (*MEGA*,I/3,515 and 516). This critical admiration for Ricardo's work was to carry it forward as a central source in the evolution of the critique of political economy. In the *Principles*, as Marx saw it in the light of his critical *telos*, political economy had reached its 'scientific' apogee.

In the 'Comments on James Mill', Marx's initial focus was on the most obvious of capitalism's phenomena, the exchange and circulation of commodities through the mediation of money. This starting point for his critique was ultimately carried through to its final form in *Capital*, Volume I, Chapter I, where the commodity appears as the most fundamental element of capitalism and its Value[1] as an essential reflection of the place of labour in production. What is more, the present 1844 piece foreshadowed most explicitly the interdependent themes of labour alienation and commodity fetishism that reflect in Marx's critico-theoretical writings through to *Capital a continuity of concern for the human condition under capitalism.*

Marx's primary concern with exchange was to examine its implications for the participants. Exchange is a *social* process. It is a manifestation of man's social being which results from his individual need to interact with nature in a socially co-ordinated way in order to produce and so survive materially. Exchange for Marx was a category that implies much about human *being*:

> *Exchange*, both of human activity within production itself [i.e. the division of labour] and of *human products* against one another, is equivalent to *species-activity* and species-spirit, the real, conscious and true mode of existence of which is *social* activity and *social* enjoyment. Since *human* nature is the *true community* of men, by manifesting their nature men *create*, produce, the *human community*, the social entity, which is no abstract universal power opposed to the single individual, but is the essential nature of each individual, his own activity, his own life, his own spirit, his own wealth. Hence this *true community* does not come into being through reflection, it appears owing to the *need* and *egoism* of individuals, i.e., it is produced directly by their life activity itself. (CW,3,216–17)

This is a profound passage in which man's existence as a *species-being* (*Gattungswesen*), that is, his *human identity*, is linked directly to his *individual* involvement in the economic process of exchange. His individual being is facilitated by the *social community* (*Gemeinwesen*) and by exercising his nature, that is, his essential life activity, he helps to create the set of social relations that comprise the social community. Thus, Marx had grasped very early on in the development of his thought the fundamental significance of *material* (economic) activity for an understanding of man's individual and social existence. And, in this ontology, it is very much *labour* that is the essence of man's being, as Marx recognised later in the 'Comments'.

From this point Marx went on to warn that the community has the capacity to be a *negative* influence on man's being:

> It does not depend on man whether this community exists or not; *but as long as man does not recognise himself as man, and therefore has not organised the world in a human way* [emphasis added], this *community* appears in the form of *estrangement* because its *subject*, man, is a being estranged from himself. (CW,3,217)

Thus, as man *is*, so is the community. Individual men *are* the community. If man is estranged or alienated² from himself, then *his* society is only a caricature of a really *human* community in which his true species-life could be realised. The consequence of this has several dimensions: labour is an activity of torment, the products of labour stand as alien objects, and his bond with other men is not based on essential, human criteria. Man has become the less than human victim of his own creations and his production appears as 'the production of his nullity' (*CW*,3,217).

Now in Marx's interpretation of political economy at this point, the community of men, the manifestation of man's natural activity, appears as exchange and trade. Society is essentially a system of exchanges, a commercial society, in which each participant is a 'merchant'. It is the case, then, that 'political economy *defines* the *estranged* form of social intercourse as the *essential* and *original* form corresponding to man's nature' (*CW*,3,217). That is, political economy portrays man's social relations as those of property owner, with the commodity as the mediating object, for there is no access to these relations except through participation in exchange. Property in a commodity is the dominating means to man's individual and social being.

In this role, the crucial characteristic of property is that it be *alienated* – *disposed of* – for this signifies actual entry into exchange. Such disposal is dependent upon the existence of an appropriate set of mutual material needs, each being for man a *necessity* for the completion of his existence and the realisation of his nature (*CW*,3,218). *Social motivation* is purely materialistic and the *social bond* is manifested as a mutuality of material needs – a *'reciprocity* in *alienation'* (*CW*,3,218).

Associated with the process of exchange are *money* and *credit* and Marx considered the nature and significance of each in turn. Both are mediations designed to facilitate exchange and both were found by Marx to exacerbate the already negative human implications of the process.

As a medium of exchange, money represents a generalised *externalisation (objectification)* of the specific results of man's productive activity; that is, a manifestation of the exchange value embodied in the commodity as a result of labour. Marx sensed that money acts as a dominant *social* force in and of itself in spite of its purely *material* roots. The effect of money is to accentuate the

41

degree of remoteness and alienation from his products that man feels in the exchange process, for by acting as a mediation, money breaks the mutuality of the exchange relation based on immediate need that exists in a barter situation. Moreover, money also accentuates the social isolation that man experiences in that his relations to other men are now doubly mediated by the commodity and its generalised exchange value form, money.

Marx reinforced his interpretation of the situation of man in an exchange system by considering the ethical and humanistic implications of *credit*. Credit represents a system of commercial interactions in which the *'worth'* of a man must be assessable. This assessment of 'worth' Marx found to be dehumanising in the sense that the *general morality* of the man becomes linked to his *credit* worthiness. Here, then, is another projection of man's qualities into the commercial field independently of his human attributes. Marx expressed the view that 'One ought to consider how vile it is to *estimate* the value of man in *money*, as happens in the credit relationship', for '*Credit* is the *economic* judgement of the *morality* of a man' (CW,3,215). However, he found an irony in this 'vile' extension of the exchange system. Man himself attains a currency in the exchange process that had been denied him in exchange mediated directly by money in that *he* is now the medium of exchange rather than metal or paper. But this restoration of a human core in exchange is an illusion because the actual mediation is man's *morality* projected outside of himself. Man must now suffer the indignity of *moral* scrutiny in order to have his *commercial* worth established. As Marx put it so clearly,

Human individuality, human *morality* itself, has become both an object of commerce and the *material* in which money exists. Instead of money . . . it is my own personal existence, my flesh and blood, my social virtue and importance, which constitutes the material, corporeal form of the *spirit of money*. Credit no longer resolves the value of money into money but into human flesh and the human heart. (CW,3,215)

By means of an enquiry into the nature of the exchange (circulation) phenomenon that probed beneath its appearances, Marx exposed its essence to be decidedly negative in *human* terms. In all of its dimensions, exchange involves men in relationships based only on *material* concerns. The result is a society in which *human being* is not given any priority. Through money and credit, the commodity mediation between men in this commercial society is made even more alienating. Beyond the satisfaction of his material needs, entry into exchange has no human return for man. He is isolated from his fellow man and from his own product with which he obtains entry to the process and to society itself. Even at the level of exchange, then, man is alienated. Marx would soon go on to provide a more elaborate account of this central component of his critique of capitalism.

So far, Marx had not given much attention to the role of *labour* in an exchange society. It was evident to him, though, that it is indeed at the root of the *existence, preservation* and *valuation* of private property in man-made products. These products are the *objects* of the exchange process.

Marx's concern was, as before, with the *human* ramifications of the *nature* and *form* of the labour and its results. He interpreted labour that produced commodities only for exchange as '*labour to earn a living*' (CW,3,219). That 'living' implies the worker's involvement in the exchange process itself and in the production process to which it is necessarily attached. Thus, labour as the mediation between man and nature in the process of material survival is now given added dimensions. These additions dictate a constrained form of labour which nullifies its creative human potential. Labour to earn a living produces a product that is unrelated to the immediate producer's own needs or to his particular labour function. It is *alienated labour* because its product is produced for someone else by a process of production that takes no account of the *human* dimensions and consequences of labour. Marx felt that the human objective of labour *ought* to be the realisation of each man's personal traits and potentialities. Constrained labour to earn a living cannot meet these requirements because it is *forced labour* in two senses: its *motivation* is material necessity and its *form* is dictated by an externally imposed set of physical relations (CW,3,220). All that man gets from his participation in such labour is access to material subsistence. For Marx, labour activity had the capacity to deliver much more in that it was ontologically central to man's existence.

The operational form of production to which Marx referred as being responsible for the less than human situation of man in exchange society involves the specialisation and division of labour:

> Just as the mutual exchange of the products of *human activity*
> appears as *barter*, as trade, so the mutual completion and exchange
> of the activity itself appears as *division of labour*, which turns man
> as far as possible into an abstract being, a machine tool, etc., and
> transforms him into a spiritual and physical monster. (CW,3,220)

It is evident that Marx had in mind here and in his subsequent
discussions both the division of labour within a sector of production and the social division of labour between sectors of production. Within a particular sector, there is a specialisation of labour
tasks that robs the labour of anything but a machine-like form. A
pattern of mutual interdependencies brings these increments of
labour form together to produce an identifiable product for exchange. Beyond this, the inter-sector social division of labour is
based on a set of social needs that are to be met by exchanging the
material results of production. Implicit in this exchange is the
exchange of the labour activities that are involved in production.
The contradiction here is that the division of labour implies the
most individualistic form of labour which is at the same time
necessarily social, but social only through its material results.

A significant characteristic of this form of society based on
division of labour and exchange is that produced material private
property has the essential property of *equivalence in exchange
independently of its specific physical form*. To this *immediate* abstract equivalence, Marx ascribed the term *Value*[3] in the following
passages:

> The mediating process between men engaged in exchange is not a
> social or human process, not *human relationship*; it is the *abstract
> relationship* of private property to private property, and the
> expression of this *abstract* relationship is *Value*, whose actual
> existence as Value constitutes *money*. (CW,3,212–13)

> Hence the mode of existence of private property as such has
> become that of a *substitute*, of an *equivalent*. Instead of its
> immediate unity with itself, it exists now only as a relation to
> *something else*. Its mode of existence as an *equivalent* is no longer
> its specific mode of existence. It has thus become a *Value*, and

immediately an *exchange-value*. Its mode of existence as *Value* is an *alienated* designation *of itself*, different from its immediate existence, external to its specific nature, a merely *relative* mode of existence of this. (CW,3,219)

Note that Marx recognised Value as *the logical entailment of the private property–exchange system*. It is the actual expression of the form of social interdependence between men under such a system and its manifest form is money or generalised exchange value. This is a view of Value to which Marx would return and consider in detail in his future work.

Now although Marx went on to add that 'How this *Value* is more precisely determined must be described elsewhere, as also how it becomes *price*' (CW,3,219), a careful reading of the passage just quoted reveals that he had already germinated the *qualitative* notion of a link between Value, alienation and objectification. The property of equivalence in exchange is designated as Value. Its *phenomenal* expression is as an exchange value (or price), a separable category measured as a money amount. But this property stands independently of the essential *human-material* rationale for producing the thing, viz. human *need*. Thus material objectification carries with it this additional dimension of existence which becomes dominant by virtue of the form of production and exchange. The product itself, then, stands in an alienated or estranged relationship to its producer, the worker, because of the necessity that it be exchanged, that is, that it is in a relation of *relativity* to other products and the potential property of another man. As a Value, the product has an existence independent of its specific material usefulness with which the producer can identify. As Marx put it,

it has ceased to be the product of the labour of its owner, his exclusive, distinctive personality. For he has alienated it, it has moved away from the owner whose product it was and has acquired a personal significance for someone whose product it is *not*. It has lost its personal significance for the owner. (CW,3,219)

That is, the consummation of the act of exchange is the realisation of the alienated status that the product has relative to its producer.

Marx exposed one further negative implication of a society in which man's material survival depends on the division of labour and exchange. Production is tied into a system of interdependent needs and each product is calculated to satisfy the needs of others. But, this satisfaction requires that the man in need is able to back up his need with *an equivalent in exchange*. Without this, his *human* need goes unrealised as a mere aspiration, and aspirations have no place in exchange. Demand only becomes effective when it is backed by possession of an equivalent Value. Man's need, that is man himself *qua* human, has no worth unless it is *commercially* viable. *Social* relations are similarly assessed in that 'Our *mutual* value is for us the Value of our *mutual* objects. Hence for us man himself is mutually of *no value*' (CW,3,227).

In the 'Comments', then, Marx first expressed his own critical ideas about an exchange society based upon division of labour in production. It is evident that he had in mind the *capitalist* system, but its particular defining characteristics were not made explicit in any detail. His immediate concern was with the human ramifications of division of labour and exchange, with the ontological importance of *labour* being stressed as the process that results in man's alienation. This theme was taken up again in the *Paris Manuscripts*, which Marx began soon after writing the 'Comments', although the critique was then set in a much more detailed and specific analysis of the nature of capitalism.

CHAPTER 2

Marx confronts the political economy of capitalism

LABOUR AND CAPITALISM

During the drafting of the *Paris Manuscripts*, begun in the spring of 1844, Marx became convinced that primacy had to be given to the *political economy* of capitalism in formulating a complete social critique.[1] Through the works of the political economists, he developed an appreciation of the generally accepted interpretation of the nature of capitalism. Political economy provided him with an 'empirical' comprehension of the system in that its abstract analyses treated the economy as real in its own right and not as an idealist projection. Thus he wrote that 'It is hardly necessary to assure the reader conversant with political economy that my results have been attained by means of a wholly empirical analysis based on a conscientious critical study of political economy' (*CW*,3,231).[2] The image of capitalism provided by the political economists, most especially Adam Smith, became the *object* of Marx's critique in the *Paris Manuscripts*.

The approach that he adopted was initially to allow political economy to speak for itself about the nature of the capitalist system.

We have proceeded from the premises of political economy. We have accepted its language and its laws. We presupposed private property, the separation of labour, capital and land, and of wages, profit of capital and rent of land – likewise division of labour, competition, the concept of exchange value, etc. (*CW*,3,270)

Then, having utilised political economy as a medium of expression of the nature of capitalism, Marx set about a deeper and more formal critical discussion of the human implications of what he had exposed. He elaborated particularly upon the thesis that under a capitalist production regime, man is debased and *alienated* through his labour activity. Marx discovered that this alienated state has several dimensions and that its roots are to be found in the existence of private property in the means of production. Indeed, the reproduction of private property by labour ensures the continued existence of alienation. For Marx, the two most essential categories in the critique of the image of capitalism in political economy were thus established as *private property* and *labour* and he reasoned that 'we will find . . . in each [other] category, e.g., trade, competition, capital, money, only a *particular* and *developed expression* of these first elements' (CW,3,281).

Political economy itself emphasised the role of *labour* in understanding the operations of capitalism, and yet its status is reduced to that of a functional component without concern for its *human* form. As Marx read it, 'Political economy starts from labour as the real soul of production; yet to labour it gives nothing, and to private property everything' (CW,3,280). Moreover, in its treatment of labour, '*Political economy conceals the estrangement inherent in the nature of labour by not considering the direct relationship between the worker* (labour) *and production*' (CW,3,273). Thus it followed for Marx that:

On the basis of political economy itself, in its own words, we have shown that the worker sinks to the level of a commodity and becomes indeed the most wretched of commodities; that the wretchedness of the worker is in inverse proportion to the power and magnitude of his production . . . (CW,3,270)

Alienated labour becomes a *fact* of political economy and capitalism (CW,3,278). It results from the situation of labour *per se* and its isolation from its product by virtue of the appropriation rights granted to the owners of the means of production. Marx proceeded to analyse this fact in much more detail in the *Paris Manuscripts* as the central theme of his critique of capitalism.

In examining the nature of capitalism through a reading of political economy, Marx adopted as his framework the *phenomen-*

al categories of distribution and their associated *factors of production*. He was not immediately concerned with any in-depth *explanation* of this distribution pattern, but he accepted it as a key characteristic of the way capitalism is portrayed by political economy. Thus Marx's first formal investigation of capitalism appears under the headings 'Wages of labour', 'Profit of capital' and 'Rent of land'. There is, however, some discussion of the issue of distribution within this given framework and Marx emphasised especially the conflict basis of the process. In the part dealing with the 'Rent of land', Marx adumbrated the idea of *exploitation* as the source of this non-labour income, but it was not generalised to all property in the means of production or developed in any detail. When he turned his attention to the elaboration of his own critique of the system that political economy had enabled him to outline, the *distribution* status of labour is taken as an empirical fact of capitalism. Marx's ultimate concern was with the situation of labour in general, *humanistic* terms rather than only in *material* terms – that is, with labour *vis-à-vis* the realisation of individual human potential, with labour as an essential ontological process.

He began, though, under the heading 'Wages of labour' by considering the material situation of the worker under capitalism as the essential determinant of man's more general situation. Marx's main source for this discussion was Adam Smith's *Wealth of Nations*.

The wage upon which the worker and his family have to subsist is determined, in Marx's words, by 'the antagonistic struggle between capitalist and worker' (CW,3,235). This struggle is rather one-sided and 'victory' for the capitalist is probable because of his relatively stronger material and socio-legal position. Firstly, he has stored up means to subsist in the exchange value of his private property; secondly, he may well have supplementary income in the form of rent and interest; and thirdly, capitalists are able to operate through combinations whereas this is not a legally acceptable tactic for workers. The workers' only means of survival is *immediate* and *continuous* labour because he is, by definition, separated from any property in the means of production. In this sort of situation, given the maximum profit motive of the capitalist, it is inevitable, in principle at least, that the worker will be paid a minimum 'subsistence' wage.[3] This principle is modified frequently by fluctuations in the relative demand for and supply of labour. The result can be that

49

the wage is lifted above the minimum, but the more significant consequence is that finding employment for any wage becomes a matter of chance: 'The worker has to struggle not only for his physical means of subsistence; he has to struggle to get work, i.e., the possibility, the means, to perform his activity' (CW,3,237). However limited may be the material returns from working, without work the human situation is no longer of any direct *economic* relevance at all. As Marx so graphically put it,

Political economy can . . . advance the proposition that the proletarian, the same as any horse, must get as much as will enable him to work. It does not consider him when he is not working, as a human being; but leaves such consideration to criminal law, to doctors, to religion, to the statistical tables, to politics and to the poor-house overseer. (CW,3,241)

Marx's impressionistic dynamics of the situation of labour as the economy fluctuates (CW,3,237ff.) did not reveal any sustainable position of well-being for the worker. Man's situation is one of material deprivation, the degree of which depends on whether he is employed or unemployed. This situation improves in boom conditions, but such conditions carry with them other negative effects on the lot of the worker in that he is likely then to be overworked and his labour becomes increasingly machine-like as the division of labour intensifies with the rapid accumulation of capital. For Marx, the prospects for the worker were gloomy indeed: 'in a declining state of society – increasing misery of the worker; in an advancing state – misery with complications; and in a fully developed state of society – static misery' (CW,3,239).

Marx went on to reiterate the contradictory way in which political economy treated labour. While arguing that labour is the *source* of all exchange value, the political economists portray the worker as subservient to those 'privileged and idle gods', the capitalist and the landlord. In spite of his vital position in the very *raison d'être* of capitalism as the *producer* of exchange value, the worker is constantly debased and debilitated by the machine-like nature of his work. Moreover, even this humanly impoverished status allowed the worker is insecure. The worker is the victim of continuous cycles of production such that his 'price' fluctuates widely. Thus Marx concluded that 'While the interest of the worker, according to the political economists, never stands opposed to the interest of society, society always and necessarily stands opposed to the interest of the worker' (*CW*,3,240). In all of these ways, then, Marx found that the status of labour in political economy as the most essential category in production is contradicted by the actual outcome of the process under capitalism. Labour's theoretically dominant role is usurped by the capitalist and landowner as private property holders who *per se* contribute nothing operationally to the *production* of exchange value or the accumulation of capital. On the qualitative side, the situation of labour is adversely affected by the very processes which improve its contribution to production. And, as a member of *society*, any improvement in the worker's contribution would always benefit the society as a whole. The irony for Marx was that these benefits appeared to flow only from the continuous oppression of the producing members of the society.

Marx's critical comprehension of the situation of labour under capitalism was reinforced by a reading of the works of some lesser-known nineteenth century writers, especially Wilhelm Schulz-Bodmer, Constantin Pecqueur and Eugène Buret.[4] They espoused most explicitly, and in quite ethical and emotional terms, a highly critical analysis of the human dimension of capitalism. Their understanding of the system was similar to Marx's own in that they emphasised its oppressive and exploitative nature. In quoting from these works, Marx's additional commentary and interpretation was minimal as their critical stance evidently corresponded with what he wanted to convey.[5]

These writers were intent upon exposing the true nature of human labour under capitalism. They treated labour as 'abstract labour' in the sense that it is labour only to earn a material living and without any meaningful specific human quality or consequence beyond this. More than this, their image of labour under capitalism was one in which the almost wholly negative-destructive quality of such labour was emphasised. Under capitalism, man's very survival depends upon the sale of his labour services. This amounts to a universal form of prostitution: 'Prostitution of the non-owning class in all its forms' (Pecqueur, quoted *CW*,3,244), or as Marx put it, 'Prostitution is only a *specific* expression of the *general* prostitution of the labourer' (*CW*,3,295n.). This analogy emphasises that labour under capitalism, besides being *the object of trade*, has its *human dimensions*, beyond the basest pragmatism of material–

physiological survival, removed just as in the case of the sexual performance of the prostitute. Moreover, Marx noted that the selling and buying of labour services in no way offends the *ethics* of political economy for indeed trading is its essence:

You must make everything that is yours *saleable*, i.e., useful. If I ask the political economist: Do I obey economic laws if I extract money by offering my body for sale, by surrendering it to another's lust? . . . Or am I not acting in keeping with political economy if I sell my friend to the Moroccans? . . . Then the political economist replies to me: You do not transgress my laws; but see what Cousin Ethics and Cousin Religion have to say about it. My *political economic* ethics and religion have nothing to reproach you with, but – But whom am I now to believe, political economy or ethics? – The ethics of political economy is *acquisition*, work . . . (CW,3,310)

Whatever the *ethics* of the situation, workers who own no means of production, and thus no access to the resources of nature in a 'civilised' society, are placed in a position of subservient dependence upon those who do own such means:

In order to live, then, the non-owners are obliged to place themselves, directly or indirectly, *at the service* of the owners – to put themselves, that is to say, into a position of dependence upon them. (Pecqueur, quoted CW,3,243)

The *appearance* is, though, that the sale of labour is freely entered into by the worker as an exchange process and that the necessary equity of such exchange processes applies. For Marx this represented a distortion in that it gave no recognition to the fact that the worker's situation is one of continuous dependence motivated by sheer survival. He cannot rationally choose to opt out and he enters the 'exchange' at a distinct disadvantage relative to the capitalist. Thus, Buret argued that

The worker is not at all in the position of a *free seller vis-à-vis* the one who employs him . . . The capitalist is always free to employ labour, and the worker is always forced to sell it. The value of labour is completely destroyed if it is not sold every instant. Labour can neither be accumulated nor even saved, unlike true [commodities]. (quoted CW,3,245)

Two consequences follow from this state of dependence: firstly, 'the right of the unlimited exploitation of the poor by the rich is . . . universally recognized' (Schulz, quoted CW,3,242); and secondly, no matter what the nature of the work to be performed, the worker must consider himself lucky to have chanced upon work at all:

millions are able to earn a bare subsistence for themselves only by strenuous labour which shatters the body and cripples them morally and intellectually; that they are even obliged to consider the misfortune of finding *such* work a piece of good fortune. (Schulz, quoted CW,3,243)

Under these circumstances, it is quite evident that labour under capitalism has no *human dimensions* beyond material survival and lacks a *human context*. The objective of the system is 'the possession of wealth, not the happiness of men' (Buret, quoted CW,3,246). In Marx's words, capitalism and thus political economy, 'knows the worker only as a working animal – as a beast reduced to the strictest bodily needs' (CW,3,242). Its objective is to *perfect the worker* in spite of the consequence that it '*degrades the man*' (Buret, quoted CW,3,245, emphasis added).

There was, though, behind all this critical condemnation of labour under capitalism an irony that was recognised by Schulz (CW,3,242). This irony served further to emphasise the terms of the critique. It is the case that in order to pursue his *human* potentials, beyond those realisable through labour, man must have *time* at his disposal: as Schulz put it, 'for spiritual creative activity and spiritual enjoyment'. However, in spite of the massive increases in labour productivity, which has the potential to free man from material slavery, capitalism maintains it. Thus although it is the case that the 'industrial revolution' *per se* could have enabled the *human* dimension of society to develop through man's access to free time, in the specific form of a *capitalist* 'industrial revolution', this was not to be and the duration of labour did not decline. The increased dependence of the worker on the means of production for survival instead facilitates the *exploitation* of him through the now 'excessive' duration of labour time *vis-à-vis social-material needs*. In this argument, it is possible to read the rudiments of *the surplus principle of revenue* for property owners, an idea which Marx foreshadowed in the following piece:

In theory, rent of land and profit on capital are *deductions* suffered by wages. In actual fact, however, wages are a deduction which land and capital allow to go to the worker, a concession from the product of labour to the workers, to labour. (CW,3,240–1)

The reality of labour's dependence upon capital and the significance of property rights in the appropriation of products were appreciated by Marx and would later enable him to formulate his theory of surplus Value based upon the exploitation of labour.

PRIVATE PROPERTY IN THE MEANS OF PRODUCTION AND NON-LABOUR INCOME

Marx considered both capital and land as forms of private property in the means of production. He adopted two separate headings for his discussion, viz. 'Profit of capital' and 'Rent of land', but, as will become clear in this section, he realised that these are only different expressions of the role that *ownership of the means of production* plays in a capitalist economy. That role is able to be explicated through the capital form. Indeed, the landowner is only a type of capitalist in the modern organisation of production.

Under the heading 'Profit of capital', Marx's first section was entitled simply 'Capital'. As a first step in the discussion, he noted that capital is a form of 'private property in the products of other men's labour' (CW,3,246). This is an important observation in two senses. Firstly, the existence of such private property is the basis of the exploitation of labour in all its historical forms, now including the form that developed under the regime of capital. Marx was to follow up and analyse much more fully the implications of this dimension of capital. Secondly, the observation foreshadows a generalised concept of capital. *All* products of labour expropriated under capitalism were to be considered as capital whether they were in the form of means of production or commodities for sale. Later Marx would explore fully the idea that capital circulated through different *forms* in the *totality* of the reproduction process.

However, as he recognised immediately, capital is a *social force* as well. Its implications go beyond those which follow its status as a physical force or form with its origins in 'stored up labour'. The social influence of capital rests on its property-rights dimension and Marx argued that

Capital is thus the *governing power* over labour and its products. The capitalist possesses this power, not on account of his personal or human qualities, but inasmuch as he is an *owner* of capital. His power is the *purchasing* power of his capital, which nothing can withstand. (CW,3,247)

Marx gave the title 'The profit of capital' to his second section dealing with capital. The existence and maintenance of capital requires that its advance brings a revenue return to its owner. As Adam Smith made explicit, this is the essential rationale of capital, for the capitalist

would have no *interest* in employing the workers, unless he expected from the sale of their work something more than is necessary to replace the stock advanced by him as wages and he would have no interest to employ a great stock rather than a small one, unless his profits were to bear some proportion to the extent of his stock. (Adam Smith, *WN*,54, quoted *CW*,3,248)[6]

It is evident in this passage that the origin of the return to capital is to be found in a *surplus* over the advances to employ labour. Neither Smith nor Marx explicitly recognised this principle, and Marx went on directly to consider the *phenomenal form* of profit as a *rate* relative to capital advanced without any concern for the *origin* of the revenue. The surplus idea is also present in two other passages paraphrased by Marx from the *Wealth of Nations*. The most explicit reference to the idea is in the following piece, but again Marx passed it by without comment:

But land, in almost any situation, produces a greater quantity of food than what is sufficient to maintain all the labour necessary for bringing it to market. . . . *The surplus, too, is always more than sufficient to replace the stock which employed that labour, together with its profits. Something, therefore, always remains for a rent to the landlord.* (WN,164, quoted, CW,3,261)

The other passage is one in which Smith argued that the greatest rate of return to capital corresponds to the lowest rate of wages (WN,108, cited CW,3,248). This reiterated the notion that wages effectively comprise a *deduction* from the exchange value of private property in the product appropriated by the owner of the means of production (CW,3,240–1). However Marx was also made aware through his reading of the *Wealth of Nations* that the realised rate of profits can be raised by other forces, especially secret cost reductions and monopoly advantages that reduce the effects of competition (CW,3,249).

Marx's third section on capital presented an amplification of the earlier reference to the dominant power of capital in the relations of production. This section was entitled 'The rule of capital over labour and the motives of the capitalist' and it is interesting to note that even given Marx's emerging critical stance on the nature of capital, the argument in this section comprises only paraphrased passages from the work of Smith and Say. Marx did not find it necessary to embellish these pieces at all in order to make *his* point.[7]

The thrust of the argument presented is that the capitalist's decisions and operations are motivated by the maximisation of his own profit return. The effects that these decisions and operations have on *human society* are not relevant to him, especially the question of how much labour is employed. Both Smith and Say were cited to this effect, and Marx found the capitalist condemned for his self-seeking behaviour at the expense of the general interest of society in works that he took to be authoritative statements on the political economy of capitalism. Adam Smith, for example, could not have been more explicit when he wrote of the capitalists that 'This is a class of people whose interest is never exactly the same as that of society, a class of people who have generally an interest to deceive and to oppress the public' (WN,278, paraphrased CW,3,250).

The negative side of capital was examined further in Marx's fourth section entitled 'The accumulation of capitals and the competition among the capitalists'. The argument in this section again followed very closely that presented by Adam Smith in the *Wealth of Nations*. Capital accumulation has the potential to raise wages and lower profits and prices through increased competition between capitals in a particular trade. Thus Marx saw competition as restraining the monopoly inclination of capitalists to raise prices in order to protect themselves against higher wages and lower profits due to any shortages of labour during periods of capital accumulation (CW,3,250–1). The problem that Marx recognised, though, is that capital accumulation has the additional (presumably longer-term) effect of causing increases in the concentration of capital and consequent increases in the monopoly power of the capitalists. Competition would only be effective if the ownership of capital remained in many hands. Marx noted that this outcome is improbable 'if capital is left to follow its natural course' with the added contradiction that 'it is precisely through competition that the way is cleared for this natural disposition of capital' (CW,3,251).

Marx found several impressionistic reasons for the progressive concentration of capitals during accumulation (CW,3,251ff.). These were not supported by any analytical justifications. Firstly, the absolute size of large capitals grows rapidly under the influence of the uniform rate of profits on all capitals. Secondly, the dominance of larger capitals is exacerbated by the tendency of the rate of profits to fall due to increased competition for investments and the need for competitive price cutting as accumulation proceeds. At the reducing rate of profits, small capitalists find it increasingly difficult to sustain an adequate *absolute* return for their needs. The result is that small-scale capitals disappear through being forced to consume their capital. Thirdly, the process of accumulation brings with it the increasing use of large-scale machinery and the small capitalist cannot compete in terms of the cost of production. Thus, his profit position is eroded even further by being disadvantaged in the market.

Capital accumulation also brings with it the possibility of overproduction due to the unco-ordinated relation of supply to demand under competitive capitalism. Marx quoted Pecqueur and Schulz on this issue (CW,3,254ff.) to the effect that overproduction introduces an instability into the economic system. The excess of commodities relative to effective demand results in business failures and a consequent increase in the ranks of the proletariat and an increase in the number of unemployed workers. This *crisis potential of capitalism*, along with the other negative human-social effects of capital accumulation referred to above, indicated to Marx that the situation of the workers would become increasingly difficult as the capitalist economy grows. This is a theme to which he would give much more attention in the future.

When Marx turned his attention to the topic 'Rent of land', he argued that rent as a *non-labour income* reflects the outcome of a socio-economic conflict. In this conflict, the particular socio-legal position of the landowner, as an owner of private property in a means of production, gives him the right and capacity to appropriate at least part of the periodic produce. Here again, much of Marx's argument is. presented by means of quotations, especially from the works of Adam Smith and Say.

He opened his discussion with a series of paraphrased quotations from these works (CW,3,259). Say's words set the tenor of the argument: '*Landlord's right* has its origin in robbery', and this was followed by a set of aphorisms from the *Wealth of Nations*:

The landlords, like all other men, love to reap where they never sowed, and demand a rent even for the natural produce of the earth. (WN,56)

rent may be considered as the produce of those *powers of nature*, the use of which the landlord lends to the farmer. (WN,385)

The *rent of land*, . . . considered as the price paid for the use of the land, is naturally a *monopoly price*. (WN,162)

Of the three original classes, that of the landlords is the one whose revenue costs them neither labour nor care, but comes to them, as it were, of its own accord, and independent of any plan or project of their own. (WN,276–7)

From these sorts of assertions Marx drew two insights that were to have a long-lasting influence upon his critique of capitalism and its political economy. The first of these is evident in the following comment:

These propositions of Smith are important, because, given equal costs of production and capital of equal size, they reduce the rent of land to the greater or lesser fertility of the soil. *Thereby showing clearly the perversion of concepts in political economy, which turns the fertility of land into an attribute of the landlord.* (CW,3,260, emphasis added)

It is a fact of capitalism that the *owners* of the means of production, land in the present case, receive income *by virtue of that ownership alone.* That the productive powers of the means of production thus appear to be ascribed to the owner is an illusion perpetrated by political economy and which obscures the role of the socio-legal status given to private property.

The second insight that Marx drew from the issue of rent is captured in the following passage:

The rent of land is established as a result of the *struggle between tenant and landlord.* We find that the hostile antagonism of interests, the struggle, the war is recognised throughout political economy as the basis of social organisation. (CW,3,260)

Here Marx overstated the pervasiveness of the conflict idea in political economy, but the significant point is that he expressed the simple but powerful idea that in a system of economic organisation in which shares in what is produced are linked to private property rights, the distribution process must be one based on a conflict of interests – here specifically between the landowner and tenant-farmer. More for one party means less for the other and the conflict outcome can only be contained through the socio-legal relativities of power over the appropriation of the products. The owners of means of production have a unique position in this respect as the product becomes their property at the point of production, although this is not immediately and precisely evident in the above argument because of the ambiguous status of the tenant-farmer.

Marx regarded the tenant-farmer as an important transitional figure in the evolution of the capitalist mode of production. Whereas the exploitation of the feudal world of landlord–serf relations was based upon traditional obligations which masked the conflict over distribution (CW,3,266f.), in the landowner–tenant relation, the exploitation occurs because of economic-power relativities and the conflict of interests is much more evident. The tenant-farmer, though, acquires a capitalist status because he employs labour and owns instruments of production with which to work the land under his control (CW,3,263f.). In this role, the tenant-farmer's status is indicative of the destiny of the landowner as capitalism comes to dominate agriculture and its feudal trappings disappear. Thus Marx argued that

in the person of the *tenant farmer* the landlord *has* already become in essence a *common* capitalist. And this must come to pass, too, in actual fact: the capitalist engaged in agriculture – the tenant – must become a landlord, or vice versa. The tenant's *industrial hucksterism* is the *landowner's* industrial hucksterism, for the being of the former postulates the being of the latter. (CW,3,286)

In this process of transition, *land* emerges as an explicit means of production and a manifest form of capital as it gradually shakes off its traditional form and role (CW,3,288f.). The basis of land's transformation to capital is its change of status from an inalienable, entailed family possession to an exchangeable commodity:

This huckstering with landed property, the transformation of landed property into a commodity, constitutes the final overthrow of the old and the final establishment of the money aristocracy. (CW,3,266)

Marx's concern in this argument was to expose landed property as an integral part of the domination and exploitation of man under the capitalist system. He wanted to dispel any remnants of romanticism attaching to the tradition of land ownership and use as he indicated in the following important summary passage when he argued that

landed property, the root of private property, be dragged completely into the movement of private property and that it become a commodity; that the rule of the proprietor appear as the undisguised rule of private property, of capital, freed of all political tincture; *that the relationship between proprietor and worker be reduced to the economic relationship of exploiter and exploited* [emphasis added]; that all . . . personal relationship between the proprietor and his property cease, property becoming merely *objective*, material wealth. . . . (CW,3,267)

In all of this, the emphasis was upon the socio-economic dynamics of historical evolution. For Marx, the status of particular categories and forms would always be interpreted as transitional for they are but products of a stage of history. The characteristics of capitalism are no exception to this as they represent a stage in the evolution of the form and situation of labour as the essential mediation between man and nature (CW,3,285f.).

As Marx read it, this transition of capitalism, especially as it affected agriculture, had its first theoretical reflection in the writings of the physiocrats. In terms of economic theory, this involved a fundamental change in the understanding of the concept of *wealth* from the static mercantilist idea of accumulated precious metals to an emphasis on its origins in the production process *per se*. This idea was taken up and developed by Adam Smith. In its handling of production as the source of wealth, physiocracy 'represents directly the decomposition of feudal property in *economic* terms', but at the same time, it returned to prominence the role of property rights in the organisation of the process and so represented 'its *economic metamorphosis* and restoration, save that now its language is no longer feudal but economic' (CW,3,292). An important aspect of the physiocratic concept of production was that while it did not conceive of land as capital, it did imply that 'land only exists for *man* through labour, through agriculture' (CW,3,292). This essential emphasis given to labour impressed Marx, although its treatment by the physiocrats had its limitations in that only a particular form of living labour was seen as productive. In emphasising agricultural production, the physiocrats had failed to generalise either production or productive labour. Production was left bound up with nature and no concept of abstract labour in general was formed (CW,3,292). The particular theoretical advance made by Adam Smith was to bring *capital* into greater prominence as the basis for a view of production and labour in which agricultural and industrial activities were not distinguished. This enabled the *origin* and *essence* of wealth to be situated in abstract labour (CW,3,292–3). However, for Marx, the important consequence of the physiocrats' developments was the provision of a framework for the analysis of production which emphasised *labour* and *private property*, the two categories upon which he concentrated in developing his critical theory of man's alienation under capitalism.

ALIENATION AND PRIVATE PROPERTY

In formulating his ideas on alienation, Marx drew together the main themes that emerged in his humanistic outline of the nature of capitalism which he had expressed largely through the words of political economy itself. It was now his intention to develop further his own critical assessment of the situation of *man as a worker* under capitalism.

Marx's fundamental objection to the *method* of political economy was that it accepts categories derived from the most apparent facets of the structure and operations of capitalism, as they are *immediately* perceived, as *sufficient* analytical components of a comprehension of the system. Private property, the separate identification of labour, capital and land, and competition are taken as given facts. No endeavour is made to question or comprehend their origin, existence and meaning as *particulars* of capitalism. The so-called 'laws' that regularise the analytical interaction of categories are not explained. Rather, they are stated as confirmations of appearances (CW,3,270–1).

By contrast, the objective that Marx set himself involved obtaining a deeper critical insight into the origin and meaning of the categories required to provide what he reasoned to be a sufficient comprehension of capitalism. The interrelationship between the categories were to be progressively built up into a *critical explanation* of the system that would transcend the more *descriptive* qualities of political economy (CW,3,271).

Marx began his critique of the situation of the worker under capitalism from that most essential '*actual* economic fact' (CW,3,271) that man labours to produce a product that is immediately the private property of someone else and therefore estranged from the true producer. Labour under capitalism, then, is such that its *results* are only manifested in its *objective output* and this falls short of the *human potential* of the activity. Indeed, the true fulfilment of the worker – his complete *human* realisation – is prevented by this situation of his labour:

the object which labour produces – labour's product – confronts it as *something alien*, as a *power independent* of the producer. The product of labour is labour which has been embodied in an object, which has become material. . . . Labour's realisation is its objectification. Under these economic conditions this realisation of labour appears as *loss of realisation* for the workers; objectification as *loss of the object and bondage to it*; appropriation as *estrangement, as alienation.* (CW,3,272)

Now it was not the *objectification per se* to which Marx objected. This is a necessary consequence of man's action on nature through labour. It was the *form* that objectification takes under capitalism that concerned Marx. *It is objectification together with the appropriating rights of private property in the means of production which alienates man from his product.* Moreover, by recognising that labour is the essential mediation between man and nature, the implication is that the capitalist arrangement alienates man from his object, nature. The situation of the worker under capitalism destroys the *natural* outcome of this mediation, viz. direct access to the material means of survival as the immediate product of man's labour. Thus man is lifted out of nature rather than being confirmed in it, as an integral part of it (CW,3,275–6).

Marx went on to argue that this most evident alienating consequence of the capitalist labour process, man's alienation from his object in nature and from the product of his labour, entails three other dimensions of alienation. Firstly, man's labour on an alien object means a loss of identification with the act of labour itself and he is alienated from his own most essential activity as a human being; secondly, the alienated form of individual labour under capitalism does not allow man readily to identify himself as a *species-being (Gattungswesen)* and his *actual* being is less than fully human in this sense; and thirdly, the demands of individual labour under capitalism leave him isolated from his fellow man in a state of *social alienation*. These three interdependent dimensions were explained in some detail by Marx.

Man's state of self-alienation in his labour activity follows directly from the alienated status of his object. As Marx saw it, 'The product is after all but the summary of the activity, of production. If then the product of labour is alienation, production itself must be . . . the activity of alienation' (CW,3,274). Man is forced to undertake labour irrespective of its form and he must leave his expressions of *human* being to his *non-labour time*.

The worker . . . only feels himself outside his work, and in his work

63

feels outside himself. He fells at home when he is not working, and when he is working he does not feel at home. His labour is therefore not voluntary, but coerced; it is *forced labour*. . . . Its alien character emerges clearly in the fact that as soon as no physical or other compulsion exists, labour is shunned like the plague. (CW,3,274)

These human expressions pursued at home tend to be confined to the more or less autonomous and animal-like activities such as eating, drinking and procreating: 'What is animal becomes human and what is human becomes animal' (CW,3,275). Thus, man's main ontological activity, *labour*, is devoid of *human* dimensions under capitalism.

For Marx, man's existence was necessarily *social*. That is, man's way through life will be marked by relations of one form or another with his fellow men, including the very basic set of socio-economic relations which are the essence of material survival. As well as relating *to* other men, man also identifies *with* them in a genus sense. Man is a *social-being* – or *communal-being (Gemeinwesen)* – and a *species-being (Gattungswesen)*. Under capitalism, man's being in both of these senses is not realised and his alienated status is thus compounded.

Man as a *species-being* is an element *in* a part of *nature*, in the human species or genus. At the same time, his existence depends *on* nature. Nature was regarded by Marx as an inorganic extension of man's body, so crucial is it to man's survival. He lives on and through nature and must remain in a constant interchange with it if he is not to die (CW,3,276).

Two aspects of man's *natural* existence in this sense are affected by the restrictions and demands of capitalism. First of all, an essential characteristic of man's species life in nature is its inherent *freedom* (CW,3,275). As a member of his species *per se*, man's activity is naturally free from formalisation – from any externally imposed form. Such freedom of activity is not allowed under capitalism. Man's interaction with nature in order to survive, that is, his labour, has its form determined by the requirements of capital. The second aspect of man's natural life impeded by the domination of capital is the *species identity* that labour has the potential to generate. Labour as a means merely to satisfy material subsistence misses the ontological point of labour. It can be an activity of free and

conscious expression of a multitude of human dimensions: 'productive life is the life of the species. It is life–engendering life. The
whole character of a species . . . is contained in the character of its
life activity' (CW,3,276). Here, then, is the germ of the *materialistic*
interpretation of the human condition that Marx would develop
much more fully in his later work.

In addition to this species alienation through capitalist labour,
Marx recognised a dependent isolation of the worker that results in
a *social alienation* as well (CW,3,277–8). As a worker, man finds
himself producing a product which is immediately the property of
someone else and designed to meet the needs of yet someone else.
Each man becomes a means to the survival of others and there is a
dependence between men built up as a consequence of the social
division of labour. But, as a *human* being, the worker is isolated
and estranged from his fellows for his dependence is a *material* one
only and lacks any *human* content. Just as his labour is dehumanised by capitalism, so are man's social relations, an argument that
foreshadows the idea of the 'fetishism of commodities'.

Marx found the social isolation and alienation of man under
capitalism accentuated by the use of *money* in realising his material
dependence on other men through exchange (CW,3,322ff.). Money
ensures that the *human* potentialities of man are irrelevant. Primarily, it gives him access to the material means of survival produced by others and, in a one-sided way, to these others as men:

Money is the *procurer* between man's need and the object, between
his life and his means of life. But *that which* mediates *my* life for
me, also *mediates* the existence of other people for me. For me it is
the *other* person. (CW,3,322)

Thus, 'If *money* is the bond binding *me* to *human* life, binding
society to me, connecting me with nature and man, is not money
the bond of all *bonds*?' (CW,3,324). Moreover, money distorts the
form of participation of man in society in that it acts as a surrogate
for his human qualities, or even lack thereof. 'Money is the alienated *ability of mankind*. That which I am unable to do as a *man*,
and of which therefore all my individual essential powers are incap-
able, I am able to do by means of money' (CW,3,325). And, even
more graphically:

I am bad, dishonest, unscrupulous, stupid; but money is honoured, and hence its possessor. Money is the supreme good, therefore its possessor is good. Money, besides, saves me the trouble of being dishonest: I am therefore presumed honest.
... Do not I, who thanks to money am capable of *all* that the human heart longs for, possess all human capacities? Does not my money, therefore, transform all my incapacities into their contrary? (CW,3,324)

By contrast, Marx envisaged that in a *human* society in which a man's relationship to other men is unmediated, participation would be a function of the *human qualities* that the man could demonstrate (CW,3,326).

In considering Marx's explanation of the origin of alienation under capitalism, it is pertinent to recall that he found in political economy the notion that capital played a dominant role in determining the nature of the system (CW,3,247). In its operational forms, capital appears as means of production and the products of the production process. Both of these forms are maintained as the property of the capitalist by virtue of the law relating to private property. But, Marx argued, private property has its origin in and is preserved by the labour of the workers, as political economy had recognised (CW,3,290).

Marx began his analysis of alienation with the empirical observation that the product of man's labour under capitalism is the immediate property of the owner of the means of production. As a consequence, man's product is alienated from him and Marx associated this most evident dimension of alienation with the existence of private property rights. The other three dimensions of man's alienation discussed above all follow from this expropriation of man's product and for Marx, alienation could be viewed as endemic to capitalism as a consequence of the system's foundation on private property. Alienation and private property are thus linked in such a way that Marx proceeded to argue that the overcoming of alienation requires the abolition of private property in the means of production and the development of a post-capitalist mode of production based on a different principle of access to and use of these means. This reasoning provided the most essential dimension of the rationale for a proletarian revolution and the emergence of a 'communist' system characterised at least by a form of labour that is

fully free, natural and human. Thus 'communism, as fully developed naturalism, equals humanism, and as fully developed
humanism equals naturalism' (*CW*,3,296).

Having exposed the human shortcomings of capitalism and the
potential for man to transcend them, Marx faced the challenge of
elaborating his critique of political economy in order to provide a
sufficient theoretical mediation for the revolutionary process. The
methodological basis for this theoretical elaboration was developed
as a consequence of Marx's critical re-examination of his philosophical premises. He began the self-clarification of his reading of
philosophy in the *Paris Manuscripts* with several critical pieces on
Hegel's idealist dialectics as presented in the *Phenomenology of
Mind* and the *Science of Logic*. This was followed, during 1844–6,
by a reassessment of the work of Feuerbach and. other 'Young
Hegelians' in the light of Marx's investigations in the *Paris Manuscripts*. As I will argue in the next chapter, this confluence of
humanistic critique, Hegelian dialectics and the rudiments of
materialism resulted in the formulation of the method of *historical
materialism*. Marx applied this method in the subsequent evolution
of his critique of capitalism and its theoretical reflection in political
economy.

PROUDHON, PRIVATE PROPERTY AND THE CRITIQUE OF
POLITICAL ECONOMY

In the autumn of 1844, Marx left the *Paris Manuscripts* unfinished
and embarked on a work of philosophical polemic written jointly
with Engels. It was Marx who wrote Chapter 4, Section 4 of *The
Holy Family, or Critique of Critical Criticism* with which I am
immediately concerned here (*CW*,4,23ff.). In this piece, he responded defensively to Edgar Bauer's translation of and critical
commentary on parts of Pierre–Joseph Proudhon's book *Qu'est-ce
que la propriété?* (*What is Property?*), second edition of 1841 (see
CW,4,ed.n.15). The importance of the piece in the present context
is that Marx took the opportunity further to develop the critical
ideas on the role of private property that he had been considering in
the *Paris Manuscripts*. He also raised some other associated critical
ideas in the process of his discussion and in all, presented a summary of some of the most important themes that he would carry

forward in his critique of political economy.

Marx ascribed to Proudhon an important place in the ongoing critical evolution of the political economy of capitalism. Proudhon's book on property represented a 'criticism of *political economy*' (CW,4,31). It would, on this basis, be transcended by the evolving critique of political economy, but this would not detract from its *historical* significance. It came from and was made possible by earlier critical developments: 'Proudhon's criticism has as its premise the criticism of the mercantile system by the physiocrats, Adam Smith's criticism of the physiocrats, Ricardo's criticism of Adam Smith, and the works of Fourier and Saint-Simon' (CW,4,31). Marx evidently saw himself also as a stage in this dialectic of intellectual history, probably as the ultimate stage leading to the transcendence of capitalism.

The important fact that Proudhon recognised explicitly was that 'All treatises on political economy take *private property* for granted' (CW,4,31–2). He took political economy to task for this unquestioning acceptance of the origin, nature and role of private property in capitalism. For Marx, Proudhon's merit was that he

makes a critical investigation – the first resolute, ruthless, and at the same time scientific investigation – of the basis of political economy, *private property*. This is the great scientific advance he made, an advance which revolutionises political economy and for the first time makes a real science of political economy possible. (CW,4,32)

Moreover, Proudhon emphasised the *human* effects of private property, an aspect of the capitalist system only exceptionally touched on by political economy: 'He takes the *human semblance* of the economic relations seriously and sharply opposes it to their *inhuman reality*' (CW,4,33). This, perhaps excessively (although allowance must be made for the polemical context), high praise for Proudhon was based upon Marx's already expressed view that private property is at the root of man's less than human situation under capitalism. To attack private property is to discredit precisely that institution which dehumanises the mode of production through alienation.

For Marx, private property represented the ultimate origin of the most profound contradiction of the capitalist system, viz. its form of distribution that manifests itself as the simultaneous existence of great wealth (in a material and value, stock and flow sense) and abject poverty. This dichotomy coincides with the class division between property owners and the non-owning proletariat. In Marx's view, such an antithetical situation results in a dialectical tension within the system which must bring with it some change. As he put it,

Proletariat and wealth are opposites; as such they form a single whole. They are both creations of the world of private property. *The question is exactly what place each occupies in the antithesis. It is not sufficient to declare them two sides of a single whole.* (CW,4,35, emphasis added)

There is a *positive* role in this antithesis for private property in that it endeavours to preserve itself through the perpetuation of the proletariat as the source of 'free' labour. In contrast to this, the proletariat's destiny, as Marx saw it, is to emancipate itself from the domination of private property by abolishing private property *and itself.* This basic contradiction of capitalism, then, is between a potential truly-human and natural existence for man and his present actual condition of life. Marx summarised this very important argument as follows:

The propertied class and the class of the proletariat present the same human self-estrangement. But the former class feels at ease and strengthened in its self-estrangement, it recognises estrangement as *its own power* and has in it the *semblance* of a human existence. The class of the proletariat feels annihilated in estrangement; it sees in it its own powerlessness and the reality of an inhuman existence. . . .
    Within this antithesis the private property-owner is therefore the *conservative* side, the proletarian, the *destructive* side. From the former arises the action of preserving the antithesis, from the latter the action of annihilating it. (CW,4,36)

The *theoretical* argument was thus immediately identified with *practical action* by Marx. The proletariat's revolutionary action to abolish private property represents *human consciousness in action* against its dehumanised existence – a realisation of the *distinction and unity* between *thought* and *being*.

Other contradictions of capitalism were also evident to Marx in the context of his reading of Proudhon. The existence and determination of the wages of labour is one aspect of capitalism which manifests a contradiction that is masked by what is made apparent by the analyses of political economy:

> in political economy wages appear at the beginning as the proportional share of the product due to labour. Wages and profit on capital stand in the most friendly, mutually stimulating, apparently most human relationship to each other. Afterwards it turns out that they stand in the most hostile relationship, in *inverse* proportion to each other. . . . The size of wages is determined at the beginning by *free* agreement between the free worker and the free capitalist. Later it turns out that the worker is compelled to allow the capitalist to determine it, just as the capitalist is compelled to fix it as low as possible. *Freedom* of the contracting parties has been supplanted by *compulsion*. (CW,4,32–3)

The apparent harmonious, freely contracted *exchange* of labour services for wages is an illusion. It is an undeniable characteristic of competitive capitalism that it is in the capitalist's interest to keep the wage as low as possible and that the sharing between the wage and profit in net produced exchange value involves a conflict over proportions – reflected in political economy's inverse relationship between wages and profit (loosely expressed at this stage in Marx's critique). The conflict is resolved by the power of private property over the worker desperate for employment in order to survive. This argument represents a pervasive theme in Marx's critique and later it would be fundamental in his formulation of the theory of Value and surplus Value.

In a similar vein, Marx objected to the treatment of exchange value determination by political economy:

> Value is determined at the beginning in an apparently rational way, by the cost of production of an object and by its social usefulness. Later it turns out that value is determined quite fortuitously and that it does not need to bear any relation to either the cost of

production or social usefulness. (CW,4,32)

Here the idea of a juxtaposition of *objective* and *subjective* exchange value determination was stated, with the overriding determination of exchange value being the state of the market. The immediate implication of this is that neither the *objective* nor the *subjective* basis for exchange value is indicative of the nature of capitalism. Its true nature is capricious as the *market* determination of exchange value suggests and whatever rationality is ascribed to the determination process by political economy is misleading. However, the significant thing here, in terms of the evolution of Marx's critique of political economy, is that he himself had not yet appreciated the nature and relevance of the multi-dimensional origin and structure of the category 'value'.

Marx did undertake some further discussion of exchange value determination in the present piece and some subsequently important ideas were raised, although their exposition lacked coherence. He recognised that costs of *production* are at the root of the process and that these costs include direct labour, material inputs and a provision for non-labour incomes associated with the existence of property rights over the means of production and the commodities produced. Such costs exist *prior to* any allowance for the effects of competition in the realisation process (CW,4,49). What Marx did not resolve analytically was the *origin* of the non-labour incomes that appear when the commodity is sold at its cost of production. He recognised the relevance of the capital–labour relation in the following passage, but did not go on to explore the matter further at this stage. For the present, the issue remained in the form of a question:

the question why the capitalist, who himself is *nothing* but an *individual* man, and what is more, a man *paid* by profit and interest, can buy back not only the product of labour, but still more than this product. To explain this . . . [it is necessary] to explain the relationship between labour and capital, that is, to expound the essence of capital. (CW,4,52)

The direction of Marx's future critical investigations was thus made explicit.

Mixed with Marx's praise for Proudhon's critical insights into capitalism were expressions of concern over their limitations. Marx's central concern was that Proudhon's work remained only a stage in the development of a complete critique of the system in that his analysis did not extend far enough in its *independent scope.* Proudhon

does not consider the further creations of private property, e.g., wages, trade, value, price, money, etc., as forms of private property in themselves as they are considered, for example, in . . . *Outlines of a Critique of Political Economy* by F. Engels . . ., but uses these economic premises in arguing against the political economists; this is fully in keeping with his historically justified standpoint . . . (CW,4,32)

Thus his analysis remained locked into *economic* preconceptions and the categorical framework of political economy. This is especially the case with respect to the concepts of *possession* and *property.* The estrangement of man could not, in Marx's view, be transcended by the equalisation of possession advocated by Proudhon, for the very *idea* of possession preserves estrangement whatever its *form.* In espousing this reform in the distributional structure of property, Proudhon left the root cause of alienation and inhuman society untouched (CW,4,42–3). In general, then, the challenge for Marx was to provide a critique of such scope that it transcends the preconceptions of political economy and probes beneath its categorical framework and analyses in search of the essential causes of man's situation under the regime of capital.

FURTHER CRITICAL INVESTIGATIONS IN POLITICAL ECONOMY

Marx moved to Brussels in February 1845 after being expelled from France. In his first year there he continued his quite extensive and intensive studies in political economy and associated historical and political topics. This work went on during a visit to Manchester in England during the summer. The results of these studies were recorded in twelve notebooks and covered some 434 large manuscript pages. He took excerpts from one or more works of fifty-four writers, many now virtually forgotten.

These notebooks remain unpublished and guidance as to their contents can only be obtained through a summary listing of the works that Marx read (*MEGA*,I/6,597ff.). This summary does include some examples of his excerpts and comments, but these are so sketchy, fragmented and out of context that they cannot form the basis of any formal analysis. Some brief observations on this work, however, are appropriate.

It is evident that many of the works that Marx read must have extended his knowledge of the more operational aspects of capitalism as they affected the workers' situation and of some of the proposals for the reform of the system. For example, he made more or less detailed studies of Babbage's *On the Economy of Machinery and Manufactures* (1832), Ure's *Philosophy of Manufactures etc.* (1835), Bray's *Labour's Wrongs and Labour's Remedy etc.* (1839), Thompson's *An Inquiry into the Principles of the Distribution of Wealth most Conducive to Human Happiness etc.* (1824), Tooke's *A History of Prices etc.* (1838), Wade's *History of the Middle and Working Class etc.* (1833) along with several of Robert Owen's works. He also returned for the third time to the study of Buret's *De la misère des classes laborieuses en Angleterre et en France* (1840) after having made substantial excerpts from it in the Paris notebooks (*MEGA*,I/3,413 – these excerpts have not been reprinted) and quoted from it several times in the *Paris Manuscripts* (*CW*,3,244ff.).

During this period Marx also must have read and discussed with Engels the latter's book *The Condition of the Working Class in England From Personal Observation and Authentic Sources* (*CW*,4,295ff.). This intense and passionate critical analysis of the horrific conditions imposed on workers by the regime of capital in the early nineteenth century was being written during 1844–5. It was published in Leipzig in June 1845 just prior to Marx's visit to Manchester where Engels was living at the time. The contents of this work, and Marx's own observations while he was in England, probably sharpened his awareness of the stark realities of proletarian misery and deprivation during this 'boom' period of the rise of capitalism. Unfortunately, there is no extant record of Marx's reading of Engels's book to provide us with any specific indication of its initial impact on him. If he did make notes on it, as would have been characteristic of his study method, they have been lost. Perhaps it was the case, though, that Engels's exposition was so graphic that no notes were needed to remind Marx of the distressing consequences of the system that was his critical object.

Marx's Brussels and Manchester notebooks also contain the results of his studies of several texts on political economy *per se*. He made his most extensive notes from the works of Petty, McCulloch, Senior, J.S. Mill, Sismondi and Quesnay. Four of these political economists have some ongoing significance in the present context. Petty was later to figure in Marx's critique of political economy as the first *classical* writer in Britain because of his early association of labour with exchange and use value formation (*CCPE*,52). The work of Quesnay, especially his *Tableau économique* in its various formats, was to become the main analytical source of Marx's comprehension of the unity of production and circulation as the basis for explaining the 'law of motion' of capitalism. Two of the others have more enigmatic places in the evolution of Marx's critique of political economy. At the present stage, Marx had available to him J.S. Mill's *Essays on Some Unsettled Questions of Political Economy* (1844). It is evident from the few comments that have been reprinted (*MEGA*,I/6,608ff.) that, on the basis of this work, Marx was not very impressed with the younger Mill's analyses. Whatever its original rationale and justification, this attitude was to continue, and even to harden, during Marx's life and he never made any worthwhile study of Mill's developing ideas. Even more puzzling is his treatment of Sismondi. In the present notebooks there is evidence that he made an intensive study of the two volumes of the *Etudes sur l'économie politique* (1837) filling forty-one large pages with excerpts and comments. This was to be his first and last recorded study of Sismondi's work in any detail, in spite of the retrospective similarity of some of the *analytical* ideas that Marx later applied in his critique of political economy.[8]

A separate manuscript, found recently amongst Marx's papers, indicates that during this period, he also again took up the study of Friedrich List's 1841 book *Das nationale System der politischen Ökonomie, Erster Band*. This work had been referred to by Engels in his 1843 'Outlines of a critique of political economy' (*CW*,3,421) and Marx had made substantial excerpts from it in the Paris notebook series early in 1844 (*MEGA*,I/3,414 – these particular notes have not been reprinted). Now, in the early months of 1845, he returned to the work and drafted a critical review of it in an endeavour to discredit the distorted impression of capitalism that it contained (*CW*,4,265ff.). The review remained as an unfinished manuscript, but it did serve to sharpen Marx's focus on political economy as the source of the false consciousness that served to obscure the essential, dehumanising nature of capitalism. List's work was a graphic example of how far this obscurantism could be carried in defence of bourgeois ideology!

To Marx, List espoused the cause of the German bourgeoisie and defended their activities as an essential function of German nationalism. In so doing, List failed to explicate the profoundly negative *human* impact of the industrial system and avoided emphasising its fundamental characteristic of serving the material and social self-interests of the bourgeois minority.

For List, industrial production in the factory system involved harnessing available 'productive forces' in the service of the *national* spirit. In Marx's reading of this argument, List personified the bourgeois concern to avoid the appearance of pursuing self-interests. The idealism of the bourgeoisie masks the reality of the system with hypocrisy:

The empty, shallow, sentimental idealism of the German bourgeois, beneath which lies hidden (is concealed) the pettiest, dirtiest and most cowardly shopkeeper's spirit (soul), has arrived at the epoch when this bourgeois is inevitably compelled to divulge his secret. But . . . he divulges it in a truly German, highflown manner. He divulges it with an idealistic-Christian sense of shame. *He disavows wealth while striving for it. He clothes spiritless materialism in an idealistic disguise and only then ventures to pursue it.* (*CW*,4,266, emphasis added)

The bourgeois demand is that the state act in their interest by providing tariff protection from international competition on the pretext of recognising the state's more general right to interfere in economic operations. But inside this external barrier, the pursuit of individual wealth proceeds with only *nominal* concern for a nationalistic spirit. In spite of appearing to pursue a '*spiritual essence*', Marx noted that the bourgeois capitalists take the opportunity to fill their pockets with the 'worldly exchange values' they pretend to despise (*CW*,4,274). In this context, List paraded the factory system as the most effective form of organisation for a spiritually sound and harmonious society (*CW*,4,275).

In his endeavour to foster this image of the 'spiritual harmony' of capitalism, List went on to argue that political economy should concern itself with the *means* for creating wealth (as a flow of exchange value) rather than with the wealth itself and its distribution (CW,4,277). The individual returns that the bourgeoisie gain from ownership of the means of production, and the associated ideas of exchange value and distribution, are not pertinent to an interpretation of a system of nationalistic political economy. National harmony and co-operation are to be emphasised. The German bourgeois thus

shrinks from speaking about the nasty exchange values which he covets and speaks about productive forces; he shrinks from speaking about competition and speaks of a national confederation of national productive forces; he shrinks from speaking of his private interest and speaks about the national interest. (CW,4,266)

Now it was Marx's view that in all of this, List defied even the *most apparent realities of capitalism* portrayed by political economy, the 'science' of the system. On behalf of the bourgeoisie, List saw his task as the creation of an idealised and socially sterilised version of the political economy of capitalism. His strategy was to try to discredit political economy for its theoretical reflection of the *realities* of the system while leaving the realities themselves untouched (CW,4,268ff.). In response to this, Marx defended some of the political economists, in particular Adam Smith, Ricardo and Sismondi, for their exposure of the principal tenets of capitalism without prejudice. Thus he noted that

Modern political economy starts out from the social system of competition. Free labour, that is to say, indirect slavery which offers itself for sale, is its principle. Its primary propositions are division of labour and the machine. And this can be given its highest development only in the factories, as modern political economy itself admits. Thus political economy today starts out from the factories as its creative principle. It presupposes present-day social conditions. (CW,4,284)

In Marx's view, List's stress on the role of 'productive forces' to the exclusion of recognising the pursuit of exchange value and profit was misleading. For while Marx was aware of the significance of 'productive forces' for comprehending the *material* dimension of this mode of production – its ability to produce in order to satisfy man's *material* needs – it was the *human* dimension of the system that he continued to emphasise. The objective of the capitalist is to produce, appropriate and realise *exchange value*, including *profit*. In this endeavour, 'productive forces' and the production of exchange value are a unity and not legitimately treated as separable as argued by List (*CW*,4,277). In this, political economy made the correct interpretation of the realities of capitalism:

If the 'School' [of political economy] made no '*scientific elaboration*' of the theory of productive forces *alongside* and *separately* from the theory of exchange values, it acted in this way because such a separation is an arbitrary abstraction, because it is impossible and cannot go beyond general phrases. (*CW*,4,284)

This characteristic of production has implications for the form of man's labour and a major effect on his conditions of life. In particular, labour itself exists as a *commodity* with exchange value and which is bought and sold as just another input to production. The consequence of this is a neglect of man's *human being* and he is perceived only as a 'productive force'. Marx stressed this point in a series of more or less rhetorical questions:

Is it a high appreciation of man for him to figure as a 'force' alongside horses, steam and water? . . . Is the bourgeois, the factory-owner, at all concerned for the worker developing his abilities, exercising his productive capacities, fulfilling himself as a human being, and thereby at the same time fulfilling his human nature? (*CW*,4,285)

As a response, he quoted two pertinent pieces from Ure's *Philosophy of Manufactures* (1835). Ure's arguments were, firstly, that the capitalist's concern for labour centred upon *replacing it* with machines and/or reducing its cost. Secondly, he argued that because *skilled* labour is less able to be manipulated and is more self-willed, it is desirable to develop unskilled labour only as 'a component of a *mechanical system*' (*CW*,4,285). It was Marx's conclusion again that capitalism could not be a *human* system: 'The bourgeois sees in the proletarian not a *human being*, but a force capable of creating wealth, a force which moreover he can then compare with other productive forces – an animal, a machine. . . . The whole of human society becomes merely a machine for the creation of wealth' (CW,4,286).

The situation of man under capitalism is a function of the particular 'social conditions' or 'political conditions' of the day. It was Marx's argument that these conditions are based upon the existence of private property. He granted that *industrial production* could be considered in abstraction from these conditions, but as such it is not an *historically* or *humanly* complete conception:

Industry can be regarded as a great workshop in which man first takes possession of his own forces and the forces of nature, objectifies himself and creates for himself the conditions of a human existence. When industry is regarded in this way, one *abstracts* from the *circumstances* in which it operates today, and in which it exists *as industry*; one's standpoint is *not* from within the industrial epoch, but *above* it; industry is regarded not by what it is for *man* today, but by what present-day man is for *human history*, what he is historically . . . (CW,4,281)

Thus Marx rejected List's view that industry can be interpreted in abstraction from the 'political conditions' of the day. For Marx, the *human* impact of the system could only be understood with industry placed in its *historically specific* setting (CW,4,277–9).

The neglect of the human side of productive activity under capitalism had been criticised by the 'Saint-Simon School' (CW,4,282–3). As Marx had previously argued, the transcendence of man's less than human condition under capitalism requires the abolition of private property and thus of the '*industrial*' mode of production. Only then can the 'productive forces' become *human* forces. Only then can proletarian labour become *human* labour (CW,4,279). Such an abolition would be achieved by a proletarian revolution in which the proletariat realises its role as the key to *human* history.

Today . . . [the proletariat] are still the slaves of the bourgeois, and in them he sees nothing but the instruments (the bearers) of his dirty (selfish) lust for profit; tomorrow they will break their chains and reveal themselves as the bearers of human development which will blow him sky-high together with his industry, which assumes the dirty outer shell – which he regards as its essence – only until the human kernel has gained sufficient strength to burst this shell and appear in its own shape. Tomorrow they will burst the chains by which the bourgeois separates them from man and so distorts (transforms) them from a real social bond into fetters of society. (CW,4,282)

Once again, then, Marx argued against the *human* consequences of the capitalist industrial system. In his polemic against List, he emphasised the potential for theoretical interpretation to distort and/or obscure the true nature of the system with respect to the situation that it dictated for workers and their families. List's bourgeois defence of the system was all the more crass because it went beyond the relatively open superficialities of orthodox political economy and distorted or obscured even the most obvious of capitalism's characteristics. Later, of course, this political economy itself would be subjected to a sustained and detailed critique by Marx on the basis that its presentation of the system also generated a false consciousness.

CHAPTER 3

The development of historical materialism

MARX'S MATERIALIST REACTION AGAINST HEGEL'S IDEALISM

In the previous chapter, I argued that Marx's critique of the capitalist system in his Paris writings centred upon his assertion of an ontological primacy for man's labour activity. Labour activity mediates between man and nature and forms the most essential of man's survival activities. The *form* of this labour, including its institutional context, is historically specific. Capitalism is one such context and it dictates a form of labour and the objectification of its results that alienates man in the several dimensions discussed in Chapter 1. This thesis of alienation is the centrepiece of Marx's humanist critique of capitalism and it is the transcendence of alienation that is the objective of the post-capitalist communist transition.

Marx found the roots of alienation in private property, the socio-legal institution upon which capitalism is founded. Such ownership of the means of production gives the capitalists the power to determine the form of labour and thus to dominate the situation of man and the nature of his being. A situation of alienation is one in which man's existence is deformed and his potential as a *human* being is not realised. The communist transition would include the abolition of private property in the means of production and the emergent mode of production would then allow for a freedom in the determination of the form of labour activity and objectification through which each man could become fully human.

Now in this argument, it is evident that Marx ascribed to the form of man's labour activity, and to his consequent situation in the contemporary mode of production, a fundamental role in determining his mode of existence as a human being. The immediate implication of this is that *human* history is founded upon the mode of production. Thus, human history is *materially* based and Marx developed this thesis into a methodological formalisation of his critique of capitalism as a phase of history.

The *materialist* roots of Marx's critique are quite evident in the *Paris Manuscripts* where he argued that the transcendence of man's alienated existence, through the communist transition to a fully-human society, depends upon changing the form of labour and its institutional setting. The *humanism* that Marx espoused is inextricably linked to man's *materialist ontology*. The criteria used to assess the *humanity* of society are essentially *materialist*. Indeed, in *The Holy Family, or Critique of Critical Criticism* (CW,4,3ff.), written soon after the *Paris Manuscripts*, Marx explicitly identified materialism with humanism at both the theoretical and practical levels. He argued that idealism – German speculative metaphysical philosophy –

will be defeated forever by *materialism*, which has now been perfected by the work of *speculation* itself and coincides with *humanism*. But just as *Feuerbach* is the representative of *materialism* coinciding with *humanism* in the *theoretical* domain, French and English *socialism* and *communism* represent *materialism* coinciding with *humanism* in the *practical* domain. (CW,4,125)

Although this passage refers to historical developments which Marx criticised, it is evident that in arraigning idealism against his own materialism, he intended to formulate a method of analysis which keeps the situation of man and the nature of man's being to the fore in the critique of capitalism. That is, *Marx's materialism* cannot be anything but an expression of *humanism* in this sense.[1]

Consider further the logic of the transcendence analysis in the *Paris Manuscripts*. The abolition of private property in the means of production is meant to facilitate a radical change in man's situation as a worker, that is, man in his most essential endeavours to manipulate nature in order to live. This involves a change in the mode of production developed under capitalism, most especially the abolition of the factory system and of the production of products for appropriation by the capitalist and subsequent exchange in the market. It is indicated in this argument that Marx believed from the beginning of his critical studies in political economy that the nature of man's existence is primarily determined by its material basis and that this nature would be changed if the form of the material basis changed. Thus in his transcendence analysis the most essential outcome is the abolition of private property for he saw this institution as the dominating force in shaping man's material life. If it is *not* the material basis of life that so affects man's situation, then this particular mode of transcendence could not have the predicted effect of humanising society. It would be possible for other dimensions of society, unchanged by such transcendence, to continue to operate and perpetuate man's less than human situation. Examples might be the political system or the religious system. Clearly, for Marx this was not the case as he interpreted it, and the *basic* logic of causal determination ran from man's involvement in production to man's general existence. This was to form one of the most fundamental tenets of historical materialism.

Marx began clarifying the methodological premises involved in this materialist–humanist analysis during 1844–5 in the third of the *Paris Manuscripts* and in *The Holy Family* through some critical reflections upon his philosophical roots. To this end, his critique of Hegel's idealism and Feuerbach's reaction to it were to prove most productive.

Marx's critique of Hegel's work focused on its historiographical implications and comprised most essentially a rejection of the idealist–monist determination of man's situation, that is, that man's *being* is a function only of his *thought*. There was in Hegel's analysis the methodological merit of his *dialectical* interpretation of man's historical progress and Marx preserved this in his critique. Man appeared for Hegel as an *historical being* engaged in a continuous struggle with his objective world, nature, albeit predominantly at the level of the intellect. Man interacts with his *given* world and through *reason* grasps it intellectually. Through *reason*, man is a self-creating and self-conscious being able to *comprehend and to conquer in thought* the alienated, objectified world around him. As Marx put it,

Just as *entities, objects*, appear as thought-entities, so the *subject* is always *consciousness* or *self-consciousness*; or rather the object appears only as *abstract* consciousness, man only as *self-*

consciousness: the distinct forms of estrangement which make their appearance are, therefore, only various forms of consciousness and self-consciousness . . . the dialectic of pure thought is the result. (*CW*,3,332)

Hegel appreciated the ontological significance of *labour*, an idea at least suggested by political economy's focus on the labour theory of value. Marx followed Hegel in this, although he interpreted Hegel's concept of labour to be restricted to the *intellectual* form as the processes of abstract reasoning and thinking. Be this as it may, Hegel did posit the *concept of alienation* in the context of the labour process and Marx summarised the issue as follows:

Hegel's standpoint is that of modern political economy. He grasps *labour* as the *essence* of man – as man's essence which stands the test: he sees only the positive, not the negative side of labour. Labour is man's *coming-to-be for himself* within *alienation*, or as *alienated* man. The only labour which Hegel knows and recognises is *abstractly mental* labour. Therefore, that which constitutes the *essence* of philosophy – the *alienation of man who knows himself*, or *alienated* science *thinking itself* – Hegel grasps as its essence. . . . (*CW*,3,333)

Thus, man's *intellectual* labour is a *positive* process for Hegel in that it enables man to situate himself *vis-à-vis* the alien real world. Man *is* reason and man's history comprises *experiences through reason*. Reality is rational and reason is reality.[2]

In spite of the merits of Hegel's historical–dialectical interpretation of man's alienated existence, Marx's critical reactions are immediately evident in the above passages. These may be explained further through a simple comparative analysis comprising three elements: the concept of man, the concept of man's objective world, and the nature of the interaction between man and his objective world.[3]

For Hegel, man *is* self-consciousness. The substance of man's self-creative being is thought or reason. The objective world with which Hegel's man interacts is *a phenomenon of reason*, that is, of the *Absolute Spirit* in a generalised sense. For man, the real world has no autonomous, independent status. It *is* only what he *reasons* it to be. Marx quoted Hegel to this effect as follows:

For us, mind has *nature* for its *premise,* being nature's *truth* and for that reason its *absolute prius.* In this truth nature *has vanished,* and mind has resulted as the idea arrived at being-for-itself, the *object* of which, as well as the *subject,* is the *concept!* (quoted CW,3,346)

And Marx argued the point further in his own words by noting that for Hegel

only *mind* is the *true* essence of man, and the true form of mind is thinking mind, the logical, speculative mind. The *human character* of nature and of the nature created by history – man's products – appears in the form that they are *products* of abstract mind and as such, therefore, phases of *mind-thought-entities.* (CW,3,332)

Moreover, 'It is clear . . . that thinghood is . . . utterly without any *independence,* and *essentiality vis-à-vis* self-consciousness; that on the contrary it is a mere creative-something *posited* by self-consciousness' (CW,3,335–6; cf.346).

In Hegel's view of history, man interacts with his objective world through a *mental struggle* the outcome of which is *knowing*:

The way in which consciousness is, and in which something is for it, is *knowing.* Knowing is its sole act. Something therefore comes to be for consciousness insofar as the latter *knows* this *something.* Knowing is its sole objective relation. (CW,3,338)

The ultimate result, the final development of reason, is the formation of omnipotent '*Absolute Knowledge*' (CW,3,330–1). Such a level of comprehension brings with it the transcendence of the alienated objective world *in thought.* This is possible because alienation is for Hegel *only and actually a mental process and state* and can thus be overcome by reason and through knowledge: 'For Hegel the *human being* – man – equals *self-consciousness.* All estrangement of the human being is therefore *nothing* but *estrangement of self-consciousness*' (CW,3,334). Hegel's man is 'comfortable' in the world *as it is* through his ability to reason. Marx interpreted this as implying a vindication of reality whatever its form may be (CW,3,331–2). The *form* of objective reality is not at issue for Hegel because man's alienation stems from its *objectivity,* its *externality, per se* and can be transcended in thought through knowing. Thus, if '*Objectivity* as such is regarded as an *estranged* human relationship which does not correspond to the *essence of man*, to self-consciousness', then 'it is *objectivity* which is to be annulled, because it is not the *determinate* character of the object, but rather its *objective* character that is offensive and constitutes estrangement for self-consciousness' (CW,3,333 and 338).

By contrast, Marx's view of man in history presented a very different set of analytical elements. Man himself is a *natural, objective being* with a *somatic* as well as a *mental* existence. His substantive being involves him in physical *and* intellectual activity. The objective world with which he interacts has *an autonomous, independent reality* no matter what he may *think* of it. Marx summarised his vision of man in the world in these terms:

Man is directly a *natural being*. As a natural being and as a living natural being he is on the one hand endowed with *natural powers, vital powers* – he is an active natural being. These forces exist in him as tendencies and abilities – as *instincts*. On the other hand, as a natural, corporeal, sensuous, objective being he is a *suffering*, conditioned and limited creature. . . . That is to say, the *objects* of his instincts exist outside him, as *objects* independent of him; yet these objects are *objects* that he *needs* – essential *objects*, indispensable to the manifestation and confirmation of his essential powers. To say that man is a corporeal, living, real, sensuous, objective being full of natural vigour is to say that he has *real sensuous objects* as the object of his being or of his life, or that he can only *express* his life in real, sensuous objects. (CW,3,336)

The interaction between man and his objective world is an intimate and very necessary one. Man's corporeal existence and his human being generally depends upon it. Marx was here adumbrating, more or less explicitly, a *materialist ontology* in which man's being is realised through his labour activity, the manifestation of his interaction with nature.

For Marx, the alienated situation in which man finds himself under capitalism is most immediately due to the form of his labour activity. The mode of transcendence of alienation advocated by Marx is a *materially active* one in that it involves a change in form of the production process. This *active transcendence* contrasts sharply with Hegel's *transcendence through reason* alone. Hegel

had the insight to formulate the *notion* of transcendence of alienation (CW,3,341–2), but it could only be an *ideal* transcendence
which leaves the *material* source of real alienation untouched.
Hegel's dialectic of human history is manifested in abstract and
logical categories and this is the setting of alienation and its transcendence in his history. Thus, for Hegel, 'The supersession of the
alienation is . . . nothing but an abstract, empty supersession of that
empty abstraction – the *negation of the negation*' (CW,3,343;
cf.329,342).

Marx went on to reiterate this humanist–materialist critique of
Hegel's idealist theory of history in *The Holy Family*. He began in
the opening lines of the Foreword to the book by noting the
contrast between *humanism* and *idealism*: '*Real humanism* has no
more dangerous enemy in Germany than *spiritualism* or speculative
idealism, which substitutes "*self-consciousness*" for the *real individual man* . . .' (CW,4,7). Hegel's history of man as self-
consciousness – the Absolute Spirit as the *subject* of history – was
again rejected by Marx:

Hegel's conception of history presupposes an *Abstract* or *Absolute
Spirit* which develops in such a way that mankind is a mere *mass*
that bears the Spirit with a varying degree of consciousness or
unconsciousness. Within *empirical*, exoteric history, therefore,
Hegel makes a *speculative*, esoteric history, develop. The history of
mankind becomes the history of the *Abstract Spirit* of mankind,
hence a *spirit far removed* from the real man. (CW,4,85)

For Hegel, *ideas* generated through reason are ontologically
omnipotent. For Marx, they are, *per se*, sterile in any material or
practical sense: '*Ideas* can never lead beyond an old world order
but only beyond the ideas of the old world order. Ideas *cannot
carry out anything* at all. In order to carry out ideas men are needed
who can exert practical force' (CW,4,119). Here Marx reiterated
the unity of theory and practice if ideas are to be translated into
effective action. He thus threw into question the role of the philosopher, i.e., the theoretician, in history. Hegel found the philosopher a role only as the *ex post* interpreter of events in *ideal* terms.
For Hegel,

The philosopher . . . is only the organ through which the maker of history, the Absolute Spirit, arrives at self-consciousness *retrospectively* after the movement has ended. The participation of the philosopher in history is reduced to this retrospective consciousness, for the real movement is accomplished by the Absolute Spirit *unconsciously*. Hence the philosopher appears on the scene *post festum*. (CW,4,85–6)

In Marx's view, the philosopher's role was much more substantial. It is the philosopher who is to provide the *critical theory* and thus the revolutionary consciousness upon which action for change is based. It is this role that Marx envisaged for himself in his humanist–materialist critique of political economy yet to be developed.

In *The Holy Family*, Marx extended his critique of philosophy to include a consideration of the method of *materialism* as it had developed in England and France (CW,4,124ff.). Marx found this materialist doctrine, based as it was upon an empiricist epistemology, to be an *anti-idealist* approach to the theory of man's interaction with his objective world (CW,4,125).

For the materialists, man's perception of his environment is a *direct reflection* in thought of what the senses pick up from it. Thus

if all human knowledge is furnished by the senses, then our concepts, notions, and ideas, are but the phantoms of the real world, more or less divested of its sensual [material] form. Philosophy can but give names to these phantoms. (CW,4,128)

There is no role for independent, abstract reason in a doctrine that gives the senses a monistic role in the generation of ideas. Experience, perhaps through the medium of education, provides the only basis for knowledge.

In this direct influence of material reality on man's psyche, Marx found a link to the idea of a communist transition in which the transcendence process must result in a *human* context in order to enable man *to be human* through activity. He summarised this argument in the following passage:

There is no need for any great penetration to see from the teaching of materialism on the original goodness and equal intellectual endowment of men, the omnipotence of experience, habit and education, and the influence of environment on man, the justification of enjoyment, etc., *how necessarily materialism is connected with communism and socialism.* If man draws all his knowledge, sensation, etc., from the world of the senses and the experience gained in it, then what has to be done is to arrange the empirical world in such a way that man experiences and becomes accustomed to what is truly human in it and that he becomes aware of himself as man. . . . *If man is shaped by environment his environment must be made human.* (CW,4,130–1, emphasis added)

From this, Marx carried forward the idea of 'the teaching of *materialism* as the teaching of *real humanism* and the *logical* basis of *communism*' (CW,4,131;cf.125), an idea which was to prove to be essential in his formulation of historical materialism as a theory of human history.

In opposing materialism to idealism, Marx suggested in the *Paris Manuscripts* that while these two monisms are both distinct from humanism, there is a sense in which such humanism should unify the positive elements of each: 'naturalism or humanism is distinct from both idealism and materialism, and constitutes at the same time the unifying truth of both . . . only naturalism is capable of comprehending the action of world history' (CW,3,336). Neither is an appropriate methodology for human history in the form of a *monism.* Some juxtaposition of their implications is required in a complete humanism. Thus, although empirical reality as the focus of materialism is perceived through the senses directly, it is not perceived independently of reason. For Marx, *consciousness* did have some independent influence on perception, but not to the extent asserted by idealism.[4] He hinted at his appreciation of this development in *The Holy Family* when he noted that while early materialism (he cited Bacon explicitly) retained a place for independent human responses to sensory data, the method soon became *mechanical*:

In this further evolution, materialism becomes *one-sided. Hobbes* is the man who *systematises Baconian* materialism. Knowledge based on the senses loses its poetic blossom, it passes into the abstract experience of the *geometrician.* Physical motion is sacrificed to *mechanical* or *mathematical* motion; *geometry* is proclaimed to be the queen of the sciences. Materialism takes to *misanthropy.* (*CW*,4,128)

In his own materialist method, Marx was to reinstate an eclectic view of the interaction of reason and reality in human history.

THE TENETS OF HISTORICAL MATERIALISM

In his critical reflections upon his philosophical roots, Marx also reacted against the work of the 'Young Hegelians', a group with whom he had once identified.[5] It was this reaction, combined with his earlier critical studies, which enabled Marx to crystallise his method of historical materialism. This development can be traced through three works of philosophical self-clarification drafted between 1844 and 1846: *The Holy Family, or Critique of Critical Criticism* of 1844 (*CW*,4,3ff.), the eleven aphoristic pieces known as the 'Theses on Feuerbach' of 1845 (*CW*,5,3ff.), and the manuscript of *The German Ideology: Critique of Modern German Philosophy etc.* of 1845–6 (*CW*,5,19ff.).[6] The first and last of these works, both written in conjunction with Engels, contain much that is not relevant in the present context. My analysis of them is confined specifically to some particular parts of Marx's contributions in an endeavour to seek out the roots of his materialist interpretation of human history, the methodological core of his critique of political economy.

The 'Young Hegelians'[7] purported to be *critics* of Hegel's work, but Marx found that they generally retained in their writings on theology and philosophy a faith in the *independent* power of ideas. That is, they remained locked into idealist ways of thinking about the world. To a considerable extent, though, Feuerbach was an exception to this and his contribution was singled out by Marx for special, albeit still critical, attention.

At the beginning of *The German Ideology*, Marx set out in general terms his misgivings about the philosophy of the 'Young Hegelians'. His argument was that they did not really use philosophy effectively to tackle the *real* material problems of life resulting from the conditions of the production system. Their philosophical critique remained idealist, for

German criticism has, right up to its latest efforts, never left the realm of philosophy. It by no means examines its general philosophic premises, but in fact all its problems originate in a definite philosophical system, that of Hegel. Not only in its answers, even in its questions there was a mystification. (*GI,CW,5,28*, emphasis added)

The 'Young Hegelians' identified the real enemy of man as *ideas*. It was the *reform of ideas* that would emancipate man from his self-imposed oppressions, all of which were interpreted to be essentially religious. As Marx read their work, they 'are in argument with the Old Hegelians in their belief in the rule of religion, of concepts, of a universal principle in the existing world', and he concluded that

Since the Young Hegelians consider conceptions, thoughts, ideas, in fact all the products of consciousness, to which they attribute an independent existence as the real chains of man (just as the Old Hegelians declared them the true bonds of human society) it is evident that the Young Hegelians have to fight only against these illusions of consciousness. (*GI,CW,5,30*)

The attack by the 'Young Hegelians' was thus only on philosophy and not on the *real* oppressions of man originating in his *material* environment. Their attack was a 'demand to change consciousness [which] amounts to a demand to interpret the existing world in a different way, i.e. to recognise it by means of a different interpretation.' From this it followed 'that they are in no way combating the real existing world when they are combating solely the phrases of this world', and that it had 'not occurred to any one of these philosophers to inquire into the connection of German philosophy with German reality, the connection of their criticism with their own material surroundings' (*GI,CW,5,30*). Marx went on to emphasise that 'it is possible to achieve real liberation [of man] only in the real world and by real means', for ' "Liberation" is a historical and not a mental act, and it is brought about by historical conditions . . .' (*GI,CW,5,38*).

It was Bruno Bauer whom Marx cited most explicitly with respect to his ineffectiveness as a critic of idealism. In Marx's view,

Bauer and the 'Young Hegelians' had not grasped the ontological significance of the material world for man. In the *Paris Manuscripts*, Marx quoted from Bauer in the following Hegelian idealist terms: 'They [the French materialists] have not yet been able to see that it is only as the movement of self-consciousness that the movement of the universe has actually come to be for itself, and achieved unity with itself' (quoted CW,3,327). For Bauer, man's inwardly satisfied self-consciousness was still the independent *subject* of history. But, as Marx read Bauer's work, this conscious subject took on the particular form of the activity of *criticism* itself and the intellectual process of the philosopher became the centrepiece of human history. This effectively transported Hegel's *Absolute Spirit* into the more specific form of the *mind* of the critical philosopher. In Marx's view, this failed altogether to get to the root of the problems of the idealist interpretation of history. Rather it merely expressed it in a different, somewhat ludicrous, way. Marx's amusement at this endeavour is evident in the following passage which summarises his reading of Bauer:

he [Bauer] proclaims criticism to be the Absolute Spirit and *himself* to be *Criticism*. . . . *Criticism* sees itself incarnate . . . exclusively in a *handful* of chosen men, in Herr *Bauer* and his disciples. . . . No longer like the Hegelian Spirit does he make history *post festum* and in imagination. He *consciously* plays the part of the World *Spirit* in opposition to the mass of the rest of mankind . . . he invents and executes history with a purpose and after mature reflection.

On the one side is the mass [of the people] as the passive, spiritless, unhistorical, *material* element of history. On the other is *the* Spirit, *Criticism*, Herr Bruno and Co. as the active element from which all *historical* action proceeds. The act of transforming society is reduced to the *cerebral activity* of Critical Criticism.
(*HF*,CW,4,86)

Just as with Hegel, then, Marx interpreted Bauer and the 'Young Hegelians' to have had a theory of history in which man is de-activated in a material sense. History was portrayed as a process which is dictated by and takes place in *thought* – this time through the agency of the 'Young Hegelian' philosophers acting as the repository of all wisdom. Whether or not Marx accurately or completely represented the philosophy of Bauer and the 'Young Hegelians' is immaterial here in the sense that his satirical argument serves admirably to emphasise his protest against the folly of such idealism.

From amongst the 'Young Hegelians', it was his critique of Feuerbach's work that provided Marx with the most productive source for the development of his own materialist interpretation of human history.[8] Feuerbach made a distinct break from Hegel's idealism and formulated a *humanist materialism* – an anthropology – that brought *men* in the real world to prominence in philosophical analysis. Marx commented in the *Paris Manuscripts* that 'It is only with *Feuerbach* that *positive*, humanistic and naturalistic criticism begins' and that Feuerbach's writings are 'the only writings since Hègel's *Phänomenologie* and *Logik* to contain a real theoretical revolution' (CW,3,232;cf.328–9).

In Feuerbach's view, *anthropology* is the basis of all science and he wrote of this in 1843, 'The new philosophy makes man, together with nature, which is the basis of man, into the unique, universal and highest object of philosophy, that is, it makes anthropology together with physiology into the all-embracing science.'[9] Marx agreed with this *human* basis for 'science', but Feuerbach left his formulation imbedded in nature and isolated from the sociopolitical reality that mediated in man's actual relationship to nature. Marx recognised this limitation very early in his study of Feuerbach for he wrote to Arnold Ruge on 13 March 1843 that 'Feuerbach's aphorisms seem to me incorrect only in one respect, that he refers too much to nature and too little to politics. That, however, is the only alliance [i.e. with politics] by which present day philosophy can become truth' (CW,1,400). Overall, Feuerbach's anthropology remained the basis for a critique of theology and philosophy rather than for a *social* critique.

As a critique of theology and philosophy, Feuerbach's critical theory remained *contemplative*. Man the 'thinker' was Feuerbach's immediate focus rather than man the 'doer':

Feuerbach's 'conception' of the sensuous world is confined on the one hand to mere contemplation of it, and on the other to mere feeling; he posits 'Man' instead of 'real historical man'. . . . He [Feuerbach] does not see that the sensuous world around him is not a thing given direct for all eternity, remaining ever the same, but the product of industry and of the state of society; and, indeed [a product] in the sense that it is an historical product, the result of the activity of a whole succession of generations, each standing on the shoulders of the preceding one, developing its industry and its intercourse, and modifying its social system according to the changed needs. (*GI,CW,5,39*)

Man is really an historically active being who is constantly working on his natural and self-created environment. This activity is ontologically fundamental in that through activity, man *makes* and *remakes* his world and his being in its several dimensions. While Feuerbach's emphasis on man as a self-conscious being represented an advance on the psychological sterility of man in 'pure' materialist doctrine, his concept of man had its limitations, for he only conceived of man as an 'object of the senses' and not as 'sensuous activity' in a particular socio-economic situation (*GI,CW,5,41*). Such a man remains *passive*, albeit *thoughtful*, about history which for him is but a passing parade. Thus 'As far as Feuerbach is a materialist he does not deal with history, and as far as he considers history he is not a materialist. With him materialism and history diverge completely . . .' (*GI,CW,5,41*). Ironically, *idealism* does give man an *active* role in making his own history, but it is a *conscious* history only and its *subject, reason*, is detached from *real* events.

Marx had already summarised these ideas in 'Thesis I' of the 'Theses on Feuerbach', written in April 1845:

The chief defect of all previous materialism (that of Feuerbach included) is that things [*Gegenstände*], reality, sensuousness are conceived only in the form of the *object, or of contemplation*, but not as *sensuous human activity, practice*, not subjectively. Hence, in contradistinction to materialism, the active side was set forth abstractly by idealism – which, of course, does not know real, sensuous activity as such. Feuerbach wants sensuous objects, really distinct from conceptual objects, but he does not conceive human activity itself as *objective* activity. (*TF,CW,5,3*)

He supplemented this summary in the briefer 'Thesis V': 'Feuerbach, not satisfied with *abstract thinking*, wants [*sensuous*] *contemplation*; but he does not conceive sensuousness as *practical*, human-sensuous activity' (*TF,CW,5,4*).

An important extension of Marx's critique so far was that man's consciousness cannot legitimately be detached from the form of his active relationship with his environment. The way man *thinks* is a function of this activity and is, indeed, a component of man's activity considered in its *totality*. For Marx, both man's objective world *and* his thought were realities and they existed in a dialectical relationship to each other. In Marx's interpretation, the objective world was more than a concept as the *idealists* would assert, and man's thought was more than a mere composite of sensory perceptions of the objective world as the *'pure' materialists* would assert. In 'Thesis II', Marx expressed the idea that thought and practice are an inseparable unity in any meaningful understanding of the human situation:

> The question whether objective truth can be attributed to human thinking is not a question of theory but is a *practical* question. Man must prove the truth, i.e., the reality and power, the this-worldliness of his thinking in practice. The dispute over the reality or non-reality of thinking which is isolated from practice is a purely *scholastic* question. (*TF,CW,5,3*)

In 'Thesis IV', Marx focused upon Feuerbach's theological approach to man's situation, but the generation of religious ideas can be read by analogy to parallel the generation of all mental constructs. In this 'Thesis', then, Marx argued further that man's ideological world is a function of the real, or secular, world *and* can only be changed by changing its source therein:

> Feuerbach starts out from the fact of religious self-estrangement, of the duplication of the world into a religious world and a secular one. . . . But that the secular basis lifts off from itself and establishes itself as an independent realm in the clouds can only be explained by the inner strife and intrinsic contradictoriness of this secular basis. The latter must, therefore, itself be both understood in its contradiction and revolutionised in practice. (*TF,CW,5,4*)

This link between material activity and the generation of ideas became the basis of the argument in 'Thesis III' that historical change is a function of man's mental and material activity in its totality. The 'pure' materialists had, in Marx' interpretation, identified separately a group of 'educators' who are able to teach man how to change his world. What this thesis neglected was that the ideas of the 'educators' are themselves a function of the real world *and* that *all* men are 'educated' in this sense:

The materialist doctrine concerning the changing of circumstances and upbringing forgets that circumstances are changed by men and that the educator must himself be educated. This doctrine must, therefore, divide society into two parts, one of which is superior to society.

The coincidence of the changing of circumstances and of human activity or self-change can be conceived and rationally understood only as *revolutionary practice. (TF,CW,5,4)*

Here Marx again espoused the unity of theory and practice as the key to social change; in particular, *revolutionary* practice based upon a theory derived from the perception of reality through an appropriate teleological framework. Feuerbach did not appreciate this role of philosophical theory as Marx asserted at the end of 'Thesis I': 'he does not grasp the significance of "revolutionary", of "practical–critical", activity' *(TF,CW,5,3)*.

Marx's theory of man emphasised that he is a *species* and a *social* being in line with the ideas of Feuerbach. Again, though, Feuerbach's conception was limited in scope for it stressed the individuality of man, albeit in a *species* context. But, this species identity was a *natural* and *passive* one and did not express the *active social extension* of this man-to-man relationship in an historically specific *societal* context. A *societal form* is the immediate setting of man's activity and is consequently of vital ontological significance, a point that Feuerbach missed. 'Thesis VI' dealt with this issue:

Feuerbach resolves the essence of religion into the essence of *man*. But the essence of man is no abstraction inherent in each single individual. In its reality it is the ensemble of the social relations.

Feuerbach, who does not enter upon criticism of this real essence is hence obliged:

1. To abstract from the historical process and to define the religious sentiment [*Gemüt*] by itself, and to presuppose an abstract – *isolated* – human individual.

2. Essence, therefore can be regarded only as 'species', as an inner, mute, general character which unites the many individuals *in a natural way*. (*TF,CW,5,4*)

Moreover, Marx added that *ideas*, too, are societally specific in 'Thesis VII': 'Feuerbach, consequently, does not see that the "religious sentiment" is itself a social product, and that the abstract individual which he analyses belongs to a particular form of society' (*TF,CW,5,5*).

The important consequence of all this for Marx's *humanist materialism* was that an image of man as an isolated being is an image in tune with man's place in the competitive 'civil society' of capitalism, but not with man as he has the *potential* to be in a truly human, *communal* society. Thus 'Thesis IX' read, 'The highest point reached by contemplative materialism, that is materialism which does not comprehend sensuousness as practical activity, is the contemplation of single individuals and of civil society'; and Marx immediately followed this with the conclusion in 'Thesis X' that '*The standpoint of the old materialism is civil society; the standpoint of the new is human society, or social humanity*' (*TF,CW,5,5*, emphasis added). The *humanistic* dimension of Marx's materialism could not have been more clearly stated than this.

Real man's *life* in society is *practical* in the sense that it is a manifestation of his *total activity*, both intellectual and material. The intellectual side of man's activity was by no means purely metaphysical for Marx as it was for the idealists. As Marx argued in 'Thesis VIII', *reason* is perceived in activity: 'All social life is essentially *practical*. All mysteries which lead theory to mysticism find their rational solution in human practice and in the comprehension of this practice' (*TF,CW,5,5*).

The 'Theses on Feuerbach' culminate in the well-known 'Thesis XI': '*The philosophers have only* INTERPRETED *the world in various ways; the point is to* CHANGE *it*' (*TF,CW,5,5*, some emphasis added). Thus, interpretation of the world, even *critical* interpretation, can only be one phase of facilitating historical change. Reason and theory, knowing, alone cannot change the *real* world. It can only bring man to a state of self-conscious reconciliation with existent historical reality. History is actually a consequence of man's material *actions* in a dialectical interplay with his *ideas.* It is revolutionary *praxis* which will generate the communist transition to a truly *human* society.[10]

In the further development of these tenets of materialism to be found in *The German Ideology*, Marx presented a more detailed analysis of the determinants of man's material, psychological and social situation in its historical–institutional context. The dominant determining factor was, in Marx's view, the *mode of production* with its various interdependent dimensions, a thesis already evident in the *Paris Manuscripts* critique of capitalism. The analysis was now generalised to include a comprehension of pre-capitalist modes of production, but the centre of critical attention remained capitalism. Also, with respect to the critique of capitalism the analysis of production was extended to a separate consideration of the material *forces of production* and the human–social *relations of production*, including the relationship between them and their institutional consequences. Marx's immediate concern was to provide a comprehension of these more *operational* aspects of capitalism, including man's involvement and situation in its processes and the potential for changing such involvement and situation for the better. His *subject*, though, was still real, living, individual man: 'The first premise of all human history is, of course, the existence of living human individuals' (*GI,CW*,5,3). Marx's stance here was still strictly humanist, but his emphasis was now less on the ontological details of man's individual existence and more on the determinants of his life situation broadly considered.

The development of the materialist interpretation of history in *The German Ideology* began with man in his activity as a *producer* engaged in the primary material maintenance of his existence. For, as Marx recognised, the simple truth was that 'man must be in a position to live in order to be able to make history' (*GI,CW*,5,41). Man must sustain himself through *continuous* activity designed to serve at least his most essential biological needs. This gives a primacy to production, the process of modifying nature through labour in order to satisfy these needs. Production is the 'first historical act' and the most permanent and pervasive one (*GI,CW*,5,42). Man *must* meet his immediate needs and meet new needs as they develop. For Marx, this was man's most essential mode of expressing his life, for without it, his life ceases. Moreover, without procreation his life as a *species* would soon cease, so this, too, had to be considered a basic process in human history (*GI,CW*,5,42–3).

Man's activity as a producer of his individual existence and his species has both *natural* and *social* dimensions. He interacts with nature and with his fellow man in an organised way to ensure the continuation of human life. The *form* of his organisation of his activity has a profound effect on the nature of man's existence. It dominates what he *is*, that is, his *being* and his *situation* in a material, social and psychological sense. The mode of production is much more than a mere *physical* mediation in man's life. 'Rather it is a definite form of activity . . ., a definite form of expressing . . . life, a definite *mode of life* . . .' (*GI,CW,5*,31). In all its dimensions, man's being is dominated by the material conditions of his life. Marx included here man's *consciousness*, his intellectual life, arguing that the 'phantoms formed in the brains of men are . . . necessarily . . . sublimates of their material life-process' (*GI,CW,5*,36). Thus, '*It is not consciousness that determines life, but life that determines consciousness*' (*GI,CW,5*,37, emphasis added). Moreover, because man's life is always set in a *social* context, the determination of his consciousness is 'from the very beginning a social product, and remains so as long as men exist at all' (*GI,CW,5*,44). Man's social existence and his consciousness are, then, highly interdependent facets of his being.

Man expresses his consciousness and his intellectual life through the creation of *institutional forms* which evolve in a mutual interdependence with his *ideology*. This system of institutions and ideas was described by Marx as the '*superstructure*' of society and it sits on the foundation of man's organisation of his production system (*GI,CW,5*,35–6).

In Marx's materialist interpretation of history, then, society comprised two interdependent structural components and an assessment of man's life situation requires an appreciation of his place in both, viz. the system of production (the 'base') and the institutional–ideological system (the 'superstructure'). This situation will be more or less human depending upon the detailed conditions that exist in these historically specific systems.

Consider first the system, or mode, of production. In the *Paris Manuscripts*, Marx presented the capitalist production process in terms of the form of labour activity and objectification that it involves and he focused on its consequences for man in the form of alienation in its several dimensions. The operational form that production takes was referred to in terms of the division of labour and its relationship to the socio-legal institution of private property rights which perpetuates the mode of production. In *The German Ideology*, the *structural form* of the mode of production was emphasised through its two summary dimensions, viz. the material *forces of production* and the human–social *relations of production*.

The *forces of production* comprise the operational structure of the production and circulation of commodities which satisfy man's material needs. Marx recognised that the most fundamental characteristic of the capitalist production process determining the form of its operations is the division of labour (*GI,CW,5,32*). He paid most attention to the *social* division of labour between sectors of production. This form of the division necessarily entails the development of an exchange-circulation process to complement production in the totality of the capitalist mode of production. Marx also mentioned the physical specialisation and division of labour *within* lines of production, but he did not go on to explore its important relationship to the use of machinery and the consequent ramifications for the *form* of labour under capitalism.

It was evident to Marx that production is more than a material process. It is immediately a *social* process as well and he used the category *relations of production* as the summary reference to this aspect of the mode of production. Most obviously, production based on the social and physical division of labour involves man in a relationship with other men in order to produce through co-operation and in order to meet all his material needs through exchange. These are the relational implications of the production-circulation unity that comprises the *forces of production*. However, for Marx these were the least significant aspects of the *relations of production* at this stage, in spite of the fact that later they were to be more fully developed as the basis for the existence of Value and the 'fetishism of commodities'. The important dimension that he developed here was the *class structure* that the relations involve as a consequence of private property rights. It was through an analysis of these rights as they influence the relations of production that the *mutual interdependence* of the mode of production and the 'superstructure' of legal and political institutions and ideology became evident to Marx.

There is an interdependence between the *forces* and *relations* of production that is manifested as the relationship between the social division of labour and private property rights over the means of production and products. Throughout history, this division of labour, the property system and the *relations of production* have existed in an interdependent relationship. Marx surveyed the historical development of this relationship briefly using four stages – tribal, city-state or communal, feudal and bourgeois capitalist (*GI,CW,5*,32ff. and 63ff.) – and concluded that 'These different forms [of production] are just so many forms of the organisation of labour, and hence of property' (*GI,CW,5*,74). In this development process, each successive stage brings a social structure that increasingly involves a *class division* based on the criterion of ownership. The class division becomes most distinct in the nineteenth century capitalist system where the *relations of production* are essentially those between the bourgeoisie who own the means of production and the propertyless workers, the proletariat. The system of private property rights here becomes the essential determinant of the social structure which arises on the basis of the form of the *relations of production*.

Now a consequence of a form of socio-economic structure based so distinctly on ownership criteria is that the fruits of production are *immediately* the sole property of the owning class. And once feudal tradition has lost is impact, there arises an open antagonism between the two classes, for what one appropriates and keeps the other cannot legally have access to. This antagonism is controlled directly by the legal system, but the effects of its presence are suppressed by the more subtle means of the *ideological system* through which man interprets his society and his situation in it. Marx argued that the dominant and pervasive system of socio-economic interpretation available in any society is that formulated by or on behalf of the ruling class: 'The ideas of the ruling class are in every epoch the ruling ideas: i.e. the class which is the ruling *material* force of society is at the same time its ruling *intellectual* force' (*GI,CW,5*,59). The basis of class rule is *economic* domination, and 'The ruling ideas are nothing more than the ideal expression of the dominant material relations, . . . hence of the relations which make the one class the ruling one . . .' (*GI,CW,5*,59). The ideology generated by the ruling class under the regime of capital inevitably *assumes* private property rights to be ordained and renders their effects to be innocuous by formulating a veneer of equity over them. This veneer is not penetrated because, in Marx's view, *there is evident in history a penchant for man to interpret the*

dominant ideology of the day as an independent, value-free entity
(*GI,CW,5,*60).

Perhaps the primary objective of Marx's work in critical theory
was to break through this almost unconscious acceptance of a 'false
consciousness'. His intention was to subject political economy, the
most dominant ideology of capitalism, to a critical dissection in
order to expose the essential roots of its forms and functions. He
hoped that this would generate an alternative proletarian consciousness in which a revolutionary emancipation from oppression
was shown to be a possibility.

In the analysis in this section an endeavour has been made not to
ascribe to Marx a mechanical, deterministic relationship between
the mode of production and the rest of society. It is the case that
while Marx's language was not very precise in this regard, he
interpreted the mode of production to be the *dominant* element in a
social structure in which all the elements are interdependent. That
is, his thesis was one of structural *consistency* rather than *causality*.
Marx did not address this issue specifically, but he made aphoristic
references in his work to the effect of the 'superstructure' in its
various dimensions on the mode of production. There existed, then,
an interdependence between these two structural and operational
'levels' of society. At one point Marx reiterated the principles of his
materialist interpretation of history giving deterministic prominence to the forces and relations of production in the formation of
social classes, the state and the various forms of consciousness. To
this brief outline he added that representation of the consequent
social totality included '*the reciprocal action of these various sides
on one another*' (*GI, CW,5,*53, emphasis added). At another point,
he argued similarly that

Industry and commerce, production and the exchange of the
necessities of life in their turn determine distribution, the structure
of the different social classes *and are, in turn, determined by it as to
the mode in which they are carried on.* . . . (*GI,CW,5,*40, emphasis
added.)

Marx concluded that his interpretation of human—social history
'*shows that circumstances make men just as much as men make
circumstances*' (*GI,CW,5,*54, emphasis added). And as Marx

argued in his 'Thesis III' on Feuerbach (*TF,CW,5,4*), men make and change their own historical situations and circumstances *and* this involves *self-conscious action*. Such consciousness is influenced by the mode of production and probably distorted by the ruling-class ideology of the day. This sort of scenario was made most explicit in Marx's theory of revolution and the communist transition out of capitalism. Historical change depends upon the effective *unity of theory and practice*. While the *practice* may be initiated in the sphere of production, the *theory* originates in the 'superstructure' as a proletarian consciousness. The impetus for revolution comes from the reaction of the proletariat when they are made aware, *through access to a detailed critique of political economy*, that they live in a society with massive material potential through its *forces of production*, but that the form of the *relations of production* acts to restrict their access to this material wealth. A social tension is the most immediate result and the *relations of production* come to be perceived as fetters on the optimal operation of the *forces of production* as assessed by their contribution to mass human welfare. (For Marx's outline of this process, see *GI,CW,5,52–3,82,438–9*.) The communist transition through revolution then brings a relief through this social tension by changing the *relations of production* and the 'superstructure' (including the dominant ideology) in such a way that the *forces of production* available are applied to *human* objectives in a *human* society. In 1859 Marx summarised these thoughts on the transition out of capitalism as follows:

> The bourgeois mode of production is the last antagonistic form of the social process of production – antagonistic not in the sense of individual antagonism but of an antagonism that emanates from the individual's social conditions of existence – but the productive forces developing within bourgeois society create also the material conditions for a solution of this antagonism. The prehistory of *human* society accordingly closes with this social formation. (*CCPE,*21–2, emphasis added)

The most essential features of the method of historical material-ism developed by Marx during his 1844–6 period of philosophical self-clarification were summarised in 1859 in the Preface to the first *published* stage in the evolution of his critical theory, *A Contribution to the Critique of Political Economy* (*CCPE*). He intended this summary to emphasise for his readers that the critical analyses that followed had a particular methodological rationale and a particular teleological *raison d'être* in his vision of what the future held for capitalism. In the present context, it is appropriate to place this summary at the original source of its ideas and at the beginning of Marx's endeavours to *apply* the method to his burgeoning critique of political economy as *the* bourgeois ideology.

After referring to the course of his studies in Paris and Brussels and his recognition of the primacy of political economy in any worthwhile critical comprehension of capitalist society, Marx wrote the following passage:

The general conclusion at which I arrived and which, once reached, became the guiding *principle of my studies* can be summarised as follows. In the *social production of their existence*, men inevitably enter into *definite relations*, which are independent of their will, namely *relations of production* appropriate to a given stage in the development of their material *forces of production*. The totality of these relations of production constitutes the economic structure of society, the *real foundation*, on which arises a legal and political *superstructure* and to which correspond definite forms of *social consciousness*. The mode of production of material life conditions the general process of social, political and intellectual life. *It is not the consciousness of men that determines their existence, but their social existence that determines their consciousness*. At a certain stage of development, the material productive forces of society come into conflict with the existing relations of production or – this merely expresses the same thing in legal terms – with the property relations within the framework of which they have operated hitherto. From forms of development of the productive forces these relations turn into their fetters. Then begins an era of *social revolution*. The changes in the economic foundation lead sooner or later to the transformation of the whole immense superstructure. (CCPE,20–1, emphasis added)

Here, then, were the central principles of the method of historical materialism that Marx had formulated and carried forward into the development of his critique of political economy. After breaking off from the writing of *The German Ideology* manuscript in the latter half of 1846, Marx soon had an opportunity to apply the method, albeit in a polemical context. Proudhon had been at work on another book and Marx was concerned over what he considered to be the highly pretentious nature of the method and substance that it contained. His reaction was to draft out and publish a critique of Proudhon's work in an endeavour to discredit it.

HISTORICAL MATERIALISM AND THE CRITIQUE OF PROUDHON'S METHOD

In *The Holy Family*, Marx had expressed some admiration for Proudhon's work in exposing the role of private property in bourgeois society. The dictum that 'property is theft!' had appealed to Marx; but more importantly, Proudhon had shown that the existence of private property should not just be taken for granted as political economy was wont to do. Its *origins* and *specific effects* were important in the critical comprehension of capitalism.

In Proudhon's latest book, *System of Economic Contradictions, or the Philosophy of Poverty*, however, Marx found much that concerned him about Proudhon's handling of the burgeoning critico-theoretical movement against capitalism. As Marx read it, the book betrayed Proudhon's shallow knowledge of political economy combined with a profound misunderstanding of the appropriate methodological implications of German idealist philosophy. This general concern was expressed by Marx in the opening passage of his main critique of Proudhon, *The Poverty of Philosophy: Answer to the 'Philosophy of Poverty' by M. Proudhon*, published in July 1847:

M. Proudhon has the misfortune of being peculiarly misunderstood in Europe. In France, he has the right to be a bad economist, because he is reputed to be a good German philosopher. In Germany, he has the right to be a bad philosopher, because he is reputed to be one of the ablest of French economists. *Being both a German and an economist at the same time, we desire to protest against this double error.* (CW,6,109, emphasis added)

In his endeavour to bring German philosophy and political economy together in a reformist critique of capitalism, Proudhon ended up with the worst of both in a potpourri of ideas that left the essential evils of the system untouched. Indeed, Marx thought Proudhon's work to be conservative and petty-bourgeois in its approach to reformist socio-economic philosophy. A critique of his work was thus needed in order to discredit the idealism and reformism on which it was based and to re-emphasise that transcendence to a truly human society requires the *material overthrow* of capitalism through *revolutionary* action. In the formulation of his programme of reform, Proudhon was engaging in an intellectual manipulation of the existing system of ideas. As Marx wrote to the Russian literary critic and journalist Pavel Annenkov, Proudhon's idealism remained obvious because

Instead . . . of regarding the politico-economic categories as abstract expressions of the real, transitory, historic social relations, M. Proudhon, owing to a mystic inversion, regards real relations merely as reifications of these abstractions. (letter of 28 December 1846, reprinted in *PP*,186–7)

Marx went on to conclude that he felt Proudhon to be 'the declared enemy of every political movement. The solution of actual problems does not lie for him in public action but in the dialectical relations of his own head' (*PP*,191).

This set the tenor of Marx's critique of Proudhon's 'economico-metaphysical method' in *The Poverty of Philosophy* (CW,6,161ff.). He found that Proudhon's analyses involved the use (and misuse) of the categorical framework provided by political economy and the idealist dialectical method of Hegel. Proudhon followed Hegel's approach in giving *reason* the *dominant* role in historical determination, at least nominally. The effect of this approach was that he separated the categories of political economy from any historical context and applied them in a *supra-historical sequence* in order to interpret contemporary reality. This logical sequence was the product of reason alone and independent of the reality itself. In this sense, Proudhon had picked up the least desirable dimension of Hegel's method with its assertion of the omnipotence of the logic and reason of analysis. Marx cited Hegel's dictum that 'Method is the absolute, unique, supreme, infinite force which no object can resist; it is the tendency of reason to find itself again, to recognise itself in every object' (quoted from the *Science of Logic*, CW,6,164) as indicative of the source of Proudhon's approach. Thus Proudhon wrote,

> We are not giving a *history according to the order in time*, but *according to the sequence of ideas*. Economic *phases* or *categories* are in their *manifestation* sometimes contemporary, sometimes invented. . . . Economic theories have nonetheless their *logical sequence* and their *serial relation in the understanding*: it is this order that we flatter ourselves to have discovered. (Proudhon, quoted CW,6,162)

Marx concluded from this that Proudhon imagined himself to be 'above' the real world and in a position to impose his personal (and arrogant) reason and logic on the order of categories in developing a critical analysis.

Marx argued that Proudhon's approach involved a vulgar misunderstanding of the nature of dialectical analysis. Proudhon's intention was to impose a *normative and contrived 'dialectic'* on the categories and relations of political economy in the form of a *good* and *bad* taxonomy. This reflected his reformist 'ideology' and could not be considered as a dialectical analysis in an Hegelian sense. Proudhon searched for a definitive formula of reform based upon the exposure and correction of the *bad* aspects of capitalism: 'he is the man in search of formulas' (CW,6,178).

Now what this approach amounted to was an emasculation of the immanent dialectic of history.

> What constitutes dialectic movement is the coexistence of two contradictory sides, their conflict and their fusion into a new category. The very setting of the problem of eliminating the bad side cuts short the dialectic movement. It is not the category which is posed and opposed to itself, by its contradictory nature, it is M. Proudhon who gets excited, perplexed and frets and fumes between the two sides of the category. (CW,6,168)

In effect, Marx went on to argue, if Proudhon's method had been applied to eliminate the *bad side* of feudal relations, the system would have been preserved, as 'All the elements which called forth the struggle would have been destroyed, and the development of the bourgeoisie nipped in the bud. *One would have set oneself the absurd problem of eliminating history*' (CW,6,174–5, emphasis added).

In this respect, the contemporary system is no different. It, too, is breeding its own antagonistic mediation that will destroy it, viz. the proletariat. The proletariat and the bourgeoisie stand materially opposed to each other, an opposition manifested in the coexistence of concentrated wealth and mass poverty. The political economists, as the theoreticians of the bourgeoisie, ignored, excused or patronised this malady. The socialist writers, as the ostensible theoreticians of the proletariat, condemned it and carried on the proletarian struggle vicariously by postulating schemes of reform; although, as Marx noted, they could do little else in the face of an as yet undeveloped proletarian revolutionary consciousness:

So long as the proletariat is not yet sufficiently developed to constitute itself as a class, and consequently so long as the very struggle of the proletariat with the bourgeoisie has not yet assumed a political character, and the productive forces are not yet sufficiently developed in the bosom of the bourgeoisie itself to enable us to catch a glimpse of the material conditions necessary for the emancipation of the proletariat and for the formation of a new society, these theoreticians are merely utopians who, to meet the wants of the oppressed classes, improvise systems and go in search of a regenerating science. (CW,6,177)

Here Marx reiterated the challenge for *his* critical theory. It must provide the theoretical basis for the development of a proletarian consciousness in which their relations with the bourgeois capitalists are correctly perceived as being *political*. That is, it must overcome the false consciousness perpetrated by political economy that the capital–labour relation is essentially an *economic* one. However, Marx emphasised that the consequent revolutionary action must come at the historically appropriate time. The transcendence of capitalism should be preceded by the complete development of its *forces of production*, for this development is the source of the *material* means by which the post-capitalist society would operate (cf.CW,6,211–12).

This critique of Proudhon's 'economico-metaphysical method' enabled Marx further to distance his own materialist method from the pervasive influences of Hegel's legacy of idealism. Indeed, *The Poverty of Philosophy* gave Marx the first real opportunity publicly to present his historical materialist method, albeit mixed up with a lot of polemic.

Moreover, in so doing, he was also able to argue the folly of reformism, even when it is dressed up with pseudo-dialectical language. Genuine change towards a *human* society could only come, he re-emphasised, through an immanently generated proletarian revolution. Such a process would necessarily involve the resolution of all contradictions affecting man's well-being through the abolition of their causes. The *unity* of theory and practice that this requires could not be *imposed* in a simplistic reformist sequence. For Marx, critical theory did not need to contain *formulae for change*. Rather it must be such as to provide the self-conscious mediation in the dialectical working out of immanent contradictions by proletarian action.

CHAPTER 4

Proudhon, propaganda and political economy

The Poverty of Philosophy also saw Marx return to the critical discussion of the categories of political economy. In this sense the work foreshadowed a period of mixed intellectual fortunes from 1847 to 1851. During this period Marx devoted considerable time and effort first of all to the propagation of his critico-theoretical work in the cause of developing a self-conscious and critically informed working class. Then, after his final exile from continental Europe in 1849, he began his life-long endeavour to delineate, fully to investigate and finally to publish his critique of political economy. For this endeavour, as it turned out, London proved to be an ideal location. Marx reread and noted many theoretical works of political economy and began his detailed study of the accumulating empirical data about the operations of English capitalism. Unfortunately, to an extent that is not entirely clear because of the paucity of extant sources, this renewed work on the critique faltered in 1852. It was then to be about five years before Marx would take up his critical project again with any determination and assessable results.

THE CRITIQUE OF PROUDHON'S VALUE THEORY

From the point of view of its discussions of political economy, *The Poverty of Philosophy* is an enigmatic work. Its *apparent* contents promise much, but in substance it delivers little that was of lasting relevance in the evolution of Marx's critique of political economy. The work carries a considerable overburden of polemic which is difficult and disappointing to remove. The titles of some of the sections suggest a potential scope and sophistication of critical analysis that is just not realised. Thus it is possible to read Marx's discussions of 'Money', 'Surplus left by labour', 'Division of labour and machinery', 'Competition and monopoly' and other topics with little intellectual reward for the present purpose. Only in one section is there material of ongoing significance, viz. that in which Marx critically assesses Proudhon's efforts to present a reformist theory of exchange value determination.

As I have already noted, Marx considered value theory in his 'Comments on James Mill' of early 1844. At that time, he argued that Value exists as a consequence of the system of production and circulation based upon private property and the division of labour. Value implies an abstract equivalence in exchange that originates in production, is independent of physical form and the essential human-material rationale for production, and manifests itself as exchange value. He had read Engels's analysis of the value concept in which the determination of exchange value was explained by an ill-defined 'combination' of a product's use value and cost of production. Neither Marx nor Engels had at this early stage recognised analytically the independent and logically prior role that *labour* played in the process of Value formation. Thus, in spite of Marx's profound insights into the *meaning* and *origin* of Value, the concept so far appeared to have significance only as the *basis* for market price determination in the context of competition.

Marx's discussion of value theory in *The Poverty of Philosophy* opened with a brief reference to the *origin* of exchange value. Ironically, Proudhon recognised correctly and clearly this origin as the following passage quoted by Marx indicates:

The capacity of all products, whether natural or industrial, to contribute to man's subsistence is specifically termed use value; their capacity to be given in exchange for one another, *exchange value*. . . . How does use value become exchange value? . . . The genesis of the idea of [exchange] value has not been noticed by economists with sufficient care. It is necessary, therefore, for us to dwell upon it. Since a very large number of the things I need occur in nature only in moderate quantities, or even not at all, I am forced to assist in the production of what I lack. And as I cannot set my hand to so many things, I shall *propose* to other men, my collaborators in various functions, to cede to me a part of their products in *exchange* for mine. (Proudhon, quoted *CW*,6,111)

Thus exchange value is a necessary epiphenomenon of a production system which operates through a social division of labour and a subsequent exchange mechanism through which the needs profile of each participant in the totality of production is met. This is the explanation for use values appearing as exchange values under capitalism. Given Marx's earlier analysis of this proposition, his sarcasm against Proudhon in the following comment was inappropriate: 'In presupposing the division of labour, you get exchange, and, consequently, exchange value. One might as well have presupposed exchange value from the very beginning' (*CW*,6,111–12). As Marx well knew, and would later develop much further, there was considerably more than a tautology in this fundamental insight.

Central to the treatment of value theory in Proudhon's book was the distinction between use value and exchange value. Proudhon stated his thesis as follows:

Economists have very well brought out the double character of value, but what they have not pointed out with the same precision is its *contradictory nature*; this is where our criticism begins. . . . It is a small thing to have drawn attention to this surprising contrast between use value and exchange value, in which economists have been wont to see only something very simple: we must show that this alleged simplicity conceals a profound mystery into which it is our duty to penetrate. . . . In technical terms, use value and exchange value stand in inverse ratio to each other. (Proudhon, quoted *CW*,6,114)

This way of interpreting the distinction as a contradictory form must have appealed to Marx, for later he would recognise this antithesis as a genuine element in the dialectic of capitalism. But, overall, the contents of the statement did not please him. In the first place, political economy had not entirely neglected the antithetical nature of use value and exchange value, and he quoted pieces from Sismondi, the Earl of Lauderdale and Ricardo as evidence of this

111

(CW,6,114–15). More importantly, though, the 'profound mystery' to which Proudhon referred was, in Marx's view, only compounded by Proudhon's attempts to 'penetrate' the use value–exchange value nexus! Proudhon was, of course, aware of use value as a necessary condition for the existence of exchange value, but he wanted to carry the nexus much further and to bring the two categories into a *synthetic* relationship after having reformulated their individual meanings. This endeavour reflected Proudhon's general approach to the 'resolution' of antitheses by imposed formula.

Marx worked through his own understanding of the market mechanism in order to get a grip on Proudhon's mystification. Market exchange value is determined by the conditions of supply and demand in a *relative* sense. Abundance and scarcity, supply in terms of its relation to demand, affects market exchange value in an inverse ratio – abundance generates a low exchange value and scarcity a high exchange value. Then he compared this 'truistic' analysis with what he found to be Proudhon's confusing interpretation of market exchange value determination.

Proudhon had failed to understand the nature of supply and demand as they related to cost of production and utility (the basis of use value). He did not recognise that the producer and the consumer interact in the market, the producer with an eye to his production costs and the consumer with an eye to his assessment of utility. Each endeavours to settle on an exchange value which reflects these respective factors, but competition dominates and the realised exchange value is that which brings effective demand into line with the available supply, independently of individual production costs and perception of use value. Proudhon had endeavoured to reconcile the existence of use value with its appearance as exchange value, a relationship that he had designated as antithetical. In this endeavour, as Marx read it, Proudhon had devised a convoluted analysis which obscured rather than amplified his original insight into the issue. Moreover, he imagined that his 'synthetic' concept of 'constituted value' effectively *resolved* the antithesis and provided the basis for his formula for economic balance and equality that he called the 'law of proportion'.

As Proudhon formulated it, 'constituted value' comprised exchange value determined by total direct and indirect labour time in production (loosely, 'cost of production'), where the measure of value is in *labour-commanded* rather than *embodied-labour* terms (CW,6,127–8). Marx's reaction to Proudhon's formulation was that it was no 'discovery'. Ricardo had already posited labour time in production as the key determinant of exchange value and measured it correctly in embodied-labour terms rather than the labour-commanded terms espoused by Adam Smith. Proudhon only mystified the issue by arguing that the labour theory somehow represented a 'synthesis' of use value and exchange value. What he did was to parade 'constituted value' as the basis for a *reform* of capitalist production and exchange when such a concept is really only a disguised version of the basic law of capitalist market exchange value determination!

After all, the determination of value by labour time – the formula M. Proudhon gives us as the regenerating formula of the future – is . . . merely the scientific expression of the economic relations of present-day society, as was clearly and precisely demonstrated by Ricardo long before M. Proudhon. (CW,6,138;cf.124)

As a formula for reform, the concept of 'constituted value' was given expression through Proudhon's complementary 'discovery', the 'law of proportion'. As Marx read it, this 'law' involved the argument that the determination of actual market exchange value by labour time in production *necessarily generates* an equality between the supply of and the demand for each commodity (CW,6,132). With exchange value measured in *labour-commanded* terms, this 'law' evidently has its origins in a loose reading of 'Say's law', although Marx did not make this point. What Proudhon had done, then, was to *invert* what is really a 'law of *disproportion*' (CW,6,135). The market situation as it was understood, e.g., by Ricardo, was summarised by Marx as follows:

Everyone knows that when supply and demand are evenly balanced, the relative value of any product is accurately determined by the quantity of labour embodied in it, that is to say, that this relative value expresses the proportional relation precisely in the sense we have . . . attached to it. [By contrast] M. Proudhon inverts the order of things. (CW,6,131)

113

Thus when allowance is made for the anarchy of capitalist production, the outcome of the competitive market process is more probably an exchange value that is above or below that determined by labour time in production because of supply and demand imbalance. Such a determination of exchange value by labour time in production cannot then be a 'formula' for 'equality' in the capitalist relations of production and exchange as Proudhon envisaged. Instead, the analysis in which Marx reacted to Proudhon's argument emphasised the destabilising implications of the supply and demand imbalances that are characteristic of the large-scale production and circulation (CW,6,137). Later his theory of the crisis-ridden 'law of motion' of capitalism would depend heavily upon the probability of overproduction inferred loosely here.

One of Marx's objections to Proudhon's 'equalitarian' application of the labour theory of value as the basis for reforming capitalism was that it was not new. In Proudhon's case, such an approach would be no more successful in abolishing the evils of capitalism than any previous argument along these lines. Marx cited as examples of 'socialist' writers who used this approach William Thompson, Thomas Hodgskin, Thomas Edmonds and John Francis Bray. He chose to quote several 'decisive passages' from Bray's book *Labour's Wrongs and Labour's Remedy etc.* of 1839 (CW,6,138ff.) in order to elaborate on this point. Marx had previously made a detailed study of this work in the winter of 1845–6 and recorded 146 excerpts from it in notebook XI of the Brussels series (*MEGA*,I/6,602). The importance of this earlier study was now to become evident in the ongoing evolution of his critique of political economy.

Marx first made the point that in Bray's book he found 'the key to the past, present and future works of M. Proudhon' (CW,6,138). By juxtaposing Bray with Proudhon, though, Marx did more than justice to Proudhon and less than justice to Bray. As will be indicated below, on the basis only of the passages that Marx quoted from Bray's book, Bray emerged as a much more sophisticated analyst and reformer, albeit utopian, than Proudhon, at least as he (Proudhon) was portrayed by Marx. Indeed, it may be concluded that in their substance, more than in their analytical setting, Bray's ideas were closer to those of *Marx* than to Proudhon's. It is not unreasonable to suggest that Marx's reading of Bray would have helped clarify some of the key points in his critique of capitalism.

114

Bray argued that reform requires first of all that the socio-political system based on private property be overthrown. More-over, he made it cler that *critical theory* would have a role to play in discrediting the current ruling ideology that upholds the system (CW,6,139).

The principle upon which the post-capitalist society was to be based in Bray's analysis was equality in exchange through a cost-of-production valuation of commodities in terms of embodied labour time. Justice in exchange would be assured if exchange values reflected only labour input (direct or indirect). Thus he wrote that

It is *labour alone which bestows value*. . . . Every man has an undoubted right to all that his honest labour can procure him. When he thus appropriates the fruits of his labour, he commits no injustice upon any other human being; for he interferes with no other man's right of doing the same with the produce of his labour.
. . .

And

Men have only two things which they can exchange with each other, namely, labour, and the produce of labour. . . . If a just system of exchanges were acted upon, the value of all articles would be determined by the *entire cost of production*; and *equal values should always exchange for equal values*. (Bray, quoted CW,6,139)

The organisation of production is to be entrusted to central plan-ning rather than to the market. The result would be a 'joint-stock system' which would

admit of *individual property* in productions in connection with a *common property* in productive powers – making every individual dependent on his own exertions, and at the same time allowing him an equal participation in every advantage afforded by nature and art. . . . (Bray, quoted CW,6,142)

In formulating his ideas, Bray made passing references to the consequences of *unequal exchanges* under capitalism, particularly where the purchase of labour services by capital is involved. The following passages reveal Bray's insight into the idea of a *surplus* in production, beyond the equivalent value paid to labour, as the origin of non-wage incomes.

We have heretofore acted upon no other than . . . [a] most unjust system of exchanges – the *workmen* have *given* the capitalist the labour of a whole year, in exchange for the value of only half a year – and from this, and not from the assumed inequality of bodily and mental powers in individuals, has arisen the inequality of wealth and power. . . . The whole transaction, therefore, plainly shews that the capitalists and proprietors do no more than give the working man, for his labour of one week, a part of the wealth which they obtained from him the week before! – which just amounts to giving him *nothing* for *something*. . . . The whole transaction . . . between the producer and the capitalist is . . . a mere farce: it is, in fact . . . no other than a barefaced though *legalised robbery*. (Bray, quoted CW,6,140)

Here Bray attributed this direct effect of unequal exchange on workers to the existence of the capital–labour, employer–employee, relationship: a relationship that quite obviously involved *exploitation*. His argument was reinforced in another piece quoted by Marx:

Under equality of exchanges, wealth cannot have, as it now has, a procreative and apparently self-generating power, such as replenishes all waste from consumption; for unless it be renewed by labour, wealth, when once consumed, is given up forever. That which is now called *profit* and *interest* cannot exist as such in connection with equality of exchanges; for producer and distributor would be alike remunerated, and the sum total of their labour would determine the value of the article created and brought to the hands of the consumer. (Bray, quoted CW,6,141)

The producer (worker) and the distributor (capitalist, perhaps entrepreneur) would thus both be paid by virtue of their *active labour time* under equal exchange. Their *total labour time* would determine the exchange value of the commodity and no surplus would be available to anyone. It is to be noticed, though, that Bray's idea of the surplus did not fully pre-empt that to be developed by Marx. *For Marx the surplus arose in spite of equal exchange of commod-*

116

ities at their embodied-labour Values. The only apparently *unequal exchange* that concerned Marx was that between the worker and the capitalist. However, once the concept of labour as a commodity was more clearly defined as *labour power*, this 'exchange' would be explained as a *partial* one in the sense that the capitalist in effect only paid for part of the living labour time that he could extract from the worker. This element of *exploitation* thus became the source of the surplus, as Bray had intimated.

Whatever Marx may have developed from his reading of Bray in later work, at present he revealed no explicit awareness of Bray's crucial insights. Marx's concern was still polemical even in his consideration of Proudhon's assertion that 'all labour must leave a surplus' (quoted, *CW*,6,152). The only part of Marx's present discussion of this issue with any lasting relevance is that he posited two characteristics of capitalism that are crucial for the existence of a surplus. Firstly, there is the fact that total production is the immediate and sole property of the capitalist. He has the legal right to dispose of it as he wishes. Secondly, the worker has access to a share in production only through the wage that the capitalist agrees to pay him. In principle, given the motives of the capitalist, this will be the minimum necessary to ensure the ongoing survival of workers as a group and their capacity to perform labour. From this second characteristic arose the question of the 'value of labour', for it is the basis of the distribution of the exchange value of production between the working class and the capitalist class.

For Marx, it seemed obvious that if labour was to be treated as a commodity, then it can be valued as a commodity through 'the labour time needed to produce all that is necessary for the maintenance of the worker' (*CW*,6,124). Here Marx quoted from Ricardo's *Principles* to this effect (*CW*,6,124–5) and once again suggested that Ricardo must be arguing with cynicism in drawing an analogy between the valuing of 'hats' and of men. However, be this as it may, the real cynicism 'is in the facts and not in the words which express the facts' (*CW*,6,125). It is a simple fact of capitalism that the treatment of labour is similar to the treatment of any other produced input to production. No euphemistic, 'humanitarian' phraseology could obliterate this fact.

Labour as a commodity must have an exchange value and this appears as the wage of the worker. The capitalist purchases labour as a commodity because it has a *use value* for him, specifically a potential to deliver *labour services*. Proudhon had expressed this point in the following way:

Labour is said to have *value* not as a commodity itself, but in view of the values which it is supposed to contain potentially. The value of labour is a figurative expression, an anticipation of the cause for the effect. (Proudhon, quoted CW,6,129)

Marx made some disparaging remarks about this passage (CW,6,130), even though Proudhon here anticipated an idea that Marx was to develop as one of the key elements in the concept of *labour power*, viz. that *as a commodity*, labour produces nothing and it exists independently of and prior to the exercise of its potential to produce value as *active* labour. As Marx put it, 'the value of labour, or labour as a commodity, produces as little as the value of wheat, or wheat as a commodity, serves as food', and 'labour [as a commodity] has value and does not produce' (CW,6,130).

WAGE LABOUR, CAPITAL AND THE MOTION OF CAPITALISM

During the autumn and winter of 1847–8 Marx was engaged in 'front line' intellectual activities associated with his membership of the Communist League. As its main theoretician, the public propagation of Marx's burgeoning critique of political economy and capitalism became a significant part of the League's programme.

Three pieces of work prepared in this context are of ongoing significance in the evolution of Marx's critique. One of these had its roots in the endeavours by Marx and Engels to establish an appropriate code of principles for the Communist League. The ultimate outline of these principles appeared as the *Manifesto of the Communist Party* in February 1848 (CW,6,477ff.). The other two works were prepared initially as material for some lectures that Marx gave to the German Workers' Association of Brussels in December 1847. One piece, the rough-drafted 'Wages' ('*Arbeitslohn*') manuscript was left unpublished (CW,6,415ff.). Marx gathered together the rest of his material for the lectures, including some of the ideas outlined in the 'Wages' manuscript, as a series of articles in the *Neue Rheinische Zeitung* during April 1849 under the title 'Wage-labour and capital' (CW,9,197ff.).[1]

In each of these works, Marx continued the development of his central intellectual theme of formulating and exposing the critical theory of man's oppressed and deformed situation under nineteenth century capitalism. As Marx saw it, capitalism had developed a massive material productive capacity under the auspices of private property and free trade, although the workers remained in a miserable and alienated situation in spite of *and* because of this development (see *Manifesto of the Communist Party*, CW,6,489–91; cf. 'Speech on the question of free trade', CW,6,461–3). In comprehending this situation, Marx applied the tenets of historical materialism giving primacy to the *forces* and *relations* of production in the analysis. He analysed man's role as a member of the working class, the proletariat, forced to sell his labour potential to the capitalist for a price called the wage in order to survive. The capital–labour relation is the key relation of production that Marx developed and he now set it in a *dynamic* context. Capitalism is a *phase* of history in that it is a society in constant dialectical motion and transition. Its progress is a function of the capital accumulation process and the changes in the *forces* and relations of production that accompany it (*Manifesto of the Communist Party*, CW,6,487). Man's situation is also dynamic and an integral component of the dialectic of capitalism. It is affected by capital accumulation, but while at first sight, and in bourgeois political economy, the appearance is that accumulation is potentially conducive to an improvement in man's situation, Marx rejected this appearance as partial and misleading. The reality as he saw it was that capital accumulation exacerbates the already miserable human-material conditions under which man exists as the ranks of the proletariat grow, the opportunities for employment decrease, and the competition between the workers acts to decrease their real wage. Such is the dialectical progress of history, though, that the increasing misery of a growing proletariat generates, with the aid of appropriate critico-theoretical guidance, an awareness among them that they have revolutionary power. Through a self-consciousness of the reasons for their situation, they can take appropriate action to abolish the system that oppresses them and replace it with one that emphasises human freedom and equity (*Manifesto of the Communist Party*, CW,6,499–500,505–6).

The central critico-theoretical piece of this period is 'Wage-labour and capital' (CW,9,197ff.). The discussion that follows concentrates upon this work[2] in which Marx developed more fully and coherently the critique of capitalism as a human-social system that he had begun in the *Paris Manuscripts*. There was now a shift of emphasis away from an immediately humanist analysis of the details of man's alienating experiences towards a more general endeavour to comprehend the material production and socio-political context in which alienation is generated. *There was no less concern in his analysis for man's total well-being and it remained the centrepiece and* raison d'être *of Marx's critique.* The analysis was couched in the categories of the classical political economists, especially Adam Smith and Ricardo, but Marx's critical and historical-materialist methodology enabled him to transcend at least their ideological limitations. The image of capitalism that emerged was quite different from that found in political economy. Marx explained his rationale for the work in this published version of his earlier lectures as follows:

From various quarters we have been reproached with not having presented the *economic relations* which constitute the material foundation of the present class struggles and the national struggles. We have designedly touched upon these relations only where they directly forced themselves to the front in political conflicts as in the *Manifesto of the Communist Party.*

Now, after our readers have seen the class struggle develop in colossal political forms in 1848, the time has come to deal more closely with the economic relations themselves on which the existence of the bourgeoisie and its class rule, as well as the slavery of the workers, are founded. (CW,9,197,198)

The tenor and objective of his analysis was thus made quite explicit.
The theme of 'Wage-labour and capital' was posited by Marx as 'the relation of *wage labour to capital*, the slavery of the worker, the domination of the capitalist' (CW,9,198). He first analysed independently the two sides of this antithetical relationship and then moved into developing the dialectical relationship between them in a setting of competitive capital accumulation, with particular emphasis on the evolution of the workers' human-material situation. The political-economic ideas formulated in 'Wage-labour

120

and capital' had been given a more historical and socio-political bias in the *Manifesto of the Communist Party*, so the two pieces together comprise a complete statement of Marx's theory of the dialectical motion and immanent self-destruction of capitalism as he understood it in 1847–8.

Under capitalism, as Marx interpreted it, labour is treated as a commodity. It thus has to have an exchange value in the market where it is sold by the worker and bought by the capitalist. The monetary expression of this exchange value is the price of labour as a commodity and is called the wage: 'the price of this peculiar commodity which has no other repository than human flesh and blood' (CW,9,201). The capitalist pays for the labour commodity out of his capital in advance of realising the exchange value of what is to be produced. The significance of this is that '*Wages are, therefore, not the worker's share in the commodity produced by him. Wages are the part of the already existing commodities with which the capitalist buys for himself a definite amount of productive labour*' (CW,9,202).

But why, Marx asked, does the worker sell his labour to the capitalist? The plain fact is that he has no viable option if he is to survive. His 'freedom' is ultimately constrained because even though he is free to leave one capitalist, and the capitalist may discharge him whenever it is no longer profitable to keep him in employment, the worker cannot be free of the capitalist *class*. They are his only means of access to material sustenance (CW,9,203). The ramifications of this position for the majority of men under capitalism are profound, for

labour is the worker's own life-activity, the manifestation of his own life. And this *life-activity* he sells to another person in order to secure the necessary *means of subsistence*. Thus his life-activity is for him only a *means* to enable him to exist. He works in order to live. He does not even reckon labour as part of his life, it is rather a sacrifice of his life. It is a commodity which he has made over to another. Hence, also, the product of his activity is not the object of his activity. What he produces for himself is not the silk that he weaves, not the gold that he draws from the mine, not the palace that he builds. What he produces for himself is wages. . . .
(CW,9,202–3)

Here Marx reiterated quite clearly his earlier humanist thesis that capitalist labour is labour 'to earn a living' only. It is not *human* labour and man becomes *alienated* as a consequence of being involved in it. His *human being* must be found outside of this most essential of all individual human activities.

In order to explain how the exchange value of labour as a commodity is determined, Marx had first to explain the determination of commodity exchange value in general terms. He focused initially on the processes of the interaction of the conditions of supply and demand in the market. Through the exercise of buyer and seller competition, the market exchange value of the commodity will be high or low under conditions of relative scarcity or abundance respectively, the rationale for the actual market exchange value established being that it clears the market. Through the mobility of capital between sectors of production, the variations in market exchange value cause adjustments in supply. Specifically, these adjustments are a response to actual profit in a particular sector being above or below a 'sound, honest, legitimate profit' (CW,9,206), or 'ordinary profits' (CW,9,207). Marx did not use the term 'profit' here with much precision, but his intention was probably to infer a *rate* of profit on capital, and a uniform general rate of profits. This supply-side adjustment is the only mechanism considered by Marx, although he made a passing reference to demand adjustments that would take place as well (CW,9,207). The adjustment mechanism centred around what Marx called here the *cost of production*, the 'central' exchange value towards which supply adjustments would drive the market exchange value when the actual market exchange value stands above or below it; that is, when the actual rate of profit stands above or below the 'ordinary' rate.

Marx's analysis of the market revealed its unstable nature under the 'anarchy' of capitalist production and circulation. He went on to argue against the equilibrium methodology of those political economists who abstract from the chaos of competition and make the cost of production the centrepiece of their analyses. Here he probably referred to the basis on which Ricardo formulated his concept of 'natural value'. In this sense, Marx found merit in the work of 'other economists' (such as Say) who emphasised the determination of exchange value by market forces (CW,9,208).

It is worth noting that at this stage in the development of his critique of political economy, Marx had not fully recognised the appropriateness of initially abstracting from market forces in analysing the determination of exchange value. He still felt that one of the problems of capitalism that must be kept to the fore in his critique was the economic chaos continuously being worked out by the process of competition. To obscure this by abstract analysis was to present a misleading vision of the system's operations. While Marx had argued that exchange value is the manifestation of Value that originates by virtue of the conditions of capitalist *production per se*, his approach had so far been to set this argument immediately in a market-analytical context.

On at least two previous occasions, Marx had made explicit critical references to the use of this method of abstraction by political economists. In his comments on Ricardo's *Principles* in the Paris notebooks of 1844, he inferred that this abstraction represented an endeavour on Ricardo's part, perhaps with some cynicism, to sterilise the exchange value determination process by removing its chaotic market elements. Such chaotic elements were deemed to be 'accidental' and Marx quipped that Ricardo 'has to assume the reality to be accidental and the abstraction to be real' (*MEGA*,I/3,502). This sort of argument was elaborated upon in the so-called 'Comments on James Mill', also written in 1844 in the Paris notebooks. Mill was berated by Marx, along with 'the school of Ricardo in general', for *isolating* the abstract law of exchange value from its opposite in the reality of the continuous interplay of competitive market forces. For Marx, such market forces could not be treated as accidental. They are, indeed, more of a 'law' of capitalism than the determination of exchange value by its essential basis in the cost of production. As Marx put it, the appropriate expression required to explain the use of abstraction in political economy would be

In political economy, law is determined by its opposite, absence of law. The true law of political economy is *chance*, from whose movement we, the scientific men, isolate certain factors arbitrarily in the form of laws. (*CW*,3,211)

Thus, Marx was not critical of the political economists just for *using* the abstract method to bring some analytical order to the chance events of capitalism. Rather, he argued that the *rationale* for

123

such analyses must be emphasised and they should not be isolated from the dimensions of reality from which temporary (although probably not arbitrary as Marx suggests) abstraction has been made.

In 'Wage-labour and capital', Marx still gave immediate emphasis to the chaotic realities of capitalist competition. He noted that it is the reliance on the disorder of the market mechanism that results in the fluctuations and crises that plague capitalism. Ironically, though, it is the process of competition that leads the system out of these maladies by generating the appropriate compensating changes (CW,9,208). In his later analyses of the 'law of motion' of capitalism, Marx would continue to recognise this important self-correcting mechanism, although he would increasingly stress that it could give the doomed system only temporary reprieves along its path to destruction. Significantly, this sort of analysis would only be attempted after a lengthy consideration of the Value and distribution issue in isolation from the effects of competition. Indeed, Marx would come to see this initial analytical stage as an absolutely essential one in formulating his critique of political economy.

The next stage in Marx's present analysis was to apply the determination of exchange value to labour as a commodity. He argued that the same analysis applied in this special case, with the market exchange value determined by supply and demand around a 'central' wage which must reflect the cost of producing labour as a commodity. This cost is derived from the exchange value of the *necessary means of subsistence* (CW,9,209). Although Marx did not comment on the ambiguity of this concept, he did refer to some *minimum* standard that would facilitate the survival of the worker and his capacity to supply active labour and to procreate (effectively, to support a family), thereby ensuring the ongoing existence of a labour force for capital to draw on. This *minimum* takes the form of a *real* (commodity) wage rather than a *nominal* (money) wage (CW,9,217).

Having considered labour in isolation, Marx turned to the other component in the capital–labour antithesis. He rejected the view found in political economy that accumulated labour in the form of means of production *is* capital. Such a view comes from an ahistorical analysis of capitalism, as he noted in this passage:

What is a Negro slave? A man of the black race. The one explanation is as good as the other.

A Negro is a Negro. He only becomes a *slave* in certain relations. A cotton-spinning jenny is a machine for spinning cotton. It becomes *capital* only in certain relations. Torn from these relationships it is no more capital than *gold* in itself is *money* or sugar the *price* of sugar. (CW,9,211)

In line with his method of historical materialism, the tenets of which he briefly summarised (CW,9,211–12), Marx went on to emphasise that capital is a *social relation of production* in that it reflects a particular situation of the forces of production (CW,9,212). Significantly also, capital is a *totality* of produced exchange values, i.e., accumulated embodied labour time taking various commodity forms. In this sense, it has an existence that is independent of its particular *material* form (later to be called 'capital-in-general'), a material form that passes through several phases in the cycle of production and circulation. But Marx reiterated that accumulated exchange value is only capital under particular historical conditions:

It is only the domination of accumulated, past, materialised labour over direct, living labour that turns accumulated labour into capital.

Capital does not consist in accumulated labour serving living labour as a means for new production. It consists in living labour serving accumulated labour as a means for maintaining and multiplying the exchange value of the latter. (CW,9,213, emphasis added)

In this piece, the means and purpose of exploitation through the employment of labour were adumbrated as the domination of labour by capital in the process of 'maintaining and multiplying the exchange value of the latter'. This *Verwertungsprozess* is the essential rationale for capitalist operations and Marx would refer to it frequently in his future writings.

The relationship between the capitalist and the worker appears to be one of *exchange*. But this exchange only makes sense if the capitalist receives more exchange value from the worker's labour activity than it costs the capitalist to purchase command over it. Thus, Marx argued that

The worker receives means of subsistence in exchange for his labour, but the capitalist receives in exchange for his means of susbsistence labour, the productive activity of the worker, the creative power whereby the worker not only replaces what he consumes but gives to the accumulated labour a greater value than it previously possessed. (*CW*,9,213;cf.220)

The *idea* of *surplus exchange value* is implicit here and it is the key to the comprehension of the capital–labour relation as one of *exploitation*. Capital and labour exist in an antithetical mutual interdependence in which capital must exploit labour and labour must submit to this exploitation (*CW*,9,214–15).

Capital accumulation, the result of the 'multiplying' part of *Verwertungsprozess*, adds further dimensions to the analysis of the capital–labour relation. Potentially, the workers and the capitalists have a common interest in capital accumulation. Under conditions of growth desired by the capitalists, it is probable that an excess demand for labour will arise and the real wage of the workers will rise as a consequence. Marx argued this coincidence of interests to be an illusion when the *relative* material position of the workers in society is considered (*CW*,9,216,218).

In more analytical terms, the opposed interests of the capitalists and workers had already been expressed in political economy as the inverse relationship between profit and wages as the relative proportions of net produced exchange value going to each class:

What, then, is *the general law which determines the fall and rise of wages and profit in their reciprocal relation?*

They stand in inverse ratio to each other. The exchange value of capital, profit, rises in the same proportion as the exchange value of labour, wages, falls, and vice versa. Profit rises to the extent that wages fall; it falls to the extent that wages rise. (*CW*,9,219)

Marx left this as an assertion and did not enter into any detailed analysis.

Marx left his readers in no doubt, however, that even under conditions of rapid capital accumulation, the most favourable to labour, the interests of the capitalists and workers remained opposed. The absolute material well-being of some workers may be raised, at least temporarily, but the essential antagonism of exploitation would still be present. *There is always a fundamental dichotomy between profit and wages in distribution.* What the capitalists retain of net produced exchange value is denied to the workers because the capitalists' immediate right to appropriate the total product is protected by the legal institution of private property. This is the political economy of the *class conflict* of capitalism that was Marx's central concern in the *Manifesto of the Communist Party.*

Other effects of capital accumulation exacerbate the dialectical tension between the class of wealth and the class of poverty. The immediate *operational* effects of accumulation were described by Marx in the 'Wages' manuscript (CW,6,430–1). Capital comprises three components: advances for raw materials, advances for the buildings, machines and power, and advances to pay wages. Notice that he already separated capital advanced to pay for labour from that advanced to purchase the material means of production. This idea was to be of great significance in the development of his theory of surplus Value where the advances for labour would be called *variable capital.* Marx asserted that the first two grow in greater proportion than the third altering the operational composition of capital. He assumed that such alteration represents changes in the *forces of production* induced by the individual capitalist's pursuit of maximum profits through lowering the costs of production under the pressure of competition. This endeavour brings only temporary gains which are soon competed away and the search for more-productive forces is renewed (CW,9,225).

Continuous competitive striving by the capitalist has several interdependent effects that impinge adversely on the situation of the workers. As machinery becomes increasingly efficient and increasingly used, the overall demand for labour decreases. Marx rejected the sanguine argument of the political economists that displaced workers would find work in producing the machinery that replaces them, mainly because machines are used to produce machines too (CW,9,226–7). Thus, as capital accumulates, it brings with it increasing competition between the workers for the available jobs. A reduction in the real wage ensues as capitalists prey on the desperation of the workers. Moreover, the nature of the work, the *form* of labour, changes with the increased division of labour that accompanies the mechanisation of production. Unskilled and undifferentiated simple labour becomes the norm and can

127

be performed by anyone, including 'cheaper' women and children! Besides increasing the monotony and general dehumanising effects of labour, and so the degree of alienation felt by the worker, the homogenisation of labour further increases the competitive pressure on him and will force him to work longer hours for less (CW,9,225–7). And, to add further to the workers' difficulties, the constant recurrence of crises that beset capitalism because of overproduction causes the concentration of capital in fewer hands as the small capitalists fail first, along with a decreasing yield on finance capital so that fewer wealth holders are able to live off their interest. Consequently, the ranks of the proletariat increase and accentuate even more the competition between proletarians for wage-paying jobs (CW,9,227–8; cf. 'Wages' manuscript, CW,6,424–5,429,432, and *Manifesto of the Communist Party,* CW,6,489–90,492–2).

All of this amounts to a summary and *impressionistic* version of what Marx would later refer to and investigate as the '*law of motion*' of capitalism. Several dimensions of the 'law' were here adumbrated: its origin in the competitive accumulation of capital, the change in the *forces of production* and composition of capital, the decrease in the demand for labour and the relative immiserisation of the proletariat, the increasing concentration in the ownership of capital, the fall in the rate of return on capital, and the fluctuating, crisis-ridden nature of the motion. However, Marx made no attempt at this time to investigate the complex analyses that would be required rigorously to support his assertions. For the purposes of rhetoric and propaganda, a simple 'all this surely requires no further explanation' (CW,9,228) replaced any such analysis. In the future, of course, Marx realised that explanation would be required and that it was not easily formulated.

MARX'S NOTES ON RICARDO'S *PRINCIPLES*, 1850–1

Of the twenty-eight notebooks that Marx filled with excerpts and comments in several years of intensive study in the early 1850s, only parts of two of them have been published. These appeared as an appendix to the German edition of the *Grundrisse* manuscript (*G(EV)*,765ff.) and included parts of notebook IV from November and December 1850 and parts of notebook VIII from April 1851, both dealing with Ricardo's *Principles*. This time Marx read the third edition (1821) of the work in English and translated his excerpts into German. The notes comprised a thorough reconsideration of most of the book as the following thematic summary indicates (*G(EV)*,1100f.).

Notebook IV

Ricardo's monetary theory
including, *inter alia*:
variations in the value of gold and silver; various effects of changes in the value of money; gold and silver money and foreign trade; interest on money; banks and currency; the relative value of money, corn and labour in rich and poor countries.

Notebook VIII

1   On value
including, *inter alia*:
definition of value; value and capital; value and wages.

2   On rent
including, *inter alia*:
critique of the rent theories of Adam Smith and Malthus; effects of the corn trade on profit and rent.

3   On natural and market price
including, *inter alia*:
difference between value and wealth; influence of demand and supply on prices; the concept of production cost; the price of corn and the price of other commodities; international trade and prices.

4   On wage-labour
including, *inter alia*:
difference between wages of labour and labour to produce commodities; influence of the accumulation of capital on wages; wages and rent; rise of the natural price of labour and the money price of commodities; influence of the price of raw produce on wages; influence of machinery on wage-labour.

5   On profit
including, *inter alia*:

129

division of cost of production between capitalists and labourers; relation between profit and wages; accumulation of capital and effects on profit and interest; various tax effects related to profits.

6   On taxes

In this work of further self-clarification, Marx made no attempt to develop any sustained critique of Ricardo's ideas. His comments were limited to brief reactions to the particular argument that he was reading at the time. Two themes that emerge in the comments are worth considering here.

Firstly, after taking excerpts from Chapter 4, 'On natural and market price', Marx once again recorded his concern about the analytical problem of abstracting from the so-called 'accidental' forces in the behaviour of capitalism (*G(EV)*,803). He referred in particular to Ricardo's analysis of exchange value formation which initially focused on the effects of production and the generation of a 'natural price' to the exclusion of the capricious market forces consequent upon imbalances in the relation of supply to *effective* demand (see also *G(EV)*,806 and 832). Clearly Ricardo's analysis of the 'natural price' was but a preliminary to the explanation of market price which allowed for these factors, but Marx seemed reluctant to grant any status to an argument which did not directly capture the real nature of the operations of capitalism. He was anxious not to give credence to an analysis that overlooked the realisation of actual exchange values, a process that he saw as being the source of capitalist instability and crisis, lest the abstracted image of stability and harmony should be interpreted as the norm. Later, of course, Marx would appreciate more fully the need for a method of presentation and explanation which proceeds from simple, abstract categories to those that more immediately represent real phenomena.

The second theme to be mentioned here arose in the context of Marx's reading of Ricardo's treatment of the relationship between wages and profits. Marx noted that Ricardo had been criticised for not explaining the *origin* of the phenomenon of profit (*G(EV)*,828f.) and he went on to suggest such an explanation. The appearance is that profit *comes from* exchange as well as being realised in it. This involved the idea of a series of transactions in which one trader cheats another by charging a price that is above his 'costs'. Marx made the point that this idea cannot serve as an explanation for *aggregate* profit because the gains of cheating would have to be offset against the losses. Rather, these sorts of transactions are more appropriately viewed as involving the redistribution of a *pre-existing surplus* which has its origins in production. In particular, the surplus arises because in the total exchange value of the commodity that exists prior to exchange, only part of the newly embodied labour time is actually paid for. This argument, not original to Marx, was to be developed into the theory of surplus value, one of the central tenets of his critique of political economy.

FROM THE CRITIQUE OF CAPITALISM TO THE CRITIQUE OF POLITICAL ECONOMY

In the period of the evolution of Marx's critical thought covered so far, there is evidence of two crucial intellectual adjustments along the way.

Firstly, he gradually shifted his attitude towards the intellectual status to be ascribed to political economy. His early studies of the subject were extensive and detailed, but the immediate consequence of these studies was an understanding of the *nature of capitalism* rather than any misgivings about the nature and intellectual status of the analyses of political economy *per se*. At this stage, he accepted such analyses as a faithful abstract reflection of the operations of the system and proceeded to use it to great effect as the *object* of his first critique of *capitalism*. This was especially evident in the *Paris Manuscripts* of 1844 where Marx used the description of capitalism provided by Adam Smith in the *Wealth of Nations* as his model.

Increasingly, however, Marx was recognising that political economy itself failed to present an adequate representation of the workings of capitalism. Its problematic was too narrow and its analyses were confined to *the confirmation of appearances*. He became aware that such appearances were deceptive in that they obscured the contradictions of the system. For Marx, it was these contradictory relationships that were the key to the dialectical motion of capitalism through time and the social and material situation of man in such motion. The contradictions de-emphasised or obscured by political economy included those between wealth and poverty, capital and labour, and use value and exchange value.

Thus it was that Marx's attention shifted from the critique of capitalism to the critique of its limited abstract reflection in political economy. He reasoned that this bourgeois ideology had as its objective the containment of dissent by explaining away the human socio-economic consequences of capitalism as natural, equitable and eternal. Marx's challenge was to discredit this false consciousness and to replace it with an alternative critical analysis in which the contradictions of the system became the central theme.

The second intellectual adjustment that Marx traversed in this period concerned the *perspective of man* taken in his critical analyses. His initial critique of capitalism itself involved the delineation of the specific dimensions of man's less than human situation under the regime. The analysis of alienation emphasised the situation of man as an *individual*; not in isolation, but as a *species* and *social* individual.

The particular dimensions of capitalism in which Marx's explanation of alienation was rooted were the social division of labour and private property in the means of production and produced commodities. As his critical analysis shifted from focusing on man *in* the capitalist economy to a concern with the comprehension of the essential nature of the economy itself, designed to transcend the false comprehension posited by political economy, so Marx's analytical focus broadened and his perspective became the consequences for *man generally* as a participant in the economy. From this emerged the socio-economic class interpretation of man's situation which Marx was to carry forward into his more formal and sophisticated critique of political economy.

Part II
Critical analyses in the *Grundrisse*

CHAPTER 5

Methodological premises for a reformulated critique of political economy

As far as can be ascertained from extant writings, by the time that Marx resolved in 1857 to begin again in earnest the drafting of his critique of political economy, it had been about a decade since he had worked on his methodological principles. During August and September of that year, he redressed this lacuna by drafting out a methodological piece headed simply 'Introduction'. The work was left in rough-drafted form and was never completed. Moreover, it was omitted from publication on the grounds that it pre-empted too much of the critique of political economy that was subsequently to be worked out. However, this in no way detracts from its significance in this study for two reasons. Firstly, Marx did not *reject* the argument of the piece even though he later emphasised some aspects of it more than others. Secondly, it is the only extant draft of Marx's own methodological position and premises developed as a consequence of his adherence to the principles of historical materialism. Indeed, it is surprising that it was not published, at least in part, for Marx's stated reasons for not doing so do not apply to some of the most important aspects of the argument that it contains.

Marx wrote under three headings in the 'Introduction' (G,69 and 83ff.):

1 Production in general
2 General relation between production, distribution, exchange and consumption
3 The method of political economy

A fourth section, 'Means (forces) of production and relations of production, relations of production and relations of circulation', was not drafted beyond a few cryptic notes (*G*,109ff.) and no outline of other planned sections (if any) was left.

In the discussions of Chapter 2 above, I considered the early formulation of Marx's methodological premises in the specific context of his critical reactions against Hegel, the 'Young Hegelians' and Proudhon. This 1844–7 period of philosophical reflection involved Marx in the critical transcendence of the idealism of Hegel's dialectic of history and the consequent emergence of a materialist dialectical method based upon man as the subject actively making his own history. This historical materialism gave ontological prominence to man's labour under particular forces and relations of production and led Marx increasingly to centre his critical theory on political economy and economic issues generally.

It was in the light of these methodological beginnings that Marx saw his first task in 1857 to be a restatement and further development of the premises that would guide his critique of political economy. As will become evident in the discussion below, in the rough-drafted present methodological statement, Marx's concern was to identify and clarify the analytical issues raised by three, highly interdependent aspects of his projected critique: firstly, its most essential critical focus or object; secondly, its framework of operational categories; and thirdly, its critical method of analysis. In this endeavour, he was influenced by a complex combination of his earlier detailed readings of political economy and a contemporaneous rereading of Hegel's *Science of Logic* (1812–16). Marx referred to the latter in a letter to Engels on 16 January 1858 saying that 'In the *method* of working it has done me great service that by mere accident . . . I have again glanced through Hegel's "Logic" ' (*MEW*,29,260). Marx still retained a great respect for the power of the logic and method of Hegel's work while rejecting its ideal substance. Indeed, it was his unrealised intention to write a study which would explicate and make accessible the demystified rational core of Hegel's contribution to method (see the above letter to Engels,*MEW*,29,260). That Hegel's influence pervaded Marx's approach to his critique of political economy is evident from the methodological discussions in the 'Introduction'. This Hegelian influence contributed to the essay being both rich in insight *and* in ambiguity.[1]

136

THE CRITICAL OBJECT OF THE CRITIQUE OF POLITICAL ECONOMY

In clarifying the choice of a critical centrepiece for his project, Marx recognised that it must be consistent with the principles of historical materialism and their implications for the determinants of man's situation in the real world. According to these principles, man's situation is most directly a function of the form of the mode of production in which he is engaged. For Marx, then, it was obvious that 'The object before us, to begin with [is] *material production*' (*G*,83).

Marx saw production as a many-sided concept. He emphasised first and foremost that it should be understood as a *social* and *historically determinate* process.

With respect to the former dimension, the point was to emphasise that man's situation in the production process could not be grasped merely by delineating his participation therein as an *isolated individual* (*G*,83f.). The *social relations of production* brought man into a situation of necessary dependence on others in order to achieve his goal of providing for his material subsistence. It made no sense, in Marx's view, to argue about the concept of an isolated man engaged in production. This is the stuff of romantic novels and not of a serious endeavour to understand the real world. Marx argued that the inclination of some political economists to utilise this image of man stemmed from the eighteenth century obsession with man as a free spirit competing with others in 'civil society' in pursuit of his own exclusive economic interests. This represented a reaction against the highly structured economic relations of feudalism in which man's identity and position was preempted by the imposed need to conform in order to live. It was Marx's point that bourgeois *society* is little different. Man as a political animal can only individuate himself in society, whether the forms and structures of that society are visible or not. In not stressing this, the political economists revealed their lack of appreciation that the historical roots of contemporary society provide the basis for the comprehension of man's situation in it.

The *historically determinate* aspect of the mode of production was important for the working out of Marx's method in the critique of political economy. He recognised the possibility of conceptualising a form of *production in general* which would present in a reasoned and consistent way the essential nature of the process in isolation from any particular historical form (G,85ff.). But, this could not be anything other than an intellectual exercise and the use of such a device could mislead in that by emphasising the ostensibly eternal, natural and harmonious dimensions of the process, it infers that it is *these* dimensions that matter most in comprehending any system. For Marx, on the contrary, these dimensions were only of concern as a means by which a critical enquiry into the peculiar nature of each historical stage could be *initiated*. For this reason, he distinguished the potentially useful '*general preconditions*' of all production from their involvement in the formulation of the category production in general. Their usefulness lies instead in helping to work out the precise nature of a particular historical stage in the evolution of the mode of production.

In Marx's case, the stage that he was concerned to pursue was contemporary nineteenth century bourgeois capitalism. He made this point specifically several times in the 'Introduction', and the idea pervades the whole of the piece and his subsequent work on the *Grundrisse* manuscript during 1857–8. As he emphasised, 'When we speak of production . . . what is meant is *always* production at a definite stage of social development – production by social individuals . . . e.g. *modern bourgeois production, which is indeed our particular theme*' (G,85, emphasis added;cf.88,105,107).

Marx clarified to some extent the principles by which these 'general preconditions' are to be devised, albeit without being too specific. Most essentially, they are categories that reflect those determinations without which there could be no production *process* at all. A second principle involves a consideration of those general factors that affect the efficiency and growth of productive capacity (G,85–6). In spite of a lack of any specific examples of these preconditions, Marx was very definite about their intellectual status.

There are characteristics which all stages of production have in common, and which are established as general ones in the mind; but the so-called *general preconditions* of all production are nothing more than these abstract moments with which no real historical stage of production can be grasped. (G,88)

In themselves, these categories are transhistorical and cannot be directly applied in critico-historical argument. The categories cannot remain historically abstract and must be enriched before any contextual use.

By emphasising that production is a social and historically determinate process, Marx distanced himself from the notion that the political economy of capitalism could be approached through a transhistorical model of production in general to which is *attached* an historically specific mode of social distribution of its results (a view ascribed by Marx to J.S. Mill,*G*,86,87). The two processes exist always as an historical and social unity, a point to which Marx returned later in the 'Introduction'.

In the meantime he noted that as with production, distribution has certain transhistorical characteristics. Firstly, it requires some form of property rights as the basis for the organisation of the post-production process. Secondly, juxtaposed to these property rights must be an appropriately formulated and administered set of legal relations. Once again, though, this transhistorical view of distribution was recognised by Marx as but a reference point for the development of a critical analysis of a particular historical mode of the process. It is pertinent to point out that in reflecting on distribution as an operational dimension of bourgeois society, the specific preconditions for the process were explicitly not *economic* in the narrow sense of the term. For Marx, the roots of distribution were to be sought in the particular socio-legal relations of any system and not in the economic relations, *whatever the appearances may be*. This fundamental insight affected very much the nature of Marx's critical reaction against the limited perceptions of the political economists in treating this category.

With *bourgeois material production* as his critico-analytical object, Marx was able to reiterate his anti-idealist stance in the comprehension of human history. This object is very definitely an *empirical* one with a manifest existence that is independent of any *thought* about it. From this premise he went on to develop his method of critical analysis. Before doing so, he elaborated further on the broader dimensions of his object as they would appear in the critique of political economy project.

A CRITICAL RECONSIDERATION OF THE OPERATIONAL CATEGORIES OF CAPITALISM

The object before Marx was the capitalist mode of production. Considered in its *totality*, the operations and perpetuation of this mode depend upon the appropriate mediation of three other operational processes, viz. distribution, exchange (circulation) and consumption. Ascertaining the logical interdependencies between these categories and production was seen by Marx as all-important in grasping the nature of capitalism, its historical motion and its human consequences. Thus it was that he set out to situate each of these operational dimensions in the composition of the totality of the mode of production and thereby to clarify the analytical framework of his critique of political economy.

From his earlier studies of political economy, Marx was aware that in its more recent developments the analysis of capitalism had centred on the four operational dimensions just referred to. The four categories, production, distribution, exchange and consumption, were juxtaposed in the initial conceptualisation of the system. This was first made *explicit* by James Mill in the Introduction to his *Elements of Political Economy* (1821).[2]

It thus appears, that four inquiries are comprehended in this science.
1st. What are the laws, which regulate the *production* of commodities:
2dly. What are the laws, according to which the commodities, produced by the labour of the community, are *distributed*:
3dly. What are the laws, according to which commodities are *exchanged for one another:*
4thly. What are the laws, which regulate *consumption*.

Marx (and James Mill) would also have read the following partitioning of the analysis in J.-B. Say's *Traité d'économie politique* (second edition, 1814):[3]

1 *De la production des richesses.*
2 *De la distribution des richesses.*
3 *De la consommation des richesses.*

As Marx read it, political economy had but 'lined up' the categories of production, distribution, exchange and consumption alongside each other. He now wanted to pursue and clarify the logic of the relations between them further (*G*,88ff.) and he began by stressing their *unity* in comprising the totality of the mode of production. This unity and its significance had not been given due consideration by political economy or its critics.

The *observation* of capitalism would reveal the 'obvious, trite notion' that

> *Production* creates the objects which correspond to the given needs; *distribution* divides them up according to social laws; *exchange* further parcels out the already divided shares in accord with individual needs; and finally, in *consumption*, the product steps outside this social movement and becomes a direct object and servant of individual need, and satisfies it in being consumed. Thus *production* appears as the point of departure, *consumption* as the conclusion, *distribution* and *exchange* as the middle.... (*G*,89, emphasis added)

As the last sentence of this piece suggests, Marx found a syllogistic logic in these relations and he went on to express their sequential interdependence in Hegelian terms. *Production* is the generality, the determinant basis of comprehending the mode of production in its totality; *consumption* is the singularity, the final conclusion of the processes that confirms their purpose; these extremes are mediated by the particularities of *distribution*, a mediation positing social norms, and *exchange*, a mediation dependent upon the chance characteristics and preferences of individuals *vis-à-vis* the commodity forms. Marx felt that as stated, this formal, syllogistic view only provided a 'shallow coherence' (*G*,89) and he proceeded to elaborate on the nature of the relationship involved. His discussion was arranged to consider in turn the relation of each of consumption, distribution and exchange (circulation) to production.

Consumption and production

Marx argued that the relationship between consumption and its origin in production involves both immediate and mediate dimensions.

Consumption has two definitions, according to the political

economists. Productive consumption is an objective process and an integral part of the analysis of production itself. Consumption proper, the subjective consumption of commodities as the end point of the economic process, is not so obviously linked to production. For Marx, the two forms of consumption were logically the same in that in both cases, production is *immediately* consumption and consumption is *immediately* production. That is, each is immediately its opposite and therefore logically cannot exist in isolation (*G*,90–1). Production *is* an act of consumption in that it is a process in which both human life forces and material means of production are consumed. Consumption *is* an act of production in that the consumption of the commodity maintains human life forces and is the very origin of the produced commodity results of production.

At the same time, there exists a *mediate* dimension of the consumption–production relationship (*G*,91–2). Production mediates consumption through the provision of its material objects in particular forms (use values) to meet particular needs. Consumption mediates production by providing the *raison d'être* of production and elevating the material results of the process to the status of commodities by rendering them needed.

Marx summarised this set of relations by using the Hegelian triad of thought:

I   immediacy: production is consumption, consumption is production;

II reflection and mediation: production mediates consumption by providing its material object, and consumption mediates production by acting as its presupposition and rationale;

III return to itself: both production and consumption complete themselves by creating their other, their opposite.

Marx found that the last tenet of this triadic representation of the consumption–production relation has a counterpart in the adoption by political economy of the 'Say's law' idea that in aggregate, production is realised by means of its own creation, aggregate consumption (*G*,93–4). He cited Heinrich Storch as one political economist who argued against this implication on the grounds that some of the aggregate net product would not be consumed but instead would be accumulated as additional means of production. This argument misrepresented the complex nature and meaning of

'Say's law',[4] a point that Marx did not seem to appreciate at this stage. Moreover, he also missed the most elementary idea that it is the net exchange value of production paid as income that provides the means for the realisation of aggregate demand comprising both provision for present consumption proper and future productive consumption. Here Marx only touched on an issue to which he was to give much more attention in the near future.

In this context Marx also raised the important methodological point of the degrees of abstraction involved in *aggregate* analysis. He ascribed to this analysis a dimension of *speculation*, although it was not made clear why (G,94). Much of Marx's own subsequent critical theory would involve such high levels of aggregation which he would then recognise as a useful initial approach to the development of the more disaggregated analyses that would be needed.

Be this as it may, Marx's conclusion from his argument was clear:

The important thing to emphasise here is only that, whether production and consumption are viewed as the activity of one or many individuals, *they appear in any case as moments of one process, in which production is the real point of departure and hence also the predominant moment.* (G,94, emphasis added)

Having worked through this mediate and immediate unity of consumption and production, Marx went on to consider the further contingent mediations involved, viz. distribution and exchange.

Distribution and its production context

At the end of the previous discussion, Marx posed the question, 'Now, does distribution stand at the side of and outside production as an autonomous sphere?' (G,94). His analysis of the category in the context of the mode of production argued for a definitely negative response to this question.

Marx had read that political economy posited the relations of distribution as a duality. The *production* categories labour, capital and land *appear* as their obverse in distribution as the origins of wage, profit (and interest) and rent incomes respectively. That is, labour, capital and land are argued simultaneously as agents of production and as 'sources' of income. In the following passage making this point, Marx dispensed with the Hegelian terminology so evident in the exposition of the consumption—production relation.

The structure of distribution is completely determined by the structure of production. Distribution is itself a product of production, not only in its object, in that only the results of production can be distributed, but also in its form, in that *the specific kind of participation in production determines the specific forms of distribution,* i.e. the pattern of participation in distribution. *It is altogether an illusion to posit land in production, ground rent in distribution etc.* (*G*,95, emphasis added.)

The points re-emphasised here are that production and distribution are an essential unity, i.e., one is immediately the other, and that within the unity, it is *production* which has the form-determining position.

Marx referred to Ricardo's appreciation of the significance of the distribution process while at the same time relating it to the exigences of production. For Ricardo, as Marx read his work, the mode of distribution represented the most evident social outcome of the form of production and provided the most appropriate immediate focus for political economy. This focus was referred to in the Preface to the *Principles*: 'To determine the laws which regulate this distribution, is the principal problem in Political Economy....'[5] As far as Marx was concerned, the social importance of distribution at this stage was that it is a phenomenal form into which each *individual* man must be fitted, largely by hereditary factors in the nineteenth century, and thereby acquire the most essential feature of his social status. This form into which he must be placed is a result of the relations of production that have developed. Under capitalism, the key consideration is that the means of production exist as forms of property, viz. capital and land. The 'distribution' of these means of production between lines of production, and the consequent 'distribution' of labour, what Marx called 'production determining distribution', enters this discussion at the material level, but it does not affect the *form* of the distribution mechanism (*G*,96–7).

Exchange (circulation) and production

Marx saw exchange (or its totality, circulation) as a contingent mediation between production and final consumption (i.e. as 'mediated by the chance characteristics of the individual' (*G*,89)), and between the 'production determining distribution' and the production process (*G*,99). In the case of the latter mediation, he argued, the links are quite evident, taking the form of the exchange process within the organisation of production itself — the circulation of intermediate commodities required for the continuity of production, largely through transactions between dealers in these commodities. Here the unity of production and exchange-circulation is obvious to the observer.

The unity between exchange and production when mediating the link to final consumption is less obvious. That a unity must exist is evident from three characteristics associated with capitalist *production*: firstly, that the social division of labour entails an exchange process; secondly, that private exchange is predicated upon private production; and thirdly, that the extent and form of exchange and circulation is a function of the degree of development and structure of production (*G*,99). Thus Marx concluded that 'Exchange in all its moments . . . appears as either directly comprised in production or determined by it' (*G*,99).

Conclusion: 'distinctions within a unity'

In these critical reconsiderations of the operational categories of the political economy of capitalism, Marx's objective was to clarify for himself the detailed structure of the object of his critique, viz. bourgeois material production. It became evident to him that this required a broadening of the concept of production *per se* to embrace those other dimensions of the system whose forms are its determinate consequences and whose functions comprise the contingent mediations of its perpetuation, viz. distribution, exchange (circulation) and consumption. The totality of the mode of production, then, comprises a unity of four distinct processes dominated by the form of production. As Marx put it,

The conclusion we reach is not that production, distribution, exchange and consumption are identical, but that they all form the members of a totality, distinctions within a unity. Production predominates not only over itself . . . but over the other moments as well. The process always returns to production to begin anew. That exchange and consumption cannot be predominant is self-evident. Likewise, distribution as distribution of products; while as distribution of the agents of production it is itself a moment of production. A definite production thus determines a definite consumption, distribution and exchange as well as *definite relations between these different moments.* Admittedly, however, *in its one-sided form,* production is itself determined by other moments. . . . Mutual interaction takes place between the different moments. This is the case with every organic whole. (G,99–100)

This, then, was the operational conception of the capitalist mode of production that Marx carried forward into his critique of political economy. It is of interest to note that the Hegelian dialectical method left its imprint on Marx's expression here and indicated that this conception was very much a *dynamic* rather than a static one. The relevant pieces are, 'The process always returns to production to begin anew', and 'Mutual interaction takes place between the different moments', both of which accord with the image of capitalism as a self-sustaining 'organic whole' in the process of motion through time.

THE CRITICAL METHOD OF THE CRITIQUE OF POLITICAL ECONOMY[6]

In considering the epistemological foundations for his critique of political economy, Marx referred initially, albeit in stylised form, to the methodological evolution evident in the writings on economic issues (G,100–1). The writings on commerce and trade of about the seventeenth century exhibited a methodology in which a discussion began with highly aggregated categories such as population, the state, and the nation. Subsequently, analytical discussion would involve the dissection of these presenting categories into simpler determinations such as division of labour, value, money. The effect of this sort of analytical induction in the history of political economy was then the gradual establishment of a set of simple categories that were considered pertinent to the explication of economic systems. These categories increasingly became the medium through which argument was presented in the works of political economy *with little reference being made to their analytical origins.* In this method of logical synthesis, knowledge was assumed to be acquired by ascending from *given* simple categories to more complex ones in order finally to grasp the phenomenal object.

Marx drew a methodological analogy from this historical development by considering the concrete concept 'population' as an immediate reflection of a phenomenon to be comprehended. This meant finding by *analysis* those simple determinants which when appropriately *arranged* and *presented* would provide a *synthetic category* 'population' which is firmly articulated to some explanatory argument giving meaningful details of its nature and composition. Marx summarised his thoughts on this methodological issue as follows:

if I were to begin with the population, this would be a chaotic conception of the whole, and I would then, by means of further determination, move analytically towards even more simple concepts, from the imagined concrete towards even thinner abstractions until I had arrived at the simplest determinations. From there the journey would have to be retraced until I had finally arrived at the population again, but this time not as the chaotic conception of a whole, but as a rich totality of many determinations and relations. (G,100)

The early writers had developed the simple categories in the first stage of this total approach but had left their intellectual potential unrealised by not pursuing the second stage of the method. Later political economists had taken up the second stage, but their insight had been limited by their acceptance of the orthodox set of categories with which they worked without questioning their adequacy. An interesting parallel can be cited here. In Hegel's *Science of Logic*, Marx would have read of this methodological duality that 'analytical cognition is merely the *apprehension* of what *is*. Synthetic cognition aims at the *comprehension* of what *is*, that is, at grasping the multiplicity of determinations in their unity.'[7] It was probably in the light of the thought behind such an argument that Marx considered that the application of *logical synthesis* forms 'obviously the scientifically correct method' (G,101) in that it provides a *comprehension* of the phenomenal rather than a mere description

147

of its reflection in the mind. Thus, 'the method of rising from the abstract to the concrete is the only way in which thought appropriates the concrete, reproduces it as the concrete in the mind' (G,101).

Marx went on once again to emphasise the distinction between his view of method, based on historical materialism, and that of the idealists such as Hegel. This meant founding knowledge of the real on the real itself and not on reason alone.

The concrete [concept] is concrete because it is the concentration of many determinations, hence unity of the diverse. It appears in the process of thinking, therefore, as a process of concentration, as a result, not as a point of departure, *even though it is the point of departure in reality and hence also the point of departure for observation and conception.* (G,101, emphasis added)[8]

Marx emphasised that the process of reason did not bring the real into existence or change it in any way. The real world has an empirical autonomy which must provide the starting point for any comprehension of the phenomena comprising it.

Now it is quite evident that Marx was traversing a process of self-clarification in these pages. He had noted that the 'scientifically correct' method involved the logical synthesis of simple, abstract categories into a reasoned concrete concept. It must have been quite obvious to him, though, that for a method *in toto* more than this would be required. The logical-synthesis approach *presupposed* the existence of an appropriate set of simple categories with which to work. Marx explicitly recognised that these had to come from somewhere and that their only legitimate source is the observation of empirical reality. Only from some pre-analytic concrete concept can its constituent determinations be *devised* and this is as much a process of *reasoning* as the subsequent synthesis.

Very early in the evolution of his critical theory, Marx noted his concern to begin with the *empirical* as given. In the Preface to the *Paris Manuscripts* of 1844, he referred to his approach in these terms:

It is hardly necessary to assure the reader conversant with political economy that my results have been attained by means of a wholly empirical analysis based on a conscientious critical study of political economy. (CW,3,231)

In these manuscripts, his empirical model of capitalism was mediated by political economy, especially that of Adam Smith's *Wealth of Nations*, and his burgeoning critical synthesis began with the categories available from this source. The formulation of historical materialism in *The German Ideology* reflected this methodological primacy of the empirical, for 'It starts out from the real premises and does not abandon them for a moment' (CW,5,37).

It is important to be clear about Marx's premises here. His approach was *empirical* rather than *empiricist*. There was still a role for reason in the process of *analysing* phenomena in the search for appropriate abstract determinations in the sense that the categories devised did not have to be immediately identifiable by sensory observations. In a way, Marx steered a middle ground of method by avoiding the extremes of the assumed omnipotence of reason as independent of any concrete reality found in idealism and the crass devotion to the scope and power of the senses which limited the potential for comprehension in empiricism.

Thus, for Marx, the critique of political economy would involve an empirical approach to the phenomena of capitalism portrayed therein, an appreciation of which was to be supplemented by his own observations. However, in the methodological discussions of the 'Introduction' this empirical dimension was not elaborated. Marx concentrated on the problem of organising the categories in developing a coherent synthetic comprehension of the phenomena of capitalism on the basis of his 'scientifically correct' method. The categories to be used were either not specified or, in the case of the examples used, taken as given in political economy. At this stage, no endeavour was made to find a means of delineating the set of categories that needed to be devised analytically prior to the application of synthetic logic. Nor was any consideration given to the vital epistemological question of assessing the *adequacy* of the category set and its logical arrangement.

Recognition of these delimitations raises the question of the relationship between the *analytic* and *synthetic* dimensions of Marx's method in the evolution of his critique of political economy. Some appreciation of this relationship is absolutely fundamental to any adequate understanding of this evolution.

With the aid of hindsight, this issue is clarified by the following important piece from the Postface to the second German edition of *Capital*, Book I:

Of course the method of presentation must differ in form from that of inquiry. The latter has to appropriate the material in detail, to analyse its different forms of development and to track down their inner connection. Only after this work has been done can the real movement be appropriately presented. (*K(PE)*,102, emphasis added)

The 'scientifically correct' method of the 'Introduction' is best interpreted as an approach to the coherent *presentation* of the explanation of capitalist phenomena. This must be preceded by a process of *inquiry* through which the determinations of the phenomena are devised and formulated as a set of abstract categories. It was this process of critical investigation that was to occupy most of the rest of Marx's life after the drafting of the 'Introduction'. At times, he set about the endeavour to develop his *logico-synthetic presentation*, particularly in the *Contribution to the Critique of Political Economy* of 1859 and *Capital*, Book I of 1867. In the writings prior to *Capital*, though, it was the clarification of categories and experiments with logical relationships that consumed Marx. He was, of course, conscious of the general direction of the projected presentation of the critique and this, to a varying degree, determined the order in which the investigations were undertaken.

It was the case, however, that Marx did not begin his investigations *tabula rasa*. In this sense at least, his intellectual filiations must not be denied, whatever may be believed about the unique dimensions of his method and categories. Political-economic thought had been developing categorical determinations of capitalist phenomena for more than a hundred years before Marx began his work. His work could not involve raw *a posteriori* analysis. Rather, he began with accumulated knowledge and through the process of *critique* he reworked the categories in accordance with his own observations, methodological premises and *telos*. This critical reassessment gave rise to new and modified categories that enabled Marx to overcome the failure of political economy fully to account for the *observed* phenomena of capitalism. He set himself the task of changing the emphasis in the pattern of observed phenomena to be explained and of getting beyond descriptive explanations that merely confirmed appearances. He aimed to do this by developing categories that were not constrained by empiricist criteria of relevance and validity.

The origin of this endeavour was not referred to by Marx, but again it can be traced to Hegel's works on logic and especially to his development of the concept of *essence*, stripped, of course, of its idealist trappings.[9]

In his discussion of the logic of being and existence, Hegel sought to delineate a set of *mediate* categories on which *immediacy* is founded. These mediate categories comprise the *essence* that is to be found by reflection on what is apparently only immediate. This recognises the lack of self-sufficiency of the immediate in terms of the logic of existence. But grasping the immediacy of existence involves a two-way logic. The essence of existence can be exposed by reflection on the immediate once it is understood that the immediate is the *product* of mediations. Thus Hegel wrote 'that essence does not remain behind or beyond appearance.'[10] Without essence, there could be no appearance, for it makes appearance what it *is*. Logically, then, the *meaning* of the appearance must be sought in its essences, for immediate reality has *form* but not *content*. 'Laws' derived from contemplating appearances lack *explanatory* power. For Hegel, a 'law' may be known from empirical regularities but 'a proof is still required, that is, a mediation for cognition, *that the law not only operates but is necessary*. The law as such does not contain this proof and its objective necessity.'[11]

Marx had no difficulty adapting these pieces of methodological logic to his empirical-materialist premises. They became the methodological core of his critical investigations, albeit with an implicit status.

In returning now to Marx's exposition of method in the 1857 'Introduction', it must be noted that it involved only 'half' of his method *in toto*. His concern was with the process of logical synthesis by means of which the concrete concepts reflecting capitalist reality could be grasped. This raised two crucial aspects of the *given* category set and its application: firstly, which category or categories to *begin* with; and secondly, the *order* in which the rest of the categories should be arranged in order to ensure complete synthetic cognition.

With respect to the first issue, recall the earlier discussion about the general formulation of the object of Marx's critique of political economy. Bourgeois capitalist material production was deigned to be the object under scrutiny. It is the phenomena of this historical form that must be accounted for and a *start* on this had been made by political economy. Within this historical form can be discerned various general preconditions for production which are considered to be transhistorical. They can account for the existence, extent and efficiency of production *per se*, but they have no empirical content until they are enriched by being situated in a particular historical context. Marx illustrated his argument with three examples of categories with long historical standing in discussions of economic issues, viz. possession, money and labour (G,102ff.). In each case, while the category could be defined in itself, its *meaning* at any time could only be found by considering its *situation* in the contemporary context. Thus, for example, under capitalism, possession manifests itself in the particular form of private property rights over the means of production and the products produced with them. Its importance lies in its form.

As an initial gambit, Marx intended to begin the presentation of his critique with an outline of the simple, transhistorical categories of political economy. Through these categories, he could begin the process of logical synthesis by progressively enriching them with the characteristics of the capitalist mode of production. The question was, in what sequential order to present them?

To some extent, Marx thought that this question could be answered by tracing the categories in their historical development:

it may be said that the simpler category can express the dominant relations of a less developed whole, or else those subordinate relations of a more developed whole which already had a historic existence before this whole existed in the direction expressed by a more concrete category. *To that extent the path of abstract thought, rising from the simple to the combined, would correspond to the real historical process.* (G,102, emphasis added)

Such guidance is limited and must be used with caution to avoid misunderstanding. For example, Marx suggested that because the original forms of organised production and distribution centred on landed property and ground rent, it may be appropriate to begin the analysis of capitalism with such categories. But, as he quickly went on to point out, under capitalism these categories are sub-ordinated to the effects of *capital*, 'the all-dominating economic power of bourgeois society'. As such, it is capital that must 'form the starting-point as well as the finishing-point, and must be dealt with before landed property' (*G*,107). From this Marx concluded that as a general rule, it would be

unfeasible [*sic*] and wrong to let economic categories follow one another in the same sequence as that in which they were historically decisive. Their sequence is determined, rather, by their relation to one another in modern bourgeois society. . . . (*G*,107)

This left him to reflect on just what the 'sequence' was to be and he did this through a series of *plans* for the presentation of his critique of political economy. These emerged progressively during the critical investigations that led up to the drafting of *Capital*.

METHOD AND THE CRITIQUE OF POLITICAL ECONOMY PROJECT

At the end of the 'Introduction', Marx set down the first of several plans of presentation for his projected critique of political economy. It is worth quoting in full because it had such significant ongoing relevance for the direction of Marx's burgeoning critical investigations.

The order obviously has to be (1) the general, abstract determinants which obtain in more or less all forms of society, but in the above explained sense. (2) The categories which make up the inner structure of bourgeois society and on which the fundamental classes rest. Capital, wage labour, landed property. Their interrelation. Town and country. The three great social classes. Exchange between them. Circulation. Credit system (private). (3) Concentration of bourgeois society in the form of the state. Viewed in relation to itself. The 'unproductive' classes. Taxes. State debt. Public credit. The population. The colonies. Emigration. (4) The international relation of production. International division of labour. International exchange. Export and import. Rate of exchange. (5) The world market and crises. (*G*,108)

The order of presentation suggested here follows a logico-synthetic method of arrangement and argument. Marx intended to begin from the simplest 'general abstract determinants' possible, given the object of his critical study. These determinants comprised the general preconditions of all modes of production 'in the above explained sense', viz. those requirements necessary for *any* production to take place and those conditions affecting the extent and efficiency of the process (G,86–7). The purpose of these transhistorical categories was to provide a frame of reference for the subsequent discussion, part of which would involve the enrichment of these categories to give them their appropriate status in the discussion of 'the inner structure of bourgeois society' in part (2).

Marx did not delineate the determinants and categories that would be used in parts (1) and (2) as he had still to provide them through further investigations. His studies of political economy had prepared the way, but more critical work remained to be done. The same applied to the rest of the plan. This really set out the *phenomena* of capitalism that must be accounted for in his critique, with the categories to be used in the explication yet to be devised. These were the *appearances* whose *essences* had to be exposed.

After drafting out the 'Introduction', Marx began work on his critical investigations. Within about two months, in November 1857, he formulated a second, revised plan for the ultimate presentation of the critique (G,227f.). In the *Grundrisse* manuscript he had been discussing money and the process of simple circulation of commodities, initially in isolation from the production process itself. These investigations guided him towards a format of presentation in which the *most apparent simple* phenomena of capitalism were to be considered first:

In this first section, where exchange values, money, prices are looked at, commodities always appear as already present. The determination of forms is simple. We know that they express aspects of social production, but the latter itself is the precondition. However, they are *not posited* in this character [of being aspects of social production].

But by itself, it points beyond itself towards the economic relations which are posited *as relations of production*. The internal structure of production therefore forms the second section. . . . (G,227)

Here, the vague reference to the general, abstract preconditions of production was dropped. An analysis of *circulation phenomena* was to be followed by a critical study of the 'internal structure of production' which *appears* as the phenomenal relations of production. The categories needed for this 'second section' were to be developed in the next stage of the investigations which would focus on capital as the key determinant of the form of bourgeois production. The format adumbrated in the first two parts of this plan was to be retained as the basis for the layout of the 1859 *Contribution and Capital*, Book I, some eight years later.

The subsequent parts of this second plan were the same as set out in the previous one, viz. the state, international relations and the world market and crises. In both of these plans, then, the *ultimate* phenomenal form of capitalism to be accounted for in the critical theory was the *crisis*. The situation of the crisis was well expressed in the second plan:

the world market the conclusion, in which production is posited as a totality together with all its moments, but within which, at the same time, all contradictions come into play. The world market then, again, forms the presupposition of the whole as well as its substratum. Crises are then the general intimation which points beyond the presupposition, the urge which drives towards the adoption of a new historic form. (*G*,227–8)

In this projected development of the presentation, it is already evident that the sufficiency of the critique of political economy would be determined finally by its ability to account fully for *the capitalist crisis* and its origin in the *totality of its contradictions*. Only through grasping adequately that the recurrent crises are immanently generated by the very nature of capitalism itself could the proletariat acquire the 'urge' to 'drive towards the adoption of a new historic form' by means of the revolutionary abolition of the present system. In spite of his omission of the development of the totality of the contradictions implied by the state, international trade and the world market, the ultimate phenomenal objective of the critical theory in the *Capital* manuscripts remained the capitalist crisis.

Soon after this second plan was written, there appeared in the *Grundrisse* manuscript two further outlines (*G*,264,275ff.). These

155

were set in the early stages of Marx's discussions of capital, 'the all-dominating power of bourgeois society' (G,107). It was now the category *capital* which dominated the presentation of the critical project and Part I comprised a detailed analysis of the phenomenal forms directly associated with this category. The two versions of 'Part I: Capital' covered much the same contents, but the second of them was couched in the Hegelian syllogistic terminology used in the 'Introduction' when the operational categories of capitalism were discussed (G,89). Only the first version of the Part is cited fully here because the form of expression in the second was not persisted with in the subsequent investigations.

I. (1) General concept of capital. (2) Particularity of capital: circulating capital, fixed capital. (Capital as the necessaries of life, as raw material, as instrument of labour.) (3) Capital as money. II. (1) *Quantity of capital. Accumulation.* (2) *Capital measured by itself. Profit. Interest. Value of capital*: i.e. capital as distinct from itself as interest and profit. (3) *The circulation of capitals.* (α) Exchange of capital and capital. Exchange of capital with revenue. Capital and *prices.* (β) *Competition of capitals.* (γ) *Concentration of capitals.* III. Capital as credit. IV. Capital as share capital. V. *Capital as money market.* VI. Capital as source of wealth. The capitalist. (G,264)

Besides the difference in the form of expression, the second version of this plan for 'capital' did include some expansion of topic I. (1) in line with Marx's discussion of capital and labour in the manuscript:

Capital.I.*Generality*: (1) (a) Emergence of capital out of money. (b) Capital and labour (mediating itself through *alien* labour). (c) The elements of capital, dissected according to their relation to labour (Product. Raw material. Instrument of labour). (G,275)

Topics to be considered after capital were to be landed property and wage labour. Marx argued that this order of treatment had a logico-historical rationale (G,275ff.). Modern landed property and its revenue, ground rent, were the consequence of the application of capital to production using land. Feudal tribute became money rent. Wage labour emerged initially through this application of capital to landed production and spread to other sectors. Access to material subsistence was now mediated by the money wage.

Finally, the first version of the two plans developed around the category capital included reference to three further parts to deal with the state, international relations and the world market and crises. These topics had been suggested earlier, but now they were set in a *six-part* plan for the project.

These plans set the guidelines for the investigations in the *Grundrisse* manuscript. Then, having worked through these investigations, Marx again considered the arrangement of the material for presentation. His notebooks and correspondence of 1858–9 reveal this concern and the following composite plan emerged by the time the *Contribution* was published in 1859.[12] The critical project was to be presented as *six 'Books'*:

BOOK I: CAPITAL
Part 1: Capital in general
Chapter 1. The commodity
Chapter 2. Money
Chapter 3. Capital
   Section 1. Production process of capital
      (1) Transformation of money into capital
      (2) Absolute surplus value
      (3) Relative surplus value
      (4) Original accumulation
      (5) Wage-labour and capital
      (6) Appearance of the law of appropriation in simple circulation
   Section 2. Circulation process of capital
   Section 3. Capital and profit
Part 2: Competition of capitals
Part 3: Credit as capital
Part 4: Share capital
BOOK II: LANDED-PROPERTY
BOOK III: WAGE-LABOUR
BOOK IV: THE STATE
BOOK V: FOREIGN TRADE
BOOK VI: WORLD MARKET AND CRISES

One aspect of this summary plan that requires comment is the first chapter of Part 1 of Book I. In the second of the *Grundrisse* plans (*G*,227), Marx listed *exchange value* as the first phenomenon of the simple circulation process to be presented, along with money and prices in their association with the commodity. At the very end of the *Grundrisse* manuscript, he introduced a new discussion headed '(1) Value' with the comment, 'This section to be brought forward' (*G*,881). The heading 'Value' then formed the first part of each subsequent outline of the presentation of the project until the *Contribution* appeared with its 'Chapter 1. The commodity'. This shift of *title* was retained in *Capital*, Book I, as it was published.

Now the significance of this change should not be overstated. Marx was well aware of the *material primacy* of the commodity phenomenon at least from the time that he wrote the heading '(1) Value' in the *Grundrisse*. The incomplete draft passage began, 'The first category in which bourgeois wealth presents itself is that of the *commodity*' (*G*,881). Compare the opening to 'Chapter 1. The commodity' in the *Contribution*: 'The wealth of bourgeois society, at first sight, presents itself as an immense accumulation of commodities, its unit being a single commodity' (*CCPE*,27). *Capital*, Book I, opens with a very similar line under the same chapter heading: 'The wealth of societies in which the capitalist mode of production prevails appears as an immense collection of commodities; the individual commodity appears as its elementary form. Our investigation therefore begins with the analysis of the commodity' (*K(PE)*,I,125). In each case, the discussion following these openings focused on the commodity as the unity of use value and exchange value, one of the fundamental contradictions of capitalism. The change of *title* for the first chapter appears to be of little significance in comprehending the evolution of Marx's critical theory. It merely served the purpose of focusing the reader's attention directly on the most obvious and elementary materialist phenomenon of capitalism, the commodity, rather than on its embodied determination, Value.

Marx's concern for the 'six-Book' plan of presentation outlined above appears at least to have faded away with the emergence of the *overall* title for the project as *Capital: A Critique of Political Economy* (see the letter to Kugelmann, 28 December 1862, *MEW*,30,639). However, the evidence pertaining to this bibliographical reorganisation and delimiting of the scope of the critique of political economy is mixed. The methodological and substantive status of the work on *Capital* is thus left in doubt, but the indications are that it is best considered as *the unfinished climax to an ambiguous critico-theoretical project of uncertain dimensions.*[13]

THE FATE OF THE METHODOLOGICAL 'INTRODUCTION'

In the Preface to the *Contribution*, published in 1859, Marx made the following observation:

A general introduction, which I had drafted, is omitted, since on further consideration it seems to me confusing to anticipate results which still have to be substantiated, and the reader who really wishes to follow me will have to decide to ascend from the individual to the general. (*CCPE*,19, translation modified)

It must be assumed that the 'introduction' to which he referred is the one from 1857 written in notebook 'M' and discussed above. No other similar piece is known to exist.

The comment reveals three things about Marx's decision to suppress the 'Introduction'. Firstly, it was not omitted because he felt that it was *wrong* in any sense — indeed, he did not need to mention it at all if this had been the case. Rather, he now considered that it would not help the reader and might impede understanding of the development of the critical argument presented.

Secondly, this potential confusion of the reader was deigned to have its source in 'anticipated results that still have to be substantiated'. There were three themes in the 'Introduction' that he probably felt fitted this description. Firstly, he had developed the structural and operational interdependence and unity of the main categories of political economy. Instead of stating these as logical premises at the outset, he must have decided to build them up progressively in the critical theory. This general framework could then be substantiated in the context of its presentation. Secondly, the analysis in the 'Introduction' might appear to imply an uncritical acceptance of the phenomenal framework of bourgeois political economy. It was crucial for Marx to demonstrate that these phenomena were rooted in more essential and particular relationships. The latter had to be emphasised before the former were presented.

Thirdly, the 'results' that capital dominated the relations of production, and that production dominated the form of distribution, exchange and consumption had been 'anticipated' and should have been substantiated before being asserted.

The third facet of the *Contribution* comment is the most difficult to reconcile. Marx wrote that 'the reader who really wishes to follow me will have to decide to ascend from the individual to the general.' In German this piece reads, '*von dem einzelnen zum allgemeinen aufzusteigen*' (*MEW*,13,7). In the text, it flows on as a *consequent* idea from the part of the sentence dealing with anticipated results yet to be substantiated. Its context thus suggests that Marx was simply referring to the avoidance of pre-empting the critical discussions of such general phenomenal categories as production, distribution, circulation, consumption, the state, the world market and crises. The 'ascent' from simple, individual categories to more conglomerate, general categories accords with the logico-synthetic method argued in the 'Introduction' as that to be followed in the presentation of the critique of political economy.[14]

CHAPTER 6

Formulation of the critique of the theory of value and distribution

The *Grundrisse* manuscript of 1857–8 is a labyrinthine work comprising a complex multitude of intellectual passageways, some of which are incomplete and lead nowhere in the context of Marx's evolving critique of political economy.[1] In this chapter and the next, I plot a course through the mass of complicated argument in the work in an endeavour to trace its critico-theoretical core of analysis. It was this core that Marx carried forward into the further development of his critique to be considered in the next part of this study.

In the *Grundrisse*, Marx was *experimenting* with critical ideas. He was engaged in a process of investigation, a search for a set of categories that would account for the nature and motion of capitalism as a human social system. His objective was to transcend the limitations of political economy in which the empiricist categories used were immediately linked to phenomena. Such categories could only provide shallow explanations that confirm what is apparent. In this sense, political economy provided only pseudo-explanations of capitalist phenomena which failed to expose their essential nature and origin. However, it is worth reiterating that Marx was anxious to keep his investigations, and the essential categories that they enabled him to develop, in close analytical contact with the empirical phenomena to which they related. At one point, early in the text of the *Grundrisse*, he expressed his misgivings about some analysis he had been working through: 'It will be necessary later, before this question is dropped, to correct the idealist manner of the presentation, which makes it seem as if it were merely a matter of

161

conceptual determinations and of the dialectic of these concepts' (*G*,151). For Marx, conceptual formations were a means to an end and not an end in themselves. His objective was the explanation of real-world phenomena. As he went on to remind himself, '*The abstraction, or idea, however, is nothing more than the theoretical expression of those material relations which are their lord and master*' (*G*,164, emphasis added).

As it was a work of experiment and investigation, much of the argument in the *Grundrisse* lacks analytical sophistication and includes much repetition in the pursuit of self-clarification. Marx was often careless in his expressions and in some places his argument is quite confusing and lacks direction. What results he expected to flow from some of his often tedious discussions is not clear. In these situations, I have taken an intellectual 'side step' and proceeded without pursuing an interpretation. Similarly, I have avoided following up many of the digressions that the work contains *vis-à-vis* my objective of discovering the critico-analytical core whose relevance was sustained into the writings for *Capital*.

OUTLINE OF THE *GRUNDRISSE* CRITIQUE

Marx began his critical investigations in the *Grundrisse* with an analysis of the process of simple circulation of commodities. This is the most apparent of all capitalist phenomena and, as an object of analysis, it can be considered in isolation from the phenomenon of production of which it is a direct extension. In simple circulation, a *given* collection of commodities is assumed without any explanation of their origin. As Marx's investigations show, a number of important aspects of capitalism can be grasped in spite of the limited scope of this initial object, although at times he was forced to touch on some production concepts in order to give his analysis coherence. This serves as a reminder that the process of production cannot be kept out of the investigation for too long.

Thus, as Marx argued in the second *Grundrisse* plan with respect to the relations of simple circulation, 'We know that they express aspects of social production, but the latter itself is the precondition.' From this it followed that such an analysis 'points beyond itself towards the economic relations which are posited as relations of production' and that 'The internal structure of production therefore forms the second section' of the critical investigation (*G*,227). Marx followed this two-stage approach in the *Grundrisse* with the first section comprising the 'Chapter on money' (*G*,115ff.) and the transitional piece, the 'Chapter on money as capital' (*G*,239ff.). The second section was elaborated around the theme of capital in the 'Chapter on capital' (*G*,250ff.), roughly in accordance with the third *Grundrisse* plan drafted early in the chapter (*G*,264). It must be emphasised, though, that the idea of simple circulation of commodities as the first stage in the presentation of the critique *was* carried forward into the *Contribution* and *Capital*, Book I even though it was not explicit in the third plan.

Marx had explained the unity of production with the other operational categories of capitalism, viz. distribution, exchange (circulation) and consumption, in some detail in the 'Introduction' to the *Grundrisse*. In his first, more or less fully fledged endeavour to argue his critique of capitalism in the *Paris Manuscripts* of 1844, it was *distribution* which he grasped as the most evident and suitable framework from which to begin (*CW*,3,235ff.). Now, having considered in depth the nature of all four operational phenomena, he chose to begin with an analysis of circulation even though he had argued the primacy of production. This suggests that Marx was concerned to work from the simplest phenomenal categories that political economy employed to describe the appearances of capitalism towards the formulation of essential categories, most of which would be devised by an analysis of production. Having proceeded to this second stage, the essence of the forms and relations of circulation would be clearly rooted in their production origin. Marx argued the interdependence between the two phenomena in this way:

Circulation . . . does not carry within itself the principle of self-renewal. The moments of the latter are presupposed to it, not posited by it. . . . Circulation which appears as that which is immediately present on the surface of society, exists only in so far as it is constantly mediated. . . . Its immediate being is therefore pure semblance. *It is the phenomenon of a process taking place behind it.* (*G*,254–5)

Continued circulation requires that the production process renew the commodities to be exchanged. Production is, in this sense, prior to, more fundamental than, circulation. However, the two processes really presuppose each other under capitalism and are to be considered as a unity.

> We have . . . reached the point of departure again, *production* which posits, creates exchange values; but this time *production which presupposes circulation as a developed moment* and which appears as a constant process, which posits circulation and constantly returns from it into itself in order to posit it anew. . . . Production itself is here no longer present in advance of its products, i.e. presupposed; it rather appears as simultaneously bringing forth these results; but it does not bring them forth, as in the first stage, as merely leading into circulation, but as simultaneously presupposing circulation. . . . (G,255–6)

It was then through the critical analysis of production that Marx investigated the essential nature of capitalist distribution. The relations of production, centred on capital, were argued to be the origin of the observed distribution phenomena of capitalism. An understanding of distribution could only come from an investigation of the relation between capital and labour in the production process, a relation that Marx exposed as, in essence, *necessarily* founded on conflict and exploitation. Profit and wages are simultaneously phenomena of production and distribution:

> profit appears as a *form of distribution*, like wages. But since capital can grow only through the retransformation of profit into capital . . . profit is at the same time a *form of production for capital*; just exactly as wages are a mere *relation of* production from the standpoint of capital, a relation of distribution from the worker's standpoint. *This shows that the relations of distribution are themselves produced by the relations of production, and represent the latter themselves from another point of view.* (G,758, last emphasis added)

The establishment of the unity of circulation, production and distribution, along with the role of consumption, led Marx to investigate their ongoing operational consistency. Here he confronted the analysis of the motion of capitalism through time and his investigations revealed that the qualitative and quantitative conditions for continuous stable reproduction and growth as the outcome of the unity of the *four* operational phenomena are very stringent indeed. Such stringent requirements are in contradiction with the anarchistic nature of capitalist decision making and Marx found himself investigating the crisis potential of capitalism even though this phenomenon was not due to be considered until the very end of the project in its form of *presentation*. From this investigation emerged some logical premises for the formulation of a 'law of motion' of capitalism which accounted in an impressionistic way for the cycles of recession and recovery that the system experienced.

Apropos Marx's argument in the *Contribution* Preface with regard to the omission of the methodological 'Introduction', the above discussion illustrates the source of his concern about it being 'confusing to anticipate results which still have to be substantiated' (*CCPE*,19). He evidently felt that a comprehension of the more complex capitalist phenomena such as reproduction and the crisis would be facilitated by a progressive comprehension of the apparently more elementary phenomena such as the commodity and Value.

COMMODITIES AND VALUE IN SIMPLE CIRCULATION

In order that commodities could be exchanged, could circulate in a sequence of exchanges, Marx argued that their individual physical form and subjective use value must be subsumed under a 'common substance' which would render them objectively comparable. This transformation into 'value symbols' involves 'making abstraction from the matter they are composed of and all their natural qualities' (*G*,142). For Marx, taking his cue from political economy, the 'substance' of Value common to all commodities was embodied human labour time: 'Every commodity (product or instrument of production) is = the objectification of a given amount of labour time' (*G*,140). But this embodied labour time is only the *essence* of Value and does not actually appear in the form of exchange value. It was quite evident to Marx that in the process of exchange, abstract Value appears as a *price* expressed in *money* terms (*G*,140). Thus, 'The value relation between A and B is expressed by

165

means of the proportion in which they are exchanged for a quantity of a third commodity' viz. money, a real mediation, and *'they are not exchanged for a value-relation'* (*G*,140, emphasis added). Price and Value are qualitatively distinct in that the former is an *external relation* of the commodity to money while the latter is an *immediate, internal* dimension of the commodity itself that exists by virtue of it having been socially produced. Marx made the point that

the commodity *is not price*, in the way in which its social substance stamped it as exchange value; this quality is not *immediately* co-extensive with it; but is mediated by the commodity's comparison with money; the commodity *is* exchange value, but it *has* a price. (*G*,190;cf.167)

Moreover, Marx was concerned to emphasise the distinction between price as the direct money expression of embodied labour Value and *market* price actually realised in the exchange process. An additional mediation entered into the determination of the latter, viz. the interplay of supply and demand. The 'real value' of a commodity exists *notionally* as an 'average' price when supply and demand are equal:

The *market value* is always different, is always below or above this average value of a commodity. Market value equates itself with real value by means of its constant oscillations, never by means of an equation with real value as if the latter were a third party, but rather by means of constant non-equation of itself. . . . (*G*,137)

Such an equality occurs only by coincidence in the capitalist mode of production.

The generation of Value is a *social* process in that it is a necessary mediation in the operation of a mode of production based upon the social division of labour between lines of production (*G*,146). Producers exist in an essential interdependence with others and, via exchange, they are able to satisfy their material needs. *Things* are produced for exchange and exchange is actually the exchange of social labour.

The reciprocal and all-sided dependence of individuals who are indifferent to one another forms their social connection. This social bond is expressed in *exchange value*, by means of which alone each individual's own activity or his product becomes an activity and a product for him; he must produce a general product – *exchange value*. . . . (G,156–7;cf.158–9,172,205)

Capitalist commodity circulation relies on the mediation of *money*[2] as the *general* manifestation of Values that appear as prices. As Marx put it, 'In the form of *money*, all properties of the commodity as exchange value appear as an object distinct from it, as a form of social existence separated from the natural existence of the commodity' (G,145). Thus money comes into being by virtue of the social form of production and the need for circulation. It becomes involved in the operations of the mode of production in several distinct and fundamental ways. Marx stated these dimensions of involvement very carefully as '(1) measure of commodity exchange; (2) medium of exchange; (3) representative of commodities (hence the object of contracts); (4) general commodity alongside the particular commodities' (G,146). It is the 'medium of exchange' and 'general commodity' roles which his investigations were to reveal as having a profound impact on the way in which the capitalist economy operates. And here, even at this very early stage of his investigations, Marx found the potential for crisis becoming evident in the commodity–money nexus. He posed the question, 'are there not contradictions, inherent in this relation itself, which are wrapped up in the existence of money alongside commodities?' (G,147). His answer was an affirmative one and he went on to outline briefly four particular contradictions (G,147ff.).

Firstly, there was the fact that the commodity has a dual existence as simultaneously both use value and exchange value. It has an inherent physical form which gives it a range of subjective uses in satisfying human needs. By virtue of its production under capitalism, it embodies an *ideal* Value which is *potentially* realisable in exchange as a money price. This realisation in circulation, mediated by money, depends very much on 'external conditions' imposed by the pattern of demand relative to its particular, fixed use value form. The contradiction that emerges is that the production of the commodity as Value takes place in some degree of isolation from the conditions that determine its potentiality for realisation as money. And yet, it is such realisation that is the very *raison d'être* of capitalism and the source of its ongoing existence (G,147–8).

At the very end of the *Grundrisse* manuscript, Marx started to prepare a restatement of his ideas on Value in a section that he marked 'to be brought forward' (G,881–2). He began by emphasising the status of the commodity as the most obvious phenomenal manifestation of bourgeois wealth. His immediate concern then was again to take up this crucial duality of the commodity's existence as the unity of use value and exchange value. Unfortunately, the piece was left unfinished and no new ideas were developed.

Secondly, the existence of money as the medium of exchange separates the exchange of commodities into two separate and mutually independent acts, viz. purchase and sale. These acts are spatially and temporally separable as a consequence of money standing alongside commodities as a generalised form of exchange value. The continuity of circulation required for the complete realisation of produced Value may be broken by money not re-entering exchange immediately, even though that is its ultimate destiny. Marx concluded that 'It is now entirely possible that consonance may be reached only by passing through the most extreme dissonance' (G,148). This dissonance, combined with the duality of the commodity form which would often be its source, would later provide the basis for Marx's analysis of the 'realisation crisis' made apparent by a partial or general glut of commodities.

The other two contradictions were less immediately important than these two. The third involves the existence of a body of merchants whose role is to 'buy in order to sell'. These intermediaries set out to increase the facility of circulation, but, as Marx pointed out, they also increase its complexity through involving more tenuous, interdependent relations in the process. This exacerbates the 'possibility of commercial crises' (G,148–9). The fourth contradiction mentioned by Marx was that the existence of *commodity* money left it open to fluctuations in its own Value. This contradicts its role as the *general* expression of Value. The point of Marx's argument here is not especially clear (G,150–1).

THE ANALYSIS OF CIRCULATION

Circulation comprises the totality of the juxtaposed flows of commodities and money taking place in the economic system (G,186). This phenomenon arises as a consequence of the nature of capitalist production with its reliance on the social division of labour between sectors specialising in producing different use values. The immediate objective of such production, though, is not these use values as such but rather the Value that they embody. This Value, the result of labour activity in production, gives the commodity an *ideal*, an as yet unrealised, money *price*. It is the function of circulation to realise this price, or a market modified version of it, through exchange (G,196).

Two dimensions of money are directly involved in establishing this circulation. It acts as the *means of expression* of the ideal price and establishes a quantitative relation between the commodity and all others. It is thus the measure of Value that society recognises (G,187). Money also provides the *medium* through which the exchange process, the transfer of ownership of commodities, takes place (G,187,194). Marx posited the intervention of money in two stages which combine to form *one view* of the circulation process (G,214–15). The act of selling translates the *commodity* into *money* in the possession of its owner, the mediation being the *price* (G,167,193). This was expressed by Marx as C–M. The rationale for this stage is the subsequent act of purchasing another commodity with the money so obtained, expressed as M–C. The process of circulation viewed in this way then comprises the totality of actions described by 'I sell in order to buy', expressed as C–M–M–C (G,201). For Marx, this was 'the original form . . . the direct form in which circulation presents itself' (G,208). It requires that a certain *volume of money* be available in the economy. This volume is determined by two factors, viz. the money value of periodic transactions involved and the rapidity with which money circulates, i.e. its velocity of circulation (G,194). Marx added to this a 'needs of trade' view of the available money supply which contrasted with the view that the quantity of money determines the prices at which transactions take place. He did not elaborate on this assertion (G,195).

The objective of circulation is the *realisation* of the Value of a commodity in money form and this represents the fulfilment, at least in principle, of the decision to produce it, due allowance being made for market aberrations of demand and supply. Marx's argument here was that the *ideal* expression of Value in money terms as price 'is by no means determined by the same laws as the real transformation', and he added that 'Their interrelation is to be examined' (G,187). The problem is most obviously one of the incongruity of the demand pattern relative to the supply pattern in qualitative and quantitative terms. However, Marx added the crucial point that demand is only relevant to the extent that it is made *effective* by being backed by the means of purchase, i.e. 'demand that can pay money' (G,198). In more subtle terms, the problem can also be accounted for by the property of money as an independent form of generalised exchange value which can be held instead of being passed on to complete the link from C–M to M–C required if continuous circulation is to proceed (G,203).

In so far as purchase and sale, the two essential moments of circulation, are indifferent to one another and separated in place and time they by no means need to coincide.

Thus already in the quality of money as medium . . . there lies the germ of crises, or at least their possibility. . . . (G,198)

It was this property of money as the 'material representative of wealth' (G,203) which led Marx to investigate an alternative view of the circulation process which highlighted an important dimension of the capitalist system, viz. that its *immediate raison d'être* is the pursuit of greater money wealth. 'Thus, growing wealthy is an end in itself. The goal-determining activity of capital can only be that of growing wealthier, i.e. of magnification, of increasing itself' (G,270). From this point of view, 'Money is . . . not only *an* object, but is *the* object of greed' (G,222). Thus, imbedded in the circulation of commodities, C–M–M–C, is the circulation of money, expressed as M–C–C–M and representing decisions to 'buy in order to sell' (G,201). Here, 'money appears not only as *medium*, nor as *measure*, but as an end-in-itself, and hence steps outside circulation . . .' (G,215). The implication is that money can be piled up and held as a hoard of wealth (G,230 and ed.n6); that is, 'it can be *accumulated* to form a *treasure*' (G,216).

Positing money as wealth in this way fails to capture the ongoing nature of the capitalists' *production* of wealth. To do so requires the concept of *capital*. Marx found that the accumulation of money 'already latently contains its quality as *capital*' (G,216). Historically, such hoards were the origin of capital, once they were applied to the purchase of means of production.

The accumulation of gold and silver, of money, is the first historic appearance of the gathering together of capital and the first great means thereto; *but, as such, it is not yet accumulation of capital. For that, the re-entry of what has been accumulated into circulation would itself have to be posited as the moment and the means of accumulation.* (G,233, emphasis added; cf.253)

Production, then, comes into focus as the integrated process supporting ongoing circulation: 'The process of circulation must also and equally appear as the process of production of exchange values', and, 'Posited in this way, exchange value is *capital*, and circulation is posited at the same time as an act of production' (G,235;cf.217). This brought Marx's investigations to the consideration of labour as the source of Value in production and in its relation to capital.

CAPITAL AND WAGE LABOUR

Observation of the circulation process reveals that it involves a series of exchanges. Such exchanges have the appearance of being voluntary and equitable and, almost by definition, the domain of circulation is a domain of harmony. The individual pursuit of self-interest serves the needs of others through exchange and advances the well-being of all people in the society (G,241ff.). For Marx, this image of freedom and harmony did not account very well for the juxtaposed extremes of poverty and wealth of capitalism. In his investigations, he sought to substantiate his suspicion that the *essence* of the system was quite different. Such essence was not to be found in any analysis of pure circulation.

In present bourgeois society as a whole, this positing of prices and their circulation etc. appears as the surface process, beneath which, however, in the depths, entirely different processes go on, in which this apparent individual equality and liberty disappear. (G,247;cf.254–5)

What is missing in the analysis of circulation is the consideration of its foundations in production, a process that centres on the relation between labour and capital. As Marx saw it, this relation is *not* one of freedom, equity and harmony.

171

In formulating his critical views on the capital–labour relation as the basis of production, Marx first clarified the appropriate *concept* of capital in this context. It is clear that for accumulated money to operate as capital it must be advanced to purchase means of production *and* to pay for the services of labour. In the former advance, the appearance is that capital is merely a *thing* even though the means of production are recognised as accumulated past embodied labour. For Marx, the true nature of capital is found in its role as the mobiliser of 'free' labour, that is of labour without the means of producing the material to satisfy its subsistence needs. From this perspective, capital becomes a *social* category in that the possession of capital separates the class of capitalists from the class of workers (*G*,257–8,266–7,274–5).

Marx gave the form of the capital–labour relation careful critical consideration in his investigations, especially its *appearance* as one based on simple exchange. The worker offers his labour services to the capitalist who pays for them with a wage. The wage then gives the worker access to the material needs of life. Labour under capitalism is *wage labour* and all the transactions involved are apparently equitable. More is implied here than is apparent, though.

In probing this relation, Marx noted first of all that what the worker sells to the capitalist is not *immediately* his labour services but rather *his capacity to perform such services* (*G*,267;cf.272). It is this *capacity* that has exchange value while it is the services performed that are the use value of what is exchanged. A 'commodity' is clearly involved here and Marx had yet to clarify its precise nature.

In the relation between capital and wage labour, then, Marx identified two conflated components that needed separate explication. Firstly, the relation involves the sale of the 'commodity labour' for a price called the wage. Secondly, the result of the sale is the transfer to the capitalist of control over the use value of this 'commodity', viz. 'labour as value-positing activity, as productive labour; i.e. . . . *the productive force which maintains and multiplies capital*' (*G*,274, emphasis added). The use value of the 'commodity labour' has the very special property of being able to *create* Value and the apparent exchange is a vital one for the capitalist. For Marx, only the first component of the capital–labour relation could be considered as an exchange in the usual sense. Its second component required a different interpretation (*G*,275).

The 'commodity labour' has a Value determined in the usual way in embodied labour terms. In this case, the 'commodity' to be reproduced is the 'capacity of . . . bodily existence' (*G*,282) of the worker and his capacity to deliver the use value of his 'commodity' on a continuous basis. Here Marx referred for the first time to this 'commodity' as *labour power* (*G*,282–3) and he retained this category throughout the development of his critique of political economy. However, he had yet to grasp its analytical significance more fully.

CAPITAL IN PRODUCTION AND THE GENERATION OF VALUE AND SURPLUS VALUE

Marx's *concept* of capital emphasised that it has *social* ramifications as the basis of the class division between workers and capitalists and as the determinant of the nature of the relations of production. The *application* of the concept in much of his critical analyses required him to go on to consider the particular *forms* of capital in order to comprehend its situation and role in the process of production. It may be helpful, therefore, to introduce this section with a brief outline of these various forms and their interdependence. The outline is most readily expressed in two diagrams. Marx's development, meaning and application of the forms shown will be considered progressively in the rest of this chapter and in the next chapter.

In each diagram, the size of the aggregate stock of capital is represented by the width of the block. The depth of each layer has no significance. Marx referred to the aggregate capital as *capital-in-general* and he usually measured it in Value terms, directly expressed in monetary units. Much of his analysis focused on capital-in-general, but each of the other forms was applied when required as his investigations proceeded.

The two diagrams reflect Marx's two views of the necessary subdivision of capital in general. Firstly, Figure 6.1 shows the various dimensions of the *operational* involvement of capital in the *aggregate* production, circulation and distribution of commodities and Value. Note that Marx identified constant capital with the instruments of labour and raw material inputs to production.

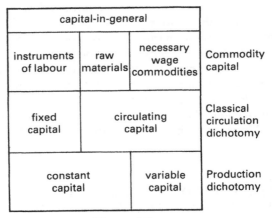

Figure 6.1

Variable capital is that which is applied to pay wages and is spent by workers on wage commodities. In this division of capital, Marx *added* to the division developed by classical political economy between fixed and circulating capital, a division appropriately used in the analysis of the circulation and turnover of capital.[3]

Secondly, Figure 6.2 refers to the allocation of aggregate capital-in-general between the different sectors of production. This allocation reflects the broad principle of the social division and specialisation of labour, the basic principle of organisation of capitalist production. By way of example, the production system is divided into five sectors, each employing a different proportion of the total capital. It is worth noting that *each* of the sector capitals may be divided according to the operational division in Figure 6.1. In this sense, the two divisions overlap. This was to be especially important for Marx's development of the analysis of Value and distribution.

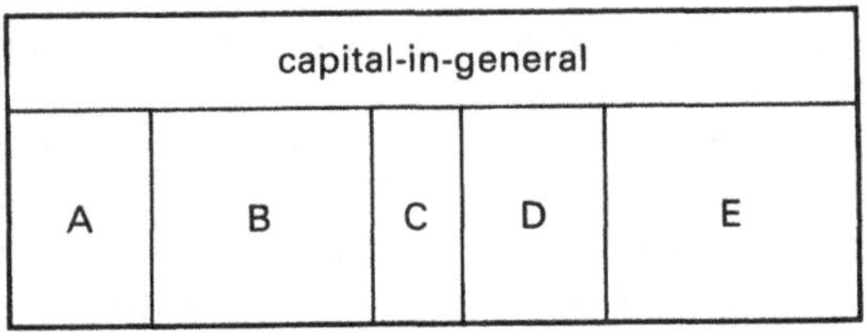

capital-in-general				
A	B	C	D	E

Figure 6.2

Marx began his more detailed consideration of production with an analysis of the *physical* aspects of the process. 'We now proceed to the relation of capital to labour as capital's use value. Labour is not only the *use value* which confronts capital, but, rather, it is *the use value* of capital itself' (G,297). In isolation, the worker represents a potential capacity only, 'a resource in the bodiliness of the worker' (G,298). This capacity can only be turned into real activity through labour being commanded by capital. But it is only *living labour* which can activate capital. Thus, 'Through the exchange with the worker, capital has appropriated labour itself; labour has become one of its moments, which now acts as a fructifying vitality upon its merely existent and hence dead objectivity' (G,298). Raw materials are the object of the 'form-positing purposive activity of labour' (G,298), while instruments of labour are 'the objective means which subjective activity inserts between itself as an object, as its conductor' (G,298–9).

Marx recognised that these *material* aspects of production have no *necessary* connection with the capital-based mode of production. The exercise of living labour on passive objectified labour in the form of raw materials and instruments of labour is not necessarily *capitalist* production. *The objectified labour is not, in itself, capital*. Marx's point in analysing the material basis of production was to demonstrate 'the simple production process itself . . . as the self propelling *content* of capital' (G,305). With this given, his concern was with *capitalist* production of commodities motivated by their Value.

The immanent motivation of capital in production, as Marx saw it, is to preserve and multiply itself both quantitatively and qualitatively.

As *use value* labour exists only for capital, and is itself the use value of capital, i.e. the mediating activity by means of which it valorises [*verwertet*] itself. Capital as that which reproduces and increases its Value . . . as a process, as the *process of valorisation* [*Verwertungsprozess*]. Therefore labour does not exist as a use value for the worker; for him it is . . . not a *power productive of wealth*. . . . (G,305)[4]

Capital uses labour as the means by which its motivation can be fulfilled. With the aid of the institution of private property, the capitalist can ensure that for the worker the labour process has quite different results. The use value of the worker's labour power, the generation of Value, can only be exercised *for capital*.

At this point, Marx began to consider the results of the production process in terms of Value generation. His initial analysis lacked sophistication, e.g., 'the price of the product is equal to the costs of production, i.e. = to the sum of the prices of the commodities consumed in the process of production' (G,313). This naive assertion did not allow for the *motive* of valorisation at all. The 'prices of the commodities consumed' were argued to be the *Values* of raw materials and that part of the instruments of labour destroyed in the production process, together with, simply, the 'Value of labour' (G,313). Marx did not use the labour power category here, and its relation to the 'Value of labour' was not discussed. However, he was possibly only concerned with the basic ability of capital to *reproduce* itself, for he added that

the production process is a production process for capital *only* to the extent that it preserves itself in this process as Value. . . . The statement that the necessary price = the sum of prices of the costs of production is . . . purely analytical. It is the presupposition of the production of capital itself. (G,313)

But, that capital should only *preserve* itself in the production process omitted its *economic rationale*. This Marx immediately recognised: 'if the act of production is merely the reproduction of the Value of capital, then it would have undergone a merely material but not an economic change, *and such a simple preservation of its Value contradicts its concept*' (G,316, emphasis added). It is in the very nature of capital to strive to multiply its Value. (Marx's earlier discussion on greed and wealth, G,222–4, is pertinent to this point.) Marx went so far as explicitly to exclude from *capitalist* production cases in which the object is not valorisation (G,317).

Marx began his analysis of valorisation with a simple arithmetical example which corresponded to the *appearances* of the phenomenon. If an original advance of capital is valued at 100 units of Value and comprises *materially* raw material = 50 units, labour = 40 units, and instruments of labour consumed = 10 units, then the immediate apparent cost of production of the resulting commodities is 100 units of Value. Marx rejected this approach: 'It is clear that it is not in fact this to which the economists refer when they speak of the determination of price by the cost of production' (*G*,315). Rather, the cost of production would include some revenue for the capitalists, say 5 units of profit and 5 units of interest. The cost of production in the example would then be 110 units of Value. But, *what is the origin of these 10 units of Value added to the input cost?* As Marx put it, how could it be explained that 'the production cost is . . . greater than the cost of production' (*G*,315)?

It may be suggested, Marx noted, that *in circulation* the improved *use value* consequent on production is realised as a higher *exchange value*. This retreat by *some* political economists from production into circulation was pointless, for only pre-existing Value could be realised in exchange. Marx's interesting conclusion was that

It is clear even empirically that if everyone sold for 10% too much, this is the same as if they all sold at the cost of production. *The surplus Value* [*Mehrwert*] would then be purely nominal, artificial, a convention, an empty phrase. (*G*,315, emphasis added)

Here, for the first time, although in passing, Marx used the category *surplus Value* to refer in general terms to the *source* of the phenomena of non-labour incomes. The *origin* of this surplus Value did not lie in circulation.

An alternative opinion espoused by some political economists was that surplus Value had some *capitalist labour* equivalent. The capitalist is 'paid for the *labour* of throwing the 100 thalers into the production process as capital, instead of eating them up' (*G*,317). Implicit in this assertion was a further alternative pseudo-explanation of the surplus Value, the 'abstinence' theory. Marx's rhetorical retort to these ideas was, 'But with what is he to be paid?' (*G*,317). The *origin* issue had not been approached, and he concluded, 'It is easy to understand how labour can increase use value; the difficulty is, how it can create exchange values greater than those with which it began' (*G*,317–18).

Marx gave the first hint of an explanation for this essential result of capitalist production in the following passage:

Suppose that the exchange value which capital pays the worker were an exact equivalent for the Value which labour creates in the production process. In that case, an increase in the exchange value of the product would be impossible. (*G*,318)

Valorisation, then, depends upon a differential between what the worker is paid and what he creates. More explicitly:

The surplus Value which capital has at the end of the production process . . . signifies, expressed in accord with the general concept of exchange value, that the labour time objectified in the product . . . is greater than that which was present in the original components of capital. *This in turn is possible only if the labour objectified in the price of labour is smaller than the living labour time purchased with it.* (*G*,321, latter emphasis added)

For Marx, the 'original components of capital' had thus far been argued as raw materials and instruments of labour consumed together with the 'Value of labour' itself. Foreshadowing a category of capital that had not been formulated so far, Marx noted that the first two of these components 'remain unchanged as Values' during production (*G*,321) in spite of any *material* change involved. These components would later be classified as '*constant capital*' for this reason.

With respect to the third component, the problem that Marx faced was to account for the differential between the Value of labour employed and the Value that labour generated in production. What looked like an exchange between capitalist and worker had to be more than a mere transfer of equal Values:

as far as the capitalist is concerned, it has to be a not-exchange. He has to obtain more value than he gives. Looked at from the capitalists' side, the exchange must be only *apparent*; i.e. must belong to an economic category other than exchange, or capital as capital and labour as labour in opposition to it would be impossible. (*G*,322)

At this stage, Marx again did not apply the term *labour power*. He used the *concept*, though, in arguing that in the exchange with capital, the worker gives up the power to use his living labour independently in return for a certain amount of objectified labour, the Value of the 'necessary' wage goods. The capitalist then exercises this living labour for as long as possible each working day, subject to some biological, institutional and, perhaps, social constraints. Thus the worker 'exchanges Value positing activity for a predetermined Value, regardless of the result of his activity' (G,323).

The 'predetermined Value' involved here is the Value of the commodity which the worker sells to the capitalist, viz. the Value of his *labour power*. This Value is basically that of the commodities needed by the worker to sustain his capacity to perform living labour from day to day, plus a margin for family survival and procreation in order that this capacity would continue to be available in the longer term.

Now if one day's living labour is, on average, required to meet this subsistence requirement then the valorisation process could not proceed. The *potential* for valorisation can only exist if less than one day's living labour is, on average, needed to produce the 'necessary' wage goods. The surplus labour above this is the *source* of surplus Value.

In quantitative terms, Marx saw capital as striving to generate the maximum possible surplus Value. Any developments in the production process, i.e. changes in the nature and composition of material capital employed, are directed towards this objective. Capital is motivated to transcend any impediments to the maximum generation of surplus Value during the development of the production process (G,334–5). These are important aspects of the dialectical evolution of the capitalist society as Marx would later show. For the present, he analysed the effects on surplus Value generation of such developments in a quite general way.

One consequence of development might be a progressive increase in the productivity of labour. This would cause a shift in the proportions of surplus labour and necessary labour in production and surplus Value could be increased. Marx's arithmetic on this issue revealed that the multiple of the labour-productivity increase exceeds the multiple of the surplus Value increase to an extent which depends upon the *initial* quantitative relation of surplus to necessary labour (G,335ff.). The greater is this initial ratio, i.e. the more developed the forces of production are to begin with, the smaller would be the marginal additions to aggregate surplus Value which flow from any given increase in labour productivity. In this analysis, then, Marx argued that the potential for additions to aggregate surplus Value decreases with the stage of development of productivity already reached when the additions are to come from further improvements in productivity alone. He referred to such gains in surplus Value as *relative surplus Value* (G,342,769).

Another feature of development might be a change in the length of the working day. In the previous case, the length of the working day was held constant. The change in labour productivity brought about a *relative* change in surplus Value generated. An increase in the working day, with productivity constant, would also increase the surplus Value generated in any period. Marx argued this to be an *absolute* increase in surplus Value (G,342,768). The distinction between *relative* and *absolute* surplus Value was to become an integral part of Marx's theory of surplus Value and its applications.

In analysing the effects of capital accumulation on the generation of surplus Value, Marx noted that they depend upon which components of the capital stock are increased and in what quantitative relativity. It was in the course of this analysis that Marx applied for the first time his distinction between capital which acts as an 'invariable Value', a 'constant Value' (G,377–8), and capital which is used to employ labour. This important distinction was further clarified and the categories *constant capital* and *variable capital* emerged (G,389) and became central in Marx's analysis of production, Value formation and distribution. Constant capital devoted to the purchase of instruments of labour and raw materials transfers its own pre-existing embodied-labour Value to the output. These material forms remain 'unchanged as Values during production' in spite of the changes in use value which occur (G,321). Variable capital enters into production as advances to pay wages, the phenomenal form of the purchase of labour power. This gives the capitalist ongoing access to the services of living labour which add to the Value of variable capital an amount of surplus Value as well as reproducing the Value of the advances made. In the application of variable capital Marx found a link to the source of surplus Value in surplus labour.

CAPITAL, SURPLUS VALUE AND PROFIT

Marx considered his development of the concept and the origin of surplus Value to be a profoundly significant one in the evolving critique of political economy. In order to emphasise this significance, he *briefly* compared and contrasted his analysis with some antecedent endeavours to relate the theory of exchange value to that of distribution (G,326ff.).[5]

Marx interpreted political economy as having advanced progressively from the limited scope of the analyses of exchange of the 'monetary system' in the sixteenth and seventeenth centuries, through the increasingly production-conscious analyses of the mercantilists and physiocrats of the seventeenth and eighteenth centuries, to the analyses of Adam Smith and David Ricardo which gave due prominence to the role of production and endeavoured to link it to distribution. As Marx saw the central problem for political economy, it was to clarify the nature and role of the capital–labour relation in the production, circulation and distribution of exchange value (G,327).

The 'monetary system' and its subsequent development as mercantilism failed to explore the *origin* of exchange value and wealth (as the aggregate *flow* of exchange value which accumulates as a stock of commodity money after realisation) to any great extent. The writers in the latter tradition did begin to grasp that the *production* of wealth involved the advancement of capital and the employment of labour, but their focus remained on the circulation of commodities as mercantile capital as the dominant operational phenomenon to be considered. They did not analyse the concept and formation of exchange value in production as such. Rather, production was considered simply as a means to an end in providing the commodities as *use values* that could enter into the all important circulation process and be realised as money (G,327–8).

The physiocrats, Marx argued, were more directly concerned with production as the integrated precondition of the circulation of commodities and money (G,329–30). For Marx, they were the 'fathers of modern economics'. Their analyses involved the advancement of capital in order to facilitate production as a central theme. This capital was conceived of as exchange value to be preserved and multiplied by the employment of labour. Their difficulty arose, in Marx's view, when they analysed the *origin* of the surplus of exchange values. The physiocrats did not link this to labour activity itself. Rather, they imposed the mediation of *nature* in the form of land and other natural environmental factors in order to explain the fact that labour is able to produce more than it consumes. Here they at least identified *productive labour* correctly, Marx felt, by linking it to the generation of a surplus (*G*,328). The problem was that they confined this *productive* activity to the *agricultural* sector and this led them to argue that *rent* is the only form in which the surplus is realised. A consequence of this view was that they gave an undue emphasis to the place of the owners of landed property in the system at the expense of those who actually advanced the capital. The capitalist had yet to rise to socio-economic dominance despite the evident importance of his capital.

This bias in the concept of production gave rise to the physiocrats' treatment of non-agricultural production as merely a process of *use value* transformation with no generation of a surplus possible. The exchange value of inputs, including labour, equalled the exchange value of outputs.

The work of Adam Smith advanced beyond such a constrained perception of production and posited a more general analysis of the origin of exchange value, including the surplus value. It was now *labour in general* which became the focus in the analysis of production (*G*,330). In Smith's analysis, though, Marx interpreted there to be a mediation analogous to that of nature in the physiocrats' work, viz. the division of labour as a 'natural force of society' (*G*,330). On this basis, Smith conceived of capital as a physical collection of means of production which enables labour to be organised for the maximum productive effect. In particular, the crucial relation between capital and labour was not fully analysed and Smith was left without an *explanation* of non-labour incomes. Instead, he simply posited the profit and rent revenues accruing to capital and land as forms of distribution and costs of production without coming to grips with their origin. Marx emphasised Smith's limitations here by reiterating his own view of distribution as essentially a socio-legal process:

Wages are actually the *only economically* justifiable, because necessary, element of production costs. Profit and rent are only *deductions* from wages, arbitrarily wrested by force in the historical process by capital and landed property, and justified by *law*, not economically. (*G*,330)

With respect to the work of David Ricardo, Marx found that it was not based upon an adequate grasp of the essential characteristic features of bourgeois capitalism as a particular historical phase in the evolution of the mode of production. Accordingly, 'wage labour and capital are again conceived of as a natural, not as a historically specific social form for the creation of wealth as use value' (*G*,331). Thus Ricardo treated the exchange value of a commodity as but a 'formal mediation of its material composition' (*G*,331) instead of as a direct consequence of the form of capitalist relations of production. And, even though Ricardo implicitly understood the analytical importance of the surplus concept, he did not link it formally to the capital–labour relation (*G*,326–7; cf. the discussion of Ricardo, 595ff.). However, whatever the limitations of Ricardo's work, it must be remembered that for Marx, he represented the apogee of the development of classical political economy and 'its complete and final expression' (*G*,884). This gave Ricardo a very significant status in the later development of Marx's critique of political economy.

For Marx, the important thing was to have situated the origin of surplus Value clearly in the production process. He related the generation of the surplus to the special social relations of production that exist under the regime of capital and to the legal relations which serve to confirm and perpetuate them.

From the viewpoint of the capitalist, it is *profit* as such that comes from advancing capital in production. Marx's surplus Value was not meant to be an empirical category in this sense:

The transformation of surplus Value into the form of profit, this method by which capital calculates surplus Value, is necessary from the standpoint of capital, regardless of how much it rests on an illusion about the nature of surplus Value, or rather veils this nature. (*G*,767)

Marx intended to lift the 'veil' and dispel the 'illusion' in order to expose what he saw as the real origin and nature of surplus Value, the source of capitalist non-labour incomes.

In the *Grundrisse*, most of the analysis of surplus Value and profit was argued around the category *capital-in-general*. That is, Marx initially abstracted from the fact that the economy comprises a multitude of different sectors of production involving capitals of varying compositions. But, as he made clear, capital-in-general is more than a convenient abstraction for analytical purposes. It is a way of looking at capital which had some substance in reality as the aggregate of the Value advanced to facilitate production (*G*,449). But, as Marx's investigations were beginning to reveal, an analysis of the production process which would account for the appearance of the phenomena of prices and profits would require the sectors of production to be made explicit.

At the level of capital-in-general, the appearance of profit was directly accounted for by Marx in the following passage.

Profit as we still regard it here, i.e. as the profit of capital *as such*, not of an individual capital at the expense of another, but rather as the *profit of the capitalist class*, concretely expressed, *can never be greater than the sum of the surplus Value.* As a sum, it is the sum of the surplus Value . . . as a proportion relative to the total Value of the capital, instead of to that part of it whose Value really grows, i.e. is exchanged for living labour. *In its immediate form, profit is nothing but the sum of the surplus Value expressed as a proportion of the total Value of the capital.* (*G*,767;cf.747,753,762)

Surplus Value acquired the status of *profit* simply by being related to *total* capital. What was not so evident was that it had been *generated*, in effect, by only one *part* of the total capital, that advanced to purchase labour power.

In order to clarify this issue, Marx introduced the distinction between two rates of return on capital (*G*,762–3). As observed by the capitalists, the rate of return appeared as a rate of profit on their individual capitals. In principle, these rates would have some relationship to the notion of a general rate of profits on aggregate capital. The other rate of return with which Marx was concerned was the rate of surplus Value. This essential category emphasised the *generation* of surplus Value through variable capital advances to purchase labour power. The introduction of this rate, Marx argued, belied the perception that the profit return on total individual or aggregate capital is actually *generated* by all of the capital.

For Marx, it was an important axiom of competitive capitalism that all individual capitals would return a uniform rate of profit, for his purposes calculated in *Value* terms.[6] This raised the issue of how such a uniform rate of profit could be explained in a situation where the compositions of the capitals varied in terms of the relative Values of variable and constant capital used. He noted that 'If capitals whose component parts are in different relations, including therefore their forces of production, nevertheless yield the same percentages on total capital, then the real surplus Value has to be very different in the different branches' (*G*,395). He used a simple example to make this relationship clear. A capital of 100 units of Value comprising 50 constant and 50 variable capital units must yield 50 per cent on its variable component in order to return 25 per cent on total capital. By contrast, with a composition of 75 constant and 25 variable, the yield on variable capital would have to be 100 per cent if a return of 25 per cent on total capital is required.

The general idea of the problem of establishing a uniform rate of profits across sectors of production with different capital compositions was first broached in the following simple arithmetical example (*G*,435). Five sectors of production were posited, each with an *immediate* percentage rate of profit on its total capital as shown here:

Sector	A	B	C	D	E
Rate of profit	15	12	10	8	5

The unweighted average rate of profit is thus 10 per cent and long-run adjustment would ensure that this rate is returned in each branch. It was clear to Marx that some redistribution of the surplus Value *vis-à-vis* its pattern of generation must be postulated in order to account for this.

A general rate of profit as such is possible only if . . . a part of the surplus Value . . . is transferred from one capitalist to another. . . . The capitalist class thus to a certain extent distributes the total surplus Value so that, to a certain degree, it [shares in it] evenly in accordance with the *size* of its capital, instead of in accordance with the surplus Value actually created by the capitals in the various branches of business. (*G*,435–6)

What he was not clear about was the *mechanism* through which this redistribution would take place.

Initially he recognised that it would involve the *prices* at which the produced commodities were actually sold, ignoring any market induced distortions. These prices would, in some way yet to be determined, diverge from the Value of the commodities. Marx hinted at this is the following passage:

The determination of prices is founded on the determination of Values, but new elements enter in. *The price, which originally appeared only as the Value expressed in money, becomes further determined as itself a specific magnitude.* (G,432, emphasis added)

With the benefit of hindsight, it is possible to see in this passage the implicit adumbration of what would later become the category *price of production*, a *modified* expression of *Value* designed to account for the realisation of the uniform rate of profits. Marx elaborated a little on this point when he referred briefly to the effects of the redistribution mechanism:

This [general rate of profits] is realised by means of the relation of prices in the different branches of business, which fall *below* the Value in some, rise *above* it in others. This makes it seem as if an equal sum of capital in unequal branches of business created *equal* . . . surplus Value. (G,436)

Such a redistribution of surplus Value to obtain a uniform *Value* rate of profits requires the formulation of modified Values which would appear as money prices. Marx did not recognise that these prices probably would not generate a uniform *money* rate of profits once the commodities comprising the compositions of capital involved were expressed in modified money price terms as well. The analytical ramifications of the articulation between Values and prices were considerable, as he would realise as his critical investigations proceeded.

Later in the *Grundrisse* manuscripts, Marx argued that profit is a *transformed* manifestation of surplus Value because it is realised in exchange by means of prices which are not proportional to Values. The analytical process by which this transformation may be explained was hinted at thus:

Presupposing the same [rate of] surplus Value, *the same surplus labour in proportion to necessary labour*, then, the *rate of profit* depends on the relation between the part of capital exchanged for living labour and the part existing in the form of raw material and means of production. (G,747)

Here Marx *assumed* a uniform rate of surplus Value without any supporting explanation. He did not consider the possibility of variations in the rate or the implications of such variations for the analysis of the relationship between the rate and the generation of the uniform rate of profit. The ideas of a uniform rate of surplus Value and a varying organic composition of capital were to be two key components in Marx's subsequent attempts to resolve analytically the articulation between surplus Value and its appearance as profit. In the *Grundrisse*, the analysis was carried no further than this.

What was missing in particular in the present context was the concept of the *price of production*. This modified Value was such that a commodity, when sold, would yield the general rate of profits on the total capital involved in its production regardless of its constant–variable composition. Now Marx realised that the 'market' price that he sought would be different from Value, but he did not demonstrate that this difference is a *systematic* one. He seemed to be aware of the problem involved in the following passage:

Since the Value posited in the production process realises its price through exchange, the price of the product appears in fact determined by the sum of money which expresses an equivalent for the total quantity of labour contained in raw material, machinery, wages and unpaid surplus labour. *Thus price still appears here merely as a formal modification of Value; as Value expressed in money*; but the magnitude of this price is presupposed in the production process of capital. Capital thereby appears as a determinant of price, so that price is determined by the advances made by capital and the surplus labour realised by it in the product. *We shall see later that price, on the contrary, appears as determining profit.* (G,761; emphasis added)

Prices and the uniform general rate of profits are mutually inter-dependent in their determination. The former *realises* the latter, but the latter must be a simultaneous determinant of the former. However, the type of analysis that Marx foreshadowed in this argument was not to emerge until the early 1860s.[7]

CHAPTER 7

The logical dimensions of the 'law of motion' of capitalism

MARX'S INTERPRETATION OF THE 'MOTION' OF CAPITALISM

Marx's vision of the historical motion, or historical dynamics, of capitalism was the result of the confluence of three influences: firstly, his critical study of Hegel's dialectical philosophy of history; secondly, his own empirical observations of the temporal instability of capitalist economic activity in the context of rapid secular technological achievement and change; and thirdly, the analytical treatment of the dynamics of the system that he studied in the writings of political economy. These three influences came together for the first time in the *Grundrisse* manuscript when Marx investigated the dialectics of capitalist progress induced by the working out of contradictions. This endeavour was directed towards the ultimate rationale of his critique of political economy in that its objective was to further his comprehension of the human situation under the operations of a mode of production dominated by capital. His premises were that, based on observation *and* intuition, conditions for the vast majority of people could only be bad under this regime and could also be shown to be destined inevitably to get worse. By exposing the *sources* of this fate in the immanent dynamic structure and operation of capitalism, Marx's idea was to reveal the revolutionary path that *could* lead to the establishment of a truly human socio-economic environment. And, he believed, it *would* be followed by the proletariat once they became self-consciously aware of the reasons for their predicament.

In earlier chapters of this study, I explained how Marx's dialectical-materialist method was developed through his critique of the idealist philosophy of history espoused by Hegel. For Marx, the theory of history was to be sought in the material foundations of human existence, a thesis argued initially by Feuerbach. The investigations into the logic of the motion of capitalism must have reinforced Marx's belief in the appropriateness of his theoretical premises.

The materialist view of history centres on individual man, acting in a collectively created social and economic structure, as its subject. Hegel's idealist *reading* of history in which reason and a world spirit determined history for man was replaced by a *theory* of history which explains events and situations as the results of human actions.[1] In particular, the situation of man in history is no longer ascribed to the work of a transcendental being. Rather, man must now take responsibility for his own historical predicaments *and has the capacity to change them*. This aspect of Marx's theory of history represented a crucial shift in the way the future of man is to be envisaged. It opened the way for the realisation of his dictum in the eleventh 'Thesis on Feuerbach' that 'The philosophers have only *interpreted* the world in various ways; the point is to *change* it' (*CW*,5,5).

For Marx, the most essential and determinant dimensions of man's actions were those directed towards obtaining the means to satisfy his material needs. The centrepiece of man's history is his productive activity; specifically, his creative interaction with nature through labour and the organisational structure within which this labour takes place. Labour is man's fundamental ontological activity. Its *form* is vital in determining his status *vis-à-vis* his human potential. As Marx argued in detail in the *Paris Manuscripts* of 1844, under the regime of capital, the organisation of production is such that man's enforced labour leaves him alienated and unable to pursue or realise most of the dimensions of his human being. The explanation for this situation, Marx reasoned, is to be found in the capitalist relations of production and the way of using human labour that is dictated by the large-scale, machine-centred mode of production into which capitalism had developed. These relations and labour forms are set in a broader operational structure which ensures their perpetuation. Marx's critical investigations were now designed to provide a comprehension of this broader socio-economic setting in the belief that such a comprehension would reveal the essential, systematic causes of man's predicament and the potential for its improvement by radical change.

In the *Manifesto of the Communist Party* published in 1848 (CW,6,477ff.), Marx posited some profound insights into the nature of the history and future of capitalist society. Now while this work was intended to be a piece of propaganda and not an academic tract, his arguments therein did foreshadow several important aspects of the conception of historical motion to be investigated more formally in the *Grundrisse* manuscript.

The centrepiece of Marx's propagandist vision in the *Manifesto* was the class struggle (CW,6,482ff.). This struggle is the phenomenal reflection of the social relations of production dictated by each historical phase of the mode of production. Throughout history, the mode of production has undergone continual change affecting its material forces and their organisation. Marx's vision was of a constant and increasing tension between the social relations and material forces of any particular production system, although he referred most specifically to feudalism and capitalism. In the case of feudalism, the outcome of this tension had been the rise to prominence of a form of productive organisation and society in which the activities and aims of the bourgeoisie were dominant. This process of transition was achieved by the gradual abolition of feudal values and traditional forms of social and economic organisation and control. The capitalism that Marx observed was the result of the subsequent development of this small-scale, bourgeois mode of production that proceeded with the rapid technological advances of the era.

Marx recognised explicitly the incredible rise in man's capacity to *produce* material wealth as a consequence of the bourgeois application, organisation and operation of capital (CW,6,489). He was just as aware, though, that this great achievement was accompanied by two, more sinister phenomena. Firstly, the proletarian majority, forced to provide the essential labour to make the system work, received a very small per capita share of its benefits. The contradiction of great wealth amid abject poverty was an observable fact. Secondly, Marx made the empirically based assertion that 'The bourgeoisie cannot exist without constantly revolutionising the instruments of production, and thereby the relations of production, and with them the whole relations of society' (CW,6,487). On the basis of this vital historical axiom, he postulated that capitalism would continue to experience fluctuations in economic activity and regular crises. These crisis situations would be corrected by compensating changes in the mode of production which would ensure that the system did not collapse (CW,6,489–90). Intuitively, Marx went on to argue, though, that the ability of capitalists to find avenues for compensating changes and reorganisations to resist the effects of economic downturns is limited. The result was predicted to be ever-deepening cyclical crises with increasingly far-reaching social effects (CW,6,490).

In this scenario, the destiny of the expanding proletarian class was set. The pattern that Marx saw emerging was similar to that which preceded the demise of feudalism. The social relations on which capitalism depended were becoming increasingly incompatible with the wealth-creating capacity of the system and the associated maldistribution of that wealth. The time was approaching when the proletariat would see its way clear to abolish the relations of production of capitalism and apply the massive forces of production in the service of human freedom and social equity (CW,6,490,496). Marx's investigations in the *Grundrisse* manuscript were directed towards giving this impressionistic prognosis a more formal, critico-analytical basis.

Marx's empirical observations of capitalism during the 1850s in London confirmed the essential substance of the vision postulated in the *Manifesto*. The system showed continuous signs of economic fluctuations involving booms and crises and he had occasion to report on this pattern in the three articles in the *Neue Rheinische Zeitung, Politisch-ökonomische Revue* during 1850 (CW,10, 257ff.,338ff., and 490ff.).

Marx undertook a review of political and economic events affecting Britain and other European countries consequent upon the boom conditions of the later 1840s. His impression was that the boom had generated an oversupply of capital and productive capacity and a resulting overproduction of commodities. That is, a general glut. This had occurred simultaneously in the industrial and agricultural sectors. If the cyclical developments followed the pattern engendered by events of 1843 to 1847, Marx predicted that the next deep crisis would occur in 1852. He found a distinct irony in the planning for the Great Exhibition of industry in 1851 taking place amidst the symptoms of the burgeoning crisis.

The bourgeoisie is celebrating this, its greatest festival, at a moment when the collapse of all its glory is at hand, a collapse which will demonstrate more conclusively than ever to it that the powers it has brought into being have grown beyond its control. (*CW*,10,500)

Once again, then, Marx reiterated his vision that the final crisis of capitalism was imminent and would emerge as a consequence of its own limitations. Even though this crisis did not eventuate, he persisted with his faith in the ultimate truth of his prognosis.

In 1857, it became apparent to Marx from his observations that, once more, Britain was about to be plunged into an economic crisis. Compared to his earlier observation, the situation apparently seemed more critical. It was his belief in this impending catastrophe that induced him to begin work in earnest on the critical investigations that were recorded in the *Grundrisse* manuscript.

Marx referred to the stimulus that he received from his perception of the imminent crisis in his correspondence of 1857. On 8 December, he wrote to Engels that he was working 'like mad', often throughout the night, on 'a synthesis' of his economic studies. The explicit reason for this mad endeavour was 'to have at least the outlines [*Grundrisse*] clear before the deluge', that is, before the final crisis of capitalism (*MEW*,29,225). Ten days later, he again referred to his work in the context of the impending final crisis. He informed Engels that he was working 'to get to the bottom of things' in preparing his 'Economics' for the public while at the same time keeping a detailed record of the trends in the crisis indicators in his notebooks (letter to Engels, 18 December 1857, *MEW*,29,232).[2] Soon after this letter to Engels, he wrote to Lassalle in the same terms: 'The present commercial crisis has induced me to devote myself in earnest to the elaboration of the basis of my "Economics" and also to prepare something on the present crisis. I am obliged to sacrifice the day with work to earn our daily living. The *real* work can only be done at night, and I am often upset by illness. . . . I have no news to report because I am living like a hermit' (21 December 1857, *MEW*,29,548). The work during the day could not have been entirely lost, it seems, because Marx was at this time writing about the crisis for the *New York Daily Tribune*.

At the theoretical level, Marx had studied the dynamics of capitalism in the analyses of the political economists. The idea of motion was presented in Adam Smith's *Wealth of Nations* as the general principle of economic growth and development. In Ricardo's *Principles*, the analysis of motion was more formalised with the relationship between growth and distribution receiving attention. For Ricardo, the falling rate of profits was linked to the possible stationary-state fate of capitalism. The physiocrats had also made motion explicit, but in a quite different sense from that in Smith's and Ricardo's work. Physiocratic concern was to present the interdependence between expenditures and production in the different sectors of the economy and the consequent money and commodity flows required to sustain the system. In all of these analyses of motion, a key role was implied or explicated for capital and the economic surplus. It was Marx's belief, though, that the role was not adequately comprehended by these writers.

Marx's investigations in the *Grundrisse* revealed that the motion just outlined comprised several, *analytically* separable dimensions. He saw these as providing the *logical essences* of the observed phenomena of capitalist motion, that is, what he would later call the 'economic law of motion' of the system (*K(PE)*,I,92).

For Marx, the motion of capitalism was fundamentally the consequence of the endeavours of *individual* capitalists to preserve and expand their capital. He considered that the most essential requirement of this endeavour is the *unity* of production and circulation. Even though he had analysed the process of simple circulation in the early stages of the *Grundrisse*, he was always aware that the process is not self-sustaining and cannot exist independently of production (*G*,217,227,235,254–5). Indeed, the very purpose of circulation is to provide the realisation of produced Value and surplus Value through commodity exchange which completes the production process. The ongoing existence and growth of capital is expressed in and dependent upon this unity: 'circulation is itself a moment of production, since capital becomes capital only through circulation . . .' (*G*,520). Later in the manuscript, Marx reiterated the point thus:

The total production process of capital includes both the circulation process proper and the actual production process. These form the two great sections of its movement, which appears as the totality of these two processes. . . . And the whole movement appears as unity of labour time and circulation time, as unity of production and circulation. This unity itself is motion, process.

Capital appears as this unity-in-process of production and circulation. . . . (G,620)

The unity of production and circulation became the central premise of Marx's investigations into the motion of capitalism. It suggested to him that several dimensions of the mode of production in which this unity is imbedded should be analysed in order to comprehend the logic and form of the motion.

Firstly, Marx was concerned to analyse more fully the process of circulation and the working out of its contradictions. These contradictions manifest themselves as various forms of misalignment between supply and demand and their implications for the *realisation* of produced Value. For Marx's vision of an expanding economy, one probability was general overproduction and he was concerned to refute the apparent implication of 'Say's law' that such a phenomenon could not occur. There was also the possibility that some individual sectors could experience overproduction because of disproportionalities in the actual pattern of production relative to the pattern of demand for commodities to be used in final consumption and as means of production.

Secondly, Marx found that the unity of production and circulation involves an immediate contradiction in that it requires capital to traverse two phases in the totality of its circulation. While involved in the production process *per se*, capital is *active* in the sense that it is directly facilitating the production of Value and surplus Value. In circulation, capital in its commodity form is deactivated and the period of this phase represents lost production time for the capitalist. However, he cannot escape the necessary unity of the two processes and his interest is best served by reducing the circulation time to a minimum, given the constraint that his commodities must reach ever-extending markets. Marx investigated the quantitative effects of this circulation time on the generation of surplus Value and extended his analysis to include the additional implications of increasing fixed capital employment in production for the turnover time of capital.

The third dimension of motion that Marx investigated was the *potential* for capitalism to reproduce itself on a constant or expanding scale without impediment. In this analysis, he established the necessary qualitative and quantitative conditions for reproduction to proceed smoothly and continuously. Here Marx adumbrated the reproduction schema as an analytical device which he would develop more fully in the future.

Fourthly, Marx analysed the process of capital accumulation and its consequences. His premise was that accumulation necessarily involved technological changes in production and the *logic* of these changes entailed that the Value rate of profits would tend to fall. This tendency was argued independently of any problems with the full realisation of Value and surplus Value that may result from impediments to circulation.

Finally, the consequence of capitalism's motion was envisaged by Marx to be a continuous sequence of ever-worsening *crises*.[3] These crises would be signalled to the capitalist by the overproduction of commodities, the failure to realise embodied Value fully and the consequent reduction in the realised rate of profits. Such consequences would result in the capitalists voluntarily or involuntarily taking decisions which would mitigate the effects involved and lead to a recovery in production, demand and profitability. For Marx, though, this recovery cycle became increasingly problematical because of *secular* trends built into the behaviour of the capitalist economy. In particular, these comprised the technologically induced fall in the *potential* rate of profits and rise in the proletarian 'reserve army of labour'. The indications were that the *social and economic* ramifications of the recessions would ultimately become so profound that the proletariat's situation would no longer be tolerable. The revolutionary abolition of the capital regime would ensue. This, then, was the ultimate message of Marx's critical analysis of motion. More than this, though, it represented the *raison d'être* of his whole critique of political economy in that the proletarian reaction could only be effective if it was founded on sound *theoretical* premises.

In the *Grundrisse*, none of these logical dimensions of the motion of capitalism, or their integration and manifestation as the crises experienced by the system, received very detailed analytical treatment. Marx's arguments were scattered and sketchy. The preliminary and experimental nature of his investigations were all too apparent in this most important aspect of his critique. The analyses that he outlined were largely impressionistic and built around unsubstantiated assertions. Especially did he give very little attention to the limitations and qualifications entailed in his arguments.

Be all this as it may, however, the extant pieces of critical analysis reveal some powerful insights into the contradiction-ridden structures and operations of capitalism. These can be presented with some degree of coherence as a clear adumbration of the form the 'law of motion' would take in Marx's later work.

THE CIRCULATION PROCESS OF CAPITAL AND ITS IMMANENT CONTRADICTIONS

In the context of his developing awareness of the crucial interdependence of production and circulation, Marx considered the phenomenon of circulation in some detail *in isolation from production*. This was but the *first stage* in the formulation of the 'law of motion' of capitalism in the *Grundrisse*, for the analysis of circulation could only be separated artificially from the other dimensions of motion.

An immediate consequence of the complexity of post-production exchanges in capitalism is the need to rely on *money* as a means of circulation. Money facilitates circulation by acting as a universal and homogeneous manifestation of exchange value. It is not constrained in *its* circulation by being embodied in any particular use-value form (*G*,145–6).

The exchange value of a thing is nothing other than the quantitatively specific expression of its capacity for serving as a *medium of exchange*. In money the *medium of exchange* becomes a thing, or, the exchange value of the thing achieves an independent existence apart from the thing. (*G*,199–200)

For Marx, the consequence of the need for capitalism to rely upon a complex circulation process, and the need for that circulation to be facilitated by money as a separate entity, was the existence of certain immanent contradictions which had the potential to disrupt the system's historical progress. Especially are these contradictions likely to impede the complete and continuous valorisation (*Verwertung*) of capital through circulation. The immediate result of production is a commodity with an *ideal* Value, part of which is transferred from capital inputs and part of which is surplus Value added by living labour. The valorisation process requires that this ideal Value be converted to a money form through exchange such that subsequent exchanges can be undertaken to replace and expand capital.

197

Valorisation comprises three components in an essential unity. Firstly, by means of 'exchange' with labour, capital is able to command living labour in production to an extent which preserves the Value of capital advanced in employing it. Secondly, because of the special form of the capital–labour relationship, the capitalist can command living labour services beyond those needed for the capital replacement. The surplus labour is potentially available to expand capital. Thirdly, the *material* result of production, the commodity with use value and exchange value, which embodies the valorisation potential, has to be realised in money form through exchange. Marx commented upon these three components:

The three processes of which capital forms the unity are external; they are separate in time and space. As such, the transition from one into the other, i.e. their unity as regards the individual capitalists, is accidental. (*G*,403)

The completion of the valorisation process, and thus the ongoing preservation of the capitalist mode of production, depends upon *chance circumstances*. The potential for failure was, as a consequence, quite evident to Marx.

Marx went on to elaborate upon the potential impediments in the circulation process. It is, most essentially, the *dual nature* of the commodity which presents the problem (*G*,147–8). The commodity is a unity of exchange value and use value, the latter being a *necessary* precondition for the *realisation* of the former. Use value is not a *sufficient* condition for the realisation of exchange value because such use value, *and* the needs for it to satisfy, can exist without exchange proceeding. As Marx put it,

whether or not the commodity is transposable into money, whether or not it can be exchanged for money, whether its exchange value can be posited for it – this depends on circumstances which initially have nothing to do with it as exchange value and are independent of that. (*G*,147)

For as he went on to recognise, 'ineffective, *non-paying needs*, i.e. a need which does not itself possess a commodity or money to give in exchange' (*G*,404), are not relevant in the valorisation of capital.

Not only does the *qualitative* demand pattern have to be appropriate, but also it has to be *quantitatively effective* in its relationship to actual production. Thus *demand*, which originates in the incomes generated by production, is a crucial factor in the valorisation process. Any impediment to the exercise of potential demand would leave unrealised part of the Value and surplus Value produced with consequent disruption to the capitalist reproduction and growth processes.

Capitalism faces, then, the potential hazard that it cannot realise in circulation the full Value of all commodities produced in any particular period of time. The key to understanding this problem is, Marx argued, that money separates the act of sale from the act of purchase (G,148,197–8). What money does, in its capacity as the medium of exchange, is to facilitate the exchange process. But once one particular exchange is completed, money provides its holder with the option of not proceeding to a subsequent exchange. That is, money becomes potentially an end in itself and is able to be held as a store of Value (G,215–16). In this sense money has the ability to *impede* circulation as an ongoing sequence of exchanges. 'Thus', wrote Marx, 'already in the quality of money as a medium, in the splitting of exchange into two acts, there lies the germ of crises, or at least their possibility . . .' (G,198).

Marx observed that the capitalist form of circulation, in which money allows the separation of purchase and sale, initiates the rise of a merchant estate (*Kaufmannsstand*) which mediates in the purchase–sale sequence (G,148–9,200). As a result, the circulation process becomes detached from production to some extent and an added potential for disruption is introduced through the increased complexity of getting the commodity from production to its ultimate consumer. Marx made the point in the following passage.

This doubling of exchange – exchange for the sake of consumption and exchange for exchange – gives rise to a new disproportion. . . . Circulation, i.e. exchange within the mercantile estate, and the point at which circulation ends, i.e. exchange between the mercantile estate and the consumers – as much as they must ultimately condition one another – are determined by quite different laws and motives, and can enter into the most acute contradiction with one another. The possibility of commercial crises is already contained in this separation. (G,149)

Marx did not elaborate to any great extent upon the ramifications of the merchant estate, but the *principle* implied is quite clear. Here is a capitalist development designed, as is the case with money, to improve the process of circulation. In this case the motive is the gains which would accrue to the merchants. The significant consequence as Marx saw it is that the development also engendered further immanent contradictions within the process which can disrupt its operation. This accentuated the potential instability in capitalist motion.

Marx also mentioned in passing that *credit* could have some effect upon the dynamics of circulation. It was his view that one means by which capital endeavoured to ensure adequate circulation for full valorisation is through the development of a *credit system* (G,416).

It thus appears as a matter of chance for production based on capital whether or not its essential condition, the continuity of the different processes which constitute its process as a whole, is actually brought about. The suspension of this chance element by capital itself is *credit*. . . . Which is why *credit* in any developed form appears in no earlier mode of production. (G,535)

At this stage, though, Marx wrote little more than this on the subject.

By its very nature, in its striving to maximise the valorisation process, capital takes steps to transcend any impediment or barrier to that process. Thus Marx wrote that 'capital is the endless and limitless drive to go beyond its limiting barrier. Every boundary [*Grenze*] is and has to be a barrier [*Schranke*] for it. Else it would cease to be capital . . .' (G,334). This was an important principle in Marx's formulation of the 'law of motion' of capitalism. The barriers to be transcended would constantly reappear as a consequence of that transcendence. The fate of capitalism is sealed in this barrier–transcendence–barrier theory of motion and Marx elaborated the *principle* in the following passage:

But from the fact that capital posits every such limit as a barrier and hence gets *ideally* beyond it, it does not by any means follow that it has *really* overcome it, and, since every such barrier contradicts its character, its production moves in contradictions which are

constantly overcome but just as constantly posited. Furthermore.
[*sic*] The universality towards which it irresistibly strives
encounters barriers in its own nature, which will, at a certain stage
of its development, allow it to be recognised as being itself the
greatest barrier to this tendency, and hence will drive towards its
own suspension. (*G*,410)

Having stated this principle, though, Marx still had a long way to
go in his endeavours to formulate from it a coherent, operational
analysis of the motion and fate of capitalism.

The barriers with which Marx was initially concerned were those
external to production:

Inside the production process, realisation [*Verwertung*] appeared
totally identical with the production of surplus labour (the
objectification of surplus time), and hence appeared to have no
bounds other than those partly presupposed and partly posited
within this process itself, but which are always posited within it as
barriers to be forcibly overcome. There now appear barriers to it
which lie *outside* it. (*G*,404)

We see in this passage that Marx was concerned also with the
barriers that were *internal* to the production process. These especially involved the dynamics of capital accumulation and will be
considered below.

For the present, it was *consumption demand* which was viewed
by Marx as the root of the barriers to adequate circulation in
support of production. This barrier has two dimensions. Firstly, the
use value of commodities must be appropriate to extant needs,
keeping in mind that such needs are quantitatively finite. Secondly,
the Value equivalent must be available for expenditure on consumption (*G*,404–5). But, just as this barrier might appear due to
failure of one or both of these conditions, so capital has to overcome it.

One way in which full valorisation might be achieved in spite of
this consumption barrier is for capital to expand its sphere of
circulation by entering new markets. Especially is this required
where capital accumulation and growth are occurring. As Marx
saw it,

A precondition of production based on capital is therefore *the production of a constantly widening sphere of circulation*, whether the sphere itself is directly expanded or whether *more points within it are created as points of production*. While circulation appeared at first as a constant magnitude, it here appears as a moving magnitude, being expanded by production itself. Accordingly, it already appears as a moment of production itself. (*G*,407)

Such expansion of circulation has negative implications as well and Marx's investigations were soon to turn to the problem of surplus Value generation in a situation of increasing capital turnover time.

From the literature on political economy, Marx drew an interesting critical comparison between the work of Ricardo and Sismondi on the issue of the possibility of the oversupply of commodities. He felt that neither writer has adequately grasped the significance of the integrated nature of the processes of production and circulation. They had not investigated the operational links between the two processes which affect the extent of *realisation* of produced commodities and the consequent degree of valorisation of capital (*G*,410–11).

For Ricardo, the ultimate objective of political economy was to explain the distributional effects of capital accumulation and development (*G*,597). In this analysis, Ricardo remained unconcerned with the potential problems for capitalism which were revealed when the analysis of production was extended to include circulation. His focus was on 'supply without regard to demand', and he

conceived production as directly identical with the self-valorisation of capital – and hence [was] . . . heedless of the barriers to consumption . . ., having in view only the development of the forces of production and the growth of the industrial population. . . . (*G*,410)

Marx commented, though, that in approaching political economy in this way, Ricardo had 'grasped the positive essence of capital more correctly and deeply' than Sismondi had done (*G*,410). Ricardo had encapsulated the way in which *the capitalists themselves* behave in their *production*-oriented decision making.

Sismondi's interpretation of capitalism gave less emphasis to this basic nature of the production process from which capitalist motion emanates. But he was more aware of the tenuous nature of the motion which does appear. Unlike Ricardo, he 'emphasised the barriers of consumption' and 'better grasped the limited nature of production based on capital, its negative one-sidedness' (G,410). Furthermore, Sismondi comprehended that the barriers are created by capital itself and that they may ultimately lead to the 'breakdown' of capitalist production in some sense. Sismondi went on to argue that the solution to this problem of capitalism is artificially to restrict production, but in Marx's view of the nature of capital any such attempt would 'necessarily be demolished by capital' (G,411).

However, Marx was able to find in Ricardo's work some awareness of the existence of barriers in the capitalist circulation process.

Ricardo . . . has a suspicion that the *exchange value* of a commodity is not a value apart from exchange, and that it proves itself as a value only in exchange; but he regards the barriers which production thereby encounters as accidental, as barriers which are overcome. He therefore conceives the overcoming of such barriers as being in the essence of capital, although he often becomes absurd in the exposition of that view. . . . (G,411)

What remained 'absurd' in Ricardo's exposition of motion was his dogmatic acceptance of the dictum posited by Say and James Mill that *general overproduction* is prevented by the *existence* of supply and its immediate consequential equivalence as demand. Marx's attitude towards this dogma was made quite clear.

This nonsense about the impossibility of overproduction (in other words, the assertion of the immediate identity of capital's process of production and its process of realisation) has been expressed in a manner which is at least sophistical, i.e. ingenious, . . . by James Mill, in the formula that supply = its own demand, that supply and demand therefore balance, which means . . . the same thing as that Value is determined by labour time, and hence that *exchange adds nothing to it*, and which forgets only that exchange does have to take place and that this depends (in the final instance) on the *use value*. (G,423)

Marx found some limited merit in the understanding of capitalism which 'Say's law' implied. This merit had two dimensions. Firstly, it *is* the case that production of Value is the potential source of demand for the commodities involved when that Value is distributed as incomes and for replacement of means of production (although Marx's present emphasis was on consumption demand only) (*G*,411–12). Secondly, the argument implicitly recognised that Value comes from production and that exchange itself adds nothing to the Value in circulation. This point was made by Marx in the above passage. Both of these dimensions gave the dictum its 'sophistical' and 'ingenious' content. They reflected a limited comprehension of two important facts about capitalism as Marx saw it. What was *not* included was the additional fact that the harmonious operation of capitalism depends upon the *exercise* of demand rather than simply upon the *potential* for it. This, Marx stressed, depends upon the nature of the use values being produced and these are unrelated to exchange values. Thus, the 'use value [of a commodity] . . . is absolutely not measured by the labour time objectified in it, but rather a measuring rod is applied to it which lies outside its nature as exchange value' (*G*,412). This 'measuring rod' is the existing needs of consumers. Note that Marx was aware in the present argument that the necessary incomes must be available to make the needs-based demand *effective* (*G*,404).

It was also the case, Marx argued, that the 'Say's law' expression of these basic features of capitalism revealed a better comprehension of the nature of the system than the 'vulgar' ideas posited by some writers who followed Ricardo. It was their approach, in endeavouring to portray the harmonious progress of capitalism, to obscure the overproduction malady by denying the specific nature of capitalist production. Marx wrote on this that

The attempts made from the orthodox economic standpoint to deny that there is *general overproduction* at any given moment are indeed childish. . . . [In] order to rescue production *based on capital* (see e.g. MacCulloch), all its specific qualities are ignored and their specific character as forms omitted, and capital is conceived as its inverse, as simple production for *immediate use value*. Totally abstracts away the essential relations. In fact, in order to cleanse it of contradictions, it is virtually dropped and negated. (*G*,411)

No supporting evidence was given for this assertion, but it did serve to emphasise again the crucial role that Marx saw for the basic nature of capital in understanding the operations of capitalism. If this nature was not interpreted 'correctly', the subsequent analysis of the system would be inaccurate, at least as a matter of logic.

The 'Say's law' principle, Marx noted, did allow for the emergence of specific disproportions between sectors of production and patterns of demand. Thus *partial* overproduction was possible while *general* overproduction was not. Marx reasoned that this view merely dodged the issue. *Any* failure to realise the Values of commodities produced through exchange constitutes *overproduction per se*. Only a matter of degree is involved (G,412). Moreover, the existence of overproduction in any degree highlights the contradictions of capitalism as Marx saw them. That *partial* overproduction can be corrected by a redistribution of productive resources *presupposes* disharmony (G,413) and implies that the disharmony can be perpetuated and exacerbated by decisions involving 'over-correction'. Competition, the basis for this corrective mechanism, is not constrained by the specific dimensions of the disproportion that exists. Political economy had failed to comprehend the disharmonious implications of competition as the manifestation of the 'inner *nature of capital*', involving as it does the continual interaction of *independent* capitals striving for maximum valorisation and individual survival (G,413–14). Marx's conclusion was that the operations of capital in production and circulation cannot prevent a continuous overproduction disequilibrium. For Marx, then,

Conceptually, *competition* is nothing other than the inner *nature of capital*, its essential character, appearing in and realised as the reciprocal interaction of many capitals with one another, the inner tendency as external necessity. . . . Capital is just as much the constant positing as the suspension of *proportionate production*. The existing proportion always has to be suspended by the creation of surplus Values and the increase of productive forces. But this demand, that production should be expanded *simultaneously* and *at once in the same proportion*, makes external demands upon capital which in no way arise out of itself; at the same time, the departure from the given proportion in one branch of production drives all of them out of it, and in unequal proportions. (G,414)

The insight contained in this passage exposed clearly the folly of the naive belief that partial overproduction is simply a temporary aberration which would be self-correcting through competition. The very nature of capital militates against this outcome. Surplus Value generation means capital accumulation and consequent changes in the forces of production. These effects constantly feed the disproportionate state of the system. The interdependent nature of the capitalist mode of production ensures the spread of any sectoral disproportion, and competition serves to sustain this state by encouraging further capital accumulation and changes in the forces of production.

According to Marx, both Malthus and Sismondi had 'correctly remarked' on the point that the aggregate demand generated by workers would not be sufficient to purchase the aggregate supply of commodities (G,413,420). Proudhon was also credited with this realisation, although his reasoning was inappropriate for it depended upon 'added-on' non-labour incomes in Value formation.

Proudhon, who certainly hears the bells ringing but never knows where, therefore sees the origin of overproduction in the fact 'that the worker cannot buy back his product'. By this he understands that interest and profit are added on to it; or that the price of the product is an overcharge on top of its real value. (G,424)

In rejecting the embodied labour theory of Value, Malthus and Sismondi had also seen the issue in much the same way. By contrast, Marx always adhered to the labour theory of Value in his discussions of overproduction.

Recognition of this constraint upon demand led Marx to consider further the capital–labour relation. Labour related to capital most directly as the exchange value of labour power purchased and the use value of living labour exercised to generate Value. An additional consideration which now came to light was the relation of capital to *labour as a consumer* (G,419–22;cf.543). The nature of capital is such that it would want to maximise consumption by workers *it did not employ* as an individual capital while minimising the consumption of workers it did so employ. Capital, then, embodies the further contradiction that, in striving to minimise the Value of labour power as dictated by real consumption patterns, it also reduces the aggregate demand for commodities produced.

In the foregoing discussion, Marx's position on the excess-commodity crisis potential of capitalism was concerned almost completely with *underconsumption*. At this stage, though, he was not intending to develop the analysis of overproduction fully. On this he wrote that 'The point here, of course, is not yet to develop overproduction specifically, but only the predisposition to it, such as it is posited in primitive form in the capital relation itself' (G,419). The most obvious and 'primitive' form of overproduction is indeed underconsumption. The development of this *particular form* of overproduction was sufficient to demonstrate the *potential* in capitalism for the malady to appear more generally. And, as Marx argued in the following passage, overproduction generally is a vital component in comprehending the motion of capitalism.

It is enough here to demonstrate that capital contains a *particular* restriction of production – which contradicts its general tendency to drive beyond every barrier to production – in order to have uncovered the foundation of *overproduction*, the fundamental contradiction of developed capital; in order to have uncovered, more generally, the fact that capital is not, as the economists believe, the *absolute* form for the development of the forces of production. . . . (G,415)

There was, however, no further development of this more general analysis of overproduction in the *Grundrisse*, although Marx's initial thoughts on the reproduction schema pointed in this direction by implication.

THE PRODUCTION–CIRCULATION UNITY AND THE GENERATION OF SURPLUS VALUE

Marx's view was that the valorisation process of capital could only be fully explained if production and circulation are treated as a unity. One particular consequence of this treatment was his recognition that the periodic generation of surplus Value depends upon the characteristics of circulation, especially the circulation time and the rate of turnover of capital embodied in the means of production. His idea was that while circulation does not itself produce a moment of *Value-determination*, for that lies exclusively in labour, its speed does determine the speed with which the production process is repeated, Values are created – thus if not *Values*, at least to a certain extent the mass of Values. Namely, the Values and surplus Values posited by the production process, multiplied by the number of repetitions of the production process in a given period of time. (*G*,538)

The fundamental principle that Marx applied in analysing this aspect of the motion of capitalism was that during any period that part of the aggregate capital advanced is not embodied in forms actually delivering or generating Value in *production*, it is effectively 'devalued'. As Marx put it, '[while] labour time appears as Value-positing activity, this circulation time of capital appears as the *time of devaluation*' (*G*,538). He went on to elaborate on this important thesis:

Capital exists as capital only in so far as it passes through the phases of circulation, the various moments of its transformation, in order to be able to begin the production process anew, and these phases are themselves phases of its valorisation – but at the same time, . . . of its *devaluation*. As long as capital remains frozen in the form of the finished product, it cannot be active as capital, it is *negated* capital. Its valorisation process is delayed in the same degree, and its Value-in-process [*prozessierender Wert*] negated. This thus appears as a loss for capital, as a relative loss of its Value, for its Value consists precisely in its valorisation process. (*G*,546)

The significance of circulation time for capital is that it acts as a *barrier*, a 'deadlock', to the maximisation of Value and surplus Value generation. In part, this is a consequence of capital's development, its endeavours to seek out more *extensive* markets (*G*,539,545).

Marx developed this idea of a 'circulation barrier' more fully later in the manuscript. His analysis first of all was devoted to the nature of capital in this particular context. This led him to formulate the categories 'circulating' capital and 'fixed' capital in a special way (*G*,618ff.). Circulation, movement *through* phases of form, is the essence of capital's involvement in the production–

circulation unity. In this sense, all capital is circulating capital and Marx explained the idea as follows:

> Circulating capital is therefore initially not a *particular* form of capital, but is rather *capital* itself, in a further developed aspect, as subject of the movement [in production-circulation] . . . which it, itself, is as its own valorisation process. In this respect, therefore, every capital is *circulating capital. (G,620)*

There is a time dimension to circulation which is determined in part by the time period that capital spends in any one phase form, e.g. as means of production or as finished commodities. During these periods it is *fixated* and *deactivated* (G,620–1). While fixated or circulating outside of the *flow* process of production, capital is not involved in generating surplus Value. The periodic generation of surplus Value by a given capital depends very much upon these characteristics of the cycle of capital (G,741).

For Marx, the circulation constraint on periodic surplus Value generation comprised two dimensions which he analysed more formally in turn: firstly, the effect of the time durations of the production and circulation *processes* themselves; and secondly, the effect of the proportional division of capital advanced into circulating and fixed components, on the usual criterion of one and more than one period return cycles.

The production–circulation cycle comprises several phases. Marx posited these as

> (1) Creation of surplus Value, or immediate production process. Its result, the product. (2) Bringing the product to market. Transformation of product into commodity. (3) (α) Entry of the commodity into ordinary circulation. . . . Its result: transformation into money. This appears as the first moment of ordinary circulation. (β) Retransformation of money into the conditions of production: money circulation. . . . (4) Renewal of the production process, which appears here as reproduction of the original capital, and production process of surplus capital. (G,619)

The number of times that surplus Value was generated in any particular period depends upon the duration of the two summary components, production time and circulation time. After struggling with some arithmetical computations, Marx devised an algebraic analysis (an approach rarely used in his writings) in which this point was considered more formally. He established that the aggregate surplus Value generated in any period can be calculated once the rate of generation in each *production* period is known and that this aggregate is inversely related to both the production and circulation times (G,652–7).[4]

In considering the effect of the division of capital into its fixed and circulating proportions on the aggregate periodic generation of surplus Value, Marx analysed three aspects of the problem, each of which affected the rate of turnover of the capital involved in the production process (G,678ff.). More specifically, his mixture of algebraic and arithmetical analysis established that the aggregate surplus Value generated in any particular period would be *decreased* if the proportion of fixed capital in total capital was increased, if the durability of the fixed capital increased, and if the turnover period of the circulating capital increased.[5]

The result of including fixed capital in production is to reduce the effective capital turnover in a given period. Marx went on to make the point that such a calculation of turnover does not mean that the fixed capital element is *replaced* in the turnover period. Replacement cycles are determined by the durability of the fixed capital concerned. He did not, however, follow through the implications of these cycles for aggregate demand in any detail, although he suggested a relationship with long-term, ten-yearly fluctuations of activity (G,720).

In these analyses of aggregate surplus Value generation and its circulation constraint, Marx recognised that he was dealing with production and circulation at the aggregate level of capital-in-general. Further development of the analysis of capitalism's motion required that he move to the many-capitals level of analysis in which the competitive interdependence between the operations of the capitals in different sectors of production are considered.

PRODUCTION AND THE ESSENTIALS OF THE REPRODUCTION OF CAPITAL

Marx was aware of the work of the physiocrats which included the first explication of an economic system in terms of the interdependence between sectors of production and the particular intersector flows of commodities and money required to ensure its ongoing operation. He had access to their works while in Brussels during 1846 and the last of his notebooks from the period included some brief excerpts from Quesnay's *Le droit naturel* and *Analyse de tableau économique* (*MEGA*,I/6,612–13; the excerpts being from the Eugène Daire edition of the physiocrats' works published in Paris in 1846).

At the time of this study, and later in the *Grundrisse*, there is no evidence that Marx appreciated the profound significance of the *Tableau* as a model of *reproduction*. He recognised it as a model which emphasised capital as the basis of production (*G*,327–8) and as an explication of the *process of circulation*. With respect to the latter point, he made the following passing remark in the *Grundrisse*: 'The circulation of capital is at the same time its becoming, its growth, its vital process. If anything needed to be compared with the circulation of blood, it was not the formal circulation of money, but the content-filled circulation of capital' (*G*,517). This was a reference to the anatomical and physiological analogy used by Quesnay to devise the *Tableau*. Marx's reading of the analysis did not see it as representing the *reproductive* integration of production and circulation, possibly because the dynamic properties of the *Tableau* were not as evident in the *Analyse* form that Marx had studied as they were in the zig-zag versions not included in the Daire edition.[6] Indeed, the latter sentence quoted above suggests that Marx quite underestimated the analytical power of the *Tableau*. And, in his own adumbration of the elements of the reproduction analysis, he made no reference to Quesnay's work at all (*G*,439ff.). The model that Marx began to develop appears to be a quite independent formulation at this stage. Later on, it was to be explicitly *integrated* with the *Tableau* (see his letter to Engels, 6 July 1863, *MEW*,30,361ff.).

It was while he was investigating the implications of a uniform general rate of profits across the various sectors of production (*G*,434ff.), that Marx devised the first principles of what was to become his schema of reproduction. As he noted later in the *Grundrisse*, the analysis of circulation at the aggregate level did not take account of the complex interdependencies between the sectors of production. Such aggregate analysis represented 'a haze under which yet another whole world conceals itself, the world of the interconnections of capital'. This *'simultaneity of the different orbits of capital'* only becomes evident once the analysis of many capitals is tackled (G,639).

The investigation of the general rate of profits caused Marx to formulate a model of production that included several different 'branches of business' (G,435). These branches all employ capital and the competition between them ensures that a uniform general rate of profits is generated. However, as well as being in competition, the branches are also highly interdependent and Marx *implied* this in his analysis of a five-branches model, although he qualified the presentation as only *possibly* to be continued later and as not belonging to the present stage of his work (G,442).

Marx presented a schema similar to that shown in Table 7.1 as the basis for his discussion (G,441).[7] The significant point is that each sector A to E (where the table ordering is Marx's own) depends for its reproduction on the other sectors in the sense that the inputs to each, viz. workers' necessaries (and thus labour), raw materials and machinery, are the outputs of other sectors. In addition, it is initially assumed that the surplus generated by each is completely spent by the capitalists on consumption of the commodity produced for them in sector D (labelled as 'Surplus-product'). This interdependence can only be realised fully if the production–circulation unity comprises a qualitatively and quantitatively appropriate set of commodities and exchanges between capitalists and capitalists and between capitalists and workers. Marx demonstrated that this is *possible* by means of some simple arithmetic, putting aside for the moment any impediments to the actual operation of the required conditions. Later Marx would refer to this case as 'simple reproduction' and the data in Table 7.1 are consistent with such a model.

Marx concluded that in the above case, the capitalists would not be serving their objective of the valorisation of capital. 'If they consumed the entire surplus, then they would have come no further at the end than they were at the beginning, and the surplus Value of their capital would not grow' (G,441). This led Marx to consider a second case in which half of the surplus generated by each capitalist is saved and applied to capital accumulation (G,441–3). This case would later be called 'expanded reproduction'.

In considering capital accumulation and the reproduction requirements, Marx did not at this stage formulate the model very

Table 7.1

		Machinery	Raw material	Labour	Surplus product
A	Raw material manufacture 1.	20	40	20	20
B	Raw material manufacture 2.	20	40	20	20
C	Machinery manufacture	20	40	20	20
E	Workers' necessaries	20	40	20	20
D	Surplus-product	20	40	20	20

clearly. He did, though, elicit some principles of the analysis which would be built upon later. The decision by capitalists to save out of surplus Value affects directly the quantitative interdependence requirements between the sectors of production. First of all, the demand for the production of sector D is halved. At the same time, the demand for the outputs of the remaining sectors are increased, with the quantitative assumption being that the replacement and additional capital compositions for each sector are the same as those already in operation. For this extension to be consistent with reproduction, again the quantitative and qualitative structure of production–circulation had to be appropriate. Marx's arithmetic on this point only went part of the way towards a formulation of the precise conditions required.

Marx drew from his analysis some significant dynamic implications for capitalism (G,443–4). It was evident to him that the reproduction conditions that apply depend on what happens to the composition of capital in use from period to period. This increases the complexity of the valorisation process and reduces the probability that it would proceed such as to generate stable growth. Moreover, the sectors would develop independently in spite of their dependence upon each other in collective operation. Such development increases the complexity of the valorisation process even further and Marx concluded that capitalism would experience recurrent disproportion crises as a consequence. These crises would appear as barriers to the progress of the system and would have to be transcended. This could occur, Marx argued, because the capitalists would be *forced* to recognise the interdependence of sectors and change their short-run decisions to compensate for the imbalances that emerge. It followed for Marx that this 'correction' process would need to be virtually continuous as each crisis, when transcended, regenerates the independent behaviours of sectors which would lead to another.

Recognition of the role that changing capital composition could have in expanded reproduction led Marx to a more detailed analysis of the qualitative effects on capital of the accumulation process. His analysis of this important dimension of the motion of capitalism was carried out at the level of capital-in-general.

THE DYNAMICS OF CAPITAL COMPOSITION AND THE RATE OF PROFITS

In the political economy that Marx had studied, one of the dominating dynamic phenomena was the tendency of the rate of profits to fall as capital accumulates. Marx, too, espoused the significance of these interdependent aspects of the motion of capitalism and he stated baldly that they represented

in every respect the most important law of modern political economy, and the most essential for understanding the most difficult relations. It is the most important law from the historical standpoint. It is a law which, despite its simplicity, has never before been grasped and, even less, consciously articulated. (G,748)

He went on to provide some brief discussion of previous endeavours to explicate the falling rate of profits as a component of the dynamics of capital.

Adam Smith had argued that as capital accumulated, there would emerge increased competition between capitalists for limited investment opportunities. This would drive down the rate of profits (G,751). David Ricardo had responded, in criticism of Smith, that while competition would act to generate a uniform rate of profit in the various branches of production, it could not itself reduce the general rate. Marx agreed with Ricardo on this principle.

Competition can permanently depress the rate of profit in all branches of industry, i.e. the average rate of profit, only if and in so far as a general and permanent fall of the rate of profit, having the force of a law, is conceivable *prior to* competition and regardless of competition. Competition executes the inner laws of capital; makes them into compulsory laws towards the individual capital, but it does not invent them. It realises them. To try to explain them simply as results of competition therefore means to concede that one does not understand them. (G,752;cf.552)

In spite of *this* agreement with Ricardo, Marx did not think Ricardo's explanation a viable one. The squeeze on the rate of profits in Ricardo's theory was the result of decreasing productivity of labour working to produce corn, the main wage commodity (G,595ff.). Marx denied that there was any empirical evidence that such a decrease in productivity ensued with the increased output of agriculture. His reading of agricultural science had shown Ricardo's assumption to be false (G,754). Moreover, Ricardo's explanation was one-sided in that it took no account of the *rising* productivity of labour in non-agricultural industry.[8]

Other writers after Ricardo had also taken up the issue of the falling rate of profits, but their efforts were, in Marx's view, even less acceptable than those of Ricardo in many cases. Marx found in the work of unspecified 'disciples' of Ricardo a marked de-emphasis of those parts of the latter's argument which implied any conflict between the participants in the capitalist system (G,754). Wakefield was cited as having retained Adam Smith's approach in which competition for limited investment opportunities would drive down the rate of profits. It was, though, Carey and especially Bastiat who received most explicit criticism from Marx for their presentation of capitalism as an harmonious set of relationships. In their work, 'The unpleasant contradictions, antagonisms within which classical economics moves, and which Ricardo emphasises with scientific ruthlessness, are thus watered down into well-to-do harmonies' (G,754). For Bastiat (G,754–8) the falling rate of profits was the consequence of a process of redistribution which gave a greater relative share of produced value to labour. While capital

215

received a greater *absolute* profit, the rate of that profit on capital advanced fell. Marx found this to be a quite superficial analysis of the issue which gave no consideration to the *production* component of the dynamics of capital accumulation. As Marx read it, Bastiat had had to assume what he set out to prove, viz. the falling rate of profits itself.

Marx sought to account for the falling rate of profits by analysing the effects of capital accumulation on the *forces* and *relations* of production while abstracting from any issues of distribution or circulation. His argument in the *Grundrisse* considered the determination of the rate of profits without referring to any change in the Value of the commodity wage and independently of a theory of rent. Moreover, the analysis proceeded in *notional* terms in the sense that the reducing rate of profits was shown to be embodied in the *immediate Value* of the commodities produced. The effects on the *realised* rate of profits allowing for any circulation problems were not considered, but would have added another dimension to the issue even at the somewhat elementary level of analysis that Marx was able to formulate at this stage of his work.

Marx's analysis of the process of surplus Value generation indicated to him that the Value rate of profits depends most directly on two dimensions of the production process (G,387n,746–7). Firstly, the *rate* of generating surplus Value per unit of *variable* capital, expressed as the ratio of surplus labour to necessary labour and later to be called the *rate of surplus Value*, is important and any change in this rate would change the rate of profits. The second factor which affects the rate of profits is the relative proportion of constant capital and variable capital comprising the capital advanced. This ratio, later to be called the *organic composition of capital*, was only expressed in vague terms by Marx. Especially throughout the *Grundrisse* he did not consider the analytical ramifications of juxtaposing this composition in *physical* and Value terms while arguing the determination of the rate of profits. Indications are that he assumed that the two ratios would always remain in direct proportion and his analyses moved between the physical and Value domains without considering the issue further (see e.g. G,380ff.).

These two variables affect the Value rate of profits in opposite directions. The rate of surplus Value has a direct, positive effect on the rate while the organic composition of capital has an inverse, negative effect on it. Marx undertook an examination of the dynamics of these two contradictory influences in an endeavour to substantiate, at least logically, the essential tendency of the rate of profits to fall as capital accumulates.

In the competitive struggle between individual capitals as each grows larger, one of the dominant considerations for the capitalist is to employ additional capital that embodies the latest, most productive technology in order to reduce the cost of production. This decision making leads to the increasing mechanisation of production, a fact that Marx took to be self evident in early nineteenth century England.[9] Thus he wrote that 'It is easy to develop the introduction of machinery out of competition and out of the law of the reduction of production costs which is triggered by competition' (G,776).

The important thing about mechanisation perceived by Marx was that it brings with it changes in the two main factors affecting the rate of profits. It involves an increase in the use of fixed capital and raw materials relative to labour employed, which Marx interpreted as a *rise* in the Value ratio of constant to variable capital. It is this rise that is the direct source of the increased labour productivity and reduced costs of production sought by the capitalist (G,380–1,389). This latter effect appears analytically as a *rise* in the rate of surplus Value.

Here capital involves itself in a contradiction. The essence of surplus Value generation is the employment of living labour in excess of the necessary labour time embodied in the Value of the commodity wage. From this point of view, the rational behaviour of the capitalist is to employ as much labour as possible while reducing the necessary component to a minimum. As Marx put it:

It is a law of capital . . . to create surplus labour . . .; it can do this only by setting *necessary labour* in motion – i.e. entering into exchange with the worker. It is its tendency, therefore, to create as much [surplus] labour as possible; just as it is equally its tendency to reduce necessary labour to a minimum. (G,399)

But, at the same time, the capitalist proceeds to introduce labour-*saving* mechanisation into the production process in spite of its contradictory implications.

217

Capital itself is the moving contradiction, [in] that it presses to reduce labour time to a minimum, while it posits labour time, on the other side, as sole measure and source of wealth. Hence it diminishes labour time in the necessary form so as to increase it in the superfluous form; hence posits the superfluous in growing measure as a condition – question of life or death – for the necessary. (*G*,706)

This interpretation of the development of capital had implications for both labour and capital itself.

As far as labour is concerned, the progressive substitution of machinery for labour in production reduces the proportion of the growing population that is required as workers. The result is a growing 'reserve' of labour (*G*,400). More than this, though, the alienating, dominating form of capital over labour becomes more pronounced in the development process. The human conditions in production thus become progressively more depressing for those still engaged in work (*G*,693–5,700–1,705). These effects on labour of the motion of capital were significant in Marx's view of the evolving socio-political force of the proletariat which accompanied the economic development of capitalism. It would be this force, born of the conditions of production, which ultimately would manifest itself in the revolutionary transition to socialism. As Marx put it, 'At a certain point, a development of the forces of material production – *which is at the same time a development of the forces of the working class* [emphasis added] – *suspends capital itself*' (*G*,543).

In analysing the implications of the increased mechanisation of production for capital, Marx was required to sort out the *relative* dynamic impact on the rate of profits of the simultaneously rising organic composition of capital and rising rate of surplus Value. His solution to this potential indeterminacy was to argue intuitively that the rising rate of surplus Value, tending to support the rate of profits in the face of the changing composition of capital, has a finite limit and must eventually stabilise. The *negative* impact of the rising organic composition of capital then becomes dominant and the rate of profits falls.

Marx found the explanation for this limitation on the rate of surplus Value in both of the two sources of the rise itself. No matter how much the productivity of the labour increases and reduces the proportion of necessary labour in total labour, the surplus is limited in an *absolute* sense by the constraint of a given (but never fixed historically) length of the working day (G,342). The other source of increasing the generation of surplus Value is by improving the *relative* productivity of labour through the increased mechanisation of the production process. Marx argued that this source of increase is limited, too. He reasoned that as technology became increasingly dominant, additional productivity increments would become more difficult to develop. That is, the rate of rise of labour productivity would fall behind the rate of rise of the organic composition of capital (G,335–6,340).

For Marx, then, given the veracity of the characteristics of the dynamics of capital accumulation just outlined, the *Value* rate of profits must fall as a matter of *logic*. His conclusion on this matter, whatever the theoretical and empirical limitations of his analyses at this stage, was quite clear:

The profit rate is . . . inversely related to the growth of relative surplus value or of relative surplus labour, to the development of the powers of production, and to the magnitude of the capital employed as [constant] capital within production. In other words, the . . . law is the *tendency of the profit rate to decline* with the development of capital. . . . (G,763)

Such a definitive assertion belied the extreme complexity of what evidently appeared to Marx to be but a simple matter!

THE MOTION OF CAPITALISM AND THE CRISIS: A SUMMARY STATEMENT[10]

Accounting for the immanent crisis potential of capitalism was the ultimate goal of Marx's investigations into the motion of the system. He made no attempt precisely to *define* the crisis, but it may be gleaned from his various references to the category that its clearest *indications*, as perceived by the capitalists, were taken to be a significant downturn in *market* prices and the *realised* rates of profit in the various sectors of production. These events would be accompanied by evidence of the overproduction of commodities relative to the *effective* demand patterns. The signal of the crisis here would be excessive accumulations of stocks of commodities. Of course, these indicators have a *qualitative* dimension as well. Defining the onset of a crisis in this sense must be more or less arbitrary and Marx's investigations did not raise this issue.

The *indicators* of the crisis give some direction as to the *cause* of the crisis, although Marx did not distinguish clearly between cause and effect in this context. But it is evident that he associated the crisis with the characteristic *essences* of the capitalist mode of production, in particular its social relations, structures and operations. The crisis is, therefore, generated immanently and not by any external factors.

Marx did not consider the relationship between the crisis, apparently a *cyclical* phenomenon that is constantly transcended by the reactions of capital, and the *secular* changes resulting from the longer-term effects of capital accumulation. It is not unreasonable to suggest, though, that he perceived these two dimensions of motion as a *unity* with their combined effects present in the ever-increasing extremes of crises that beset the system. In effect, the secular trend of the falling rate of profits carries the cyclical falls in the realised rates of profit to increasingly low points. Marx's investigations did not canvass any such combined effect explicitly.

The basic driving force behind the motion of capitalism was interpreted by Marx to be the competitive pursuit by *individual* capitalists of the maximum valorisation of their capitals. This necessarily involved capital accumulation and the endeavour to expand markets and, in these *material* senses, capital had been highly successful in its one hundred or so years of operation and development (G,325).

The driving force and its effects cannot proceed unimpeded because the capitalist mode of production is structured around and operates through a set of contradictions. Each of the dimensions of motion contains its contradictory moments and in combination, they entail the emergence of a continuous sequence of barriers which capital must transcend by adjustment if it is to survive. These barriers appear as periodic crises from which the system is able to recover by internally generated changes. Such changes would be both quantitative and qualitative, including bankruptcies, increased concentration of capital and temporary reductions in production and capital accumulation. These impediments are accentuated by the *secular* trends of the system, especially the declining general rate of profits and the growing 'reserve army' of unemployed workers that accompany the accumulation of capital.

The day-to-day operations of capitalism, in essence, involve the generation of surplus Value through the exploitation of labour. The surplus Value that the capitalists strive to maximise is embodied in commodities which must be sold for the surplus to be realised as money. Such realisation requires that a process of circulation be integrated with the process of production and that there exists sufficient effective demand of the appropriate qualitative structure to absorb the commodities produced. Ideally, this absorption should be at *actual* prices that systematically reflect underlying Values (perhaps in a modified form). All of this can proceed in such a way as to ensure consistent reproduction *as a matter of principle*. However, the anarchistic and contradictory characteristics of capitalism mitigate against this being so in practice.

Marx emphasised that capitalist production decisions are taken in isolation from circulation and the quantitative and qualitative requirements for the maximum valorisation of capital are unlikely to be present. The root of this problem is to be found most essentially in the contradiction of use value and exchange value being embodied in the commodity. The commodity is produced under conditions of the social division of labour and the necessary exchange system is facilitated by the mediation of money. This mediation aggravates the probability of circulation failure in that it separates the acts of sale and purchase and enables sellers to opt out of buying, at least temporarily, by hoarding Value in its *general* form. From this reasoning, Marx concluded that capitalism would continue to suffer realisation problems of one sort or another.

Within the production process itself, the capitalists are motivated to reduce production costs and to produce more. Capital accumulation serves both of these objectives. Each individual capitalist is engaged in a competitive struggle to keep his costs down by ensuring that his additional and replacement means of production embody the most productive technology available. This endeavour has significant implications for the potential rate of profits in the economy and for the employment of labour.

Capital accumulation brings with it a rising organic composition, reflecting the increasing use of mechanised production based on fixed capital. The labour-saving bias of such production methods contributes to a rising level of unemployment. For the capitalist,

221

these methods bring reduced production costs and a higher rate of surplus Value by increasing labour productivity. But, at the same time, the variable capital component of total capital, the *source* of surplus Value, is being relatively reduced. Increases in the rate of surplus Value increase the rate of profits. Marx's intuitively based argument was, though, that these increases were limited and would ultimately be overshadowed by the predominantly constant capital growth through which the productivity gains are achieved. The logical consequence is a secular decline in the general rate of profits, probably exacerbated by increased circulation time and slower capital turnover necessitated by the geographically larger markets required to match the growth of productive capacity.

The declining *notional* rate of profits generated in production faces the further stricture that it must be *realised* to be meaningful to the capitalists. Realisation of profit is an integral result of the sale of commodities and is affected by the impediments to circulation referred to above and which reduce market prices in periods of overproduction. The *realised* rate of profits is thus a cyclical phenomenon and its significant decline below the notional rate is experienced during crises.

In Marx's vision of the historical motion of capitalism, then, a complex of self-imposed contradictions leads the system towards its inevitable demise. His *impression* was that the severity of the crises experienced would continue to increase and that the extent of recovery would decrease. The crucial *social* ramification of the cyclical and secular *economic* experiences of capitalism was, for Marx, the expansion of the increasingly alienated and increasingly unemployed proletariat. It was thus argued to be the misery of the proletariat which would provide the ultimate *limit* to the existence of capital. Proletarian intolerance of its situation and a self-conscious awareness of the reasons for its situation were foreshadowed by Marx as the factors that would lead to the revolutionary abolition of capitalism. His own conclusion made this vision and prognosis quite clear:

the highest development of productive power together with the
greatest expansion of existing wealth will coincide with
depreciation of capital, degradation of the labourer, and a most
straitened exhaustion of his vital powers. These contradictions lead
to explosions, cataclysms, crises, in which by momentaneous

suspension of labour and annihilation of a great portion of capital the latter is violently reduced to the point where it can go on. . . . Yet, these regularly recurring catastrophes lead to their repetition on a higher scale, and finally to its [capitalism's] violent overthrow. (G,750)

CHAPTER 8

The interim development of the *Grundrisse*

During 1858 Marx turned his attention to the *presentation* of his critique of political economy. After completing notebook VII of the *Grundrisse* manuscript around the middle of the year, he attempted to set up an index of the materials from his investigations under chapter headings (see *G(EV)*,855ff. and 860ff.). A publisher for Marx's book dealing with capital-in-general had been organised earlier in the year by Lassalle and, on the basis of his index, Marx began a first draft of the work. Parts of this draft are extant (*G(EV)*,871ff.), but as Marx was not satisfied with it, he decided to write another for publication (see his letter to Lassalle, 12 November 1858, *MEW*,29,566f). He was especially troubled by his style of presentation and it was not until January 1859 that the manuscript was sent off to the publisher in its rewritten form.

It had been Marx's intention to include three chapters in the work, dealing in turn with the commodity, money and capital under the rubric of capital-in-general. In the manuscript sent to the publisher, the vital third chapter was omitted. It was promised for the near future and would form a second volume for the work. This procedure was not followed and Marx's endeavours to complete the third chapter were fraught with difficulties. The task was eventually abandoned in the early 1860s when he decided to begin the presentation of the critique of political economy again in *Capital*, Book I.

Marx made it clear in the Preface to his *A Contribution to the Critique of Political Economy* (*CCPE*) when it was eventually published in June 1859 that it comprised the first two chapters of the first part of the book *On Capital*. There were to be six books in the overall project at this stage, with those on landed property, wage labour, the state, foreign trade and the world market to follow the work on capital (*CCPE*,19). The plan for the first part of *On Capital* included three chapters: 1 The commodity; 2 Money or simple circulation; and 3 Capital-in-general. In each of these chapters, capital was to be treated as an aggregate with the second part of the book left to deal with the issue of competition between sector capitals. Two further parts were projected for *On Capital* also, one dealing with capital as credit and the other with share capital.

The *Contribution* was Marx's first formal *presentation* of the beginnings of his extensive critique of political economy. His immediate concern was with those phenomena of capitalism that are most readily observable, viz, the commodity and the simple circulation of commodities through the mediation of money. This level of interpretation directly involved the analysis of value forms as the most significant dimensions of the commodity. The interpretation and analysis also considered the role of money in the circulation process and Marx touched briefly on the potential for commercial crises which could be attributed to the form of circulation.

Marx's focus in the *Contribution* was not directly on production as such, although its presence as a unity with circulation is evident in the argument of the book. Most especially, the discussion of the commodity and value forms could not be pursued in isolation from their origin in production. These categories are social categories which reflect the particular relations of production, the social division of labour and the exploitation of labour that characterise the capitalist regime.

Included in the two chapters of the *Contribution* were three critico-historical sections in which Marx briefly set his work in its intellectual context. These sections dealt with 'Historical notes on the analysis of commodities', 'Theories of the standard of money' and 'Theories of the medium of circulation and of money'. They were designed to differentiate and distance Marx's analyses from those of his antecedents rather than to elucidate his sources. The first of these sections is emphasised below because it foreshadows most clearly the massive draft of the critical history which was to follow some two years later.[1] The other two pieces are of lesser ongoing significance.

THE COMMODITY AND ITS VALUE FORMS

Marx opened his first chapter with these words: 'The wealth of bourgeois society, at first sight, presents itself as an immense accumulation of commodities, its unit being a single commodity. Every commodity, however, has a twofold aspect – *use value* and *exchange value* [*Tauschwert*]' (CCPE,27). The commodity is the elementary form of appearance of capitalist wealth (as both a stock and a flow). Marx's intention was to dissect the commodity and to situate it in its capitalist context and link it to the relevant capitalist forms.

The commodity is perceived through the value forms it embodies as a unity. Firstly, it has a *value in use* as determined primarily by its physical form, although this may be adapted to a limited extent according to needs. Secondly, it has a *value in exchange* which sets it alongside other commodities, most apparently in a relative quantitative sense.

It is interesting to note here that throughout the *Contribution*, Marx conflated the categories Value and exchange value. While the distinction between the two had been suggested in his earlier investigations and would emerge very clearly in Chapter 1 of *Capital*, Book I, it was not made explicit in this first presentation of the analysis. Value as logically prior to its *expression* as exchange value was simply merged with the latter. The distinction that Marx emphasised in the present context was that between exchange value and its expression as money price. Thus he wrote that 'Price is the converted form in which the exchange value of commodities *appears* within the circulation process' (CCPE,66); and 'The commodity as such *is* an exchange value, the commodity *has* a price' (CCPE,69). The most essential value category in the *Contribution* was exchange value rather than Value. However, it must be stressed that in using the category exchange value, Marx's argument implies that it has the same *meaning* as Value, the logically entailed outcome of the form of the capitalist mode of production, and not the limited meaning that it took in political economy as the basis for explaining prices. Marx's analysis of the commodity and its value forms was designed to serve a critical understanding of capitalism in broad perspective rather than its price formation process.

From the appearance of the commodity, its most obvious value form is its use value. The physical constitution of the the commodity reflects the particular categories of labour that were used in its production. As Marx pointed out, this has no direct connection with the status of a *product* as a commodity. A commodity must have use value, but the existence of a use value does not make a commodity (CCPE,28). The commodity *form* is the result of a particular mode of social production in which use values are produced not immediately for that value but because they embody exchange value (including surplus exchange value). Thus, 'Use value is the immediate physical entity in which a definite economic relationship – *exchange value* – is expressed' (CCPE,28).

In the capitalist mode of production, commodities must be able to be exchanged for one another. For this to proceed, they must be *comparable* and for Marx, in the classical tradition, the basis of this comparability was to be an *objective* exchange value. As use values, commodities are heterogeneous qualitative and quantitative entities. They cannot be related to each other for the purpose of exchange without the intervention of some mediation. The essence of this mediation is to be sought in the production process in that commodities are all products of labour, that is, they represent materialised social labour (CCPE,28–9).

In appearance, this social labour takes many diverse forms and does not seem to give comparability any more than do the physical forms of the commodities that it produces. What Marx had to explain was the existence of a category of *homogeneous* social labour, or '*abstract general* labour' (CCPE,29;cf.32). His argument relating to this category proceeded in several stages. He referred first to the idea that all labour is essentially a mixture of similar functions:

This abstraction, human labour in general, *exists* in the form of average labour which, in a given society, the average person can perform, productive expenditure of a certain amount of human muscles, nerves, brain, etc. It is *simple* labour which any average individual can be trained to do and which in one way or another he has to perform. (CCPE,31)

In addition to this conceptual basis, Marx made the *empirical* generalisation that in nineteenth century capitalist production, most labour was of this form, that is, 'unskilled labour' (*CCPE*,31 and n.). Finally, he considered the puzzle of skilled labour and treated this obviously as some compound of simple labour: 'This kind of labour resolves itself into simple labour; it is simple labour raised to a higher power, so that for example one day of skilled labour may equal three days of simple labour' (*CCPE*,31). The 'laws concerning this reduction' were dismissed as not of concern, with Marx adding the circular point that the reduction itself is entailed by the logic of the embodied-labour theory of exchange value which assumes it: 'It is . . . clear that the reduction is made, for, as exchange value, the product of highly skilled labour is equivalent, in definite proportions, to the product of simple average labour . . .' (*CCPE*,31).

Marx reiterated in passing the important point about capitalism that its appearances disguise the true nature of its relations and operations. He referred here to the exchange process as appearing to be a set of relations between *things*. The social–human dimensions of exchange are obscured: 'exchange value is a relation between persons, [but] it is . . . necessary to add that it is a relation hidden by a material veil' (*CCPE*,34). One possible outcome of this appearance is the illusion that exchange value actually *originates* in the use value form of the commodity. Marx dismissed this idea (*CCPE*,36).

It *is* the case, though, Marx argued, that the *appearance* of exchange value relations is between disparate use value forms: 'The exchange value of one commodity . . . manifests itself in the use values of other commodities' (*CCPE*,38). He went on to consider in some detail the significance of the juxtapositioning of use values in an exchange value relation.

A particular quantity of a particular use value (such as one yard of linen) can have its exchange value expressed through its quantitative relation to a multitude of other particular use values (such as two pounds of coffee, eight pounds of bread, etc.). This amounts to an infinite series of exchange value relations based upon a universal equivalent (the one yard of linen) (*CCPE*,39).

The exchange value relation is commutative. The expressions involved in a series of relations can be reversed such that each of the particular use values has its exchange value expressed in terms of the universal equivalent (*CCPE*,39,46). Here the universal equivalent acquires a duality of use value. It has a particular use value form based on its physical constitution while also serving as a universal use value as the mediating expression of all exchange values (*CCPE*,47,48). The essence of the exchange value of the universal equivalent itself is its socially necessary (*CCPE*,31,32) embodied abstract labour content. Herein lies the *principle* of the *money* commodity (*CCPE*,48). For Marx, then, the category money was imbedded in the commodity form: 'the commodity is the origin of money' (*CCPE*,64). An *actual* money commodity emerges in response to the development of the exchange process to an extent that renders barter inefficient (*CCPE*,48ff.) and Marx later specified gold as *the* most appropriate commodity (*CCPE*,64).

The status and properties of the commodity form in general were considered by Marx in some detail. As the unity of use value and exchange value (*CCPE*,27,41), it does not exist *immediately*. *Mediations* are required in order to transform a mere product into a commodity. A product acquires a use value status by encountering a particular human need (or range thereof) that it can satisfy (*CCPE*,42). Such use value forms have the *potential* to become commodities in that they may be produced in anticipation of being demanded. The product that is produced as a commodity must then have the simultaneous properties of being a use value *and* a non-use value. The latter form represents its exchange value as perceived by its producer-owner: 'The commodity is a use value for its owner only in so far as it is an exchange value' (*CCPE*,42). For him, the product must be *not* a use value in its physical form.

The realisation of the physical use value of a commodity in its consumption (intermediate or final) requires that it be realised as an exchange value first. The necessary condition for this is that it is already established as a use value form (*CCPE*,43). At the point of production under capitalism, the commodity is only notionally a use value and notionally an exchange value.

All of these dimensions of the commodity have significant implications for the interpretation of the process of simple circulation. Marx would soon analyse these implications in Chapter 2 of the *Contribution*.

THE CRITICAL HISTORY OF THE ANALYSIS OF THE COMMODITY AND ITS VALUE

The theme of Marx's 'Historical notes' on the treatment of commodities in the *Contribution* (*CCPE*,52ff.) was an extremely brief critical outline of the evolution of the association between labour and value forms. In particular, the link between labour and exchange value was traced from its rudiments in the work of Petty in the late seventeenth century to its apogee in Ricardo's *Principles* early in the nineteenth century. Along with their respective French contemporaries, Boisguillebert and Sismondi, these two writers represented the chronological limits of what Marx considered to be 'classical' political economy (*CCPE*,52).

The origin of the association between labour and exchange value was, Marx argued, the emergence of the social division of labour in production and the consequent necessity for a system of exchanges. He found that early discussions of the association failed to distinguish labour as a general form from its particular forms and did not separate exchange value from its expression as money price (*CCPE*,54–5).

The problem of focusing upon specific forms of labour carried into the eighteenth century and was formalised in the work of the physiocrats. The issue that they raised was not the origin or measure of exchange value, but rather the origin of the surplus to be expressed in exchange value terms. For the physiocrats, the only productive labour in this issue was agricultural labour. The important point that Marx drew out of this work in the present context, was that the physiocrats had bypassed the fundamental question of the relation between labour and exchange value. They had proceeded directly to resolve 'a complex form of the problem before having solved its elementary form', a project analogous to the construction of 'separate habitable storeys of a building before laying the foundation stone' (*CCPE*,57). Thus Marx emphasised that political economy must proceed first and foremost from an understanding of the nature of the commodity and its exchange value.

Sir James Steuart, writing after the mid-eighteenth century, took a crucial analytical step forward when he distinguished the value forms more clearly than had been done previously. Some ambiguity remained, as Marx noted, because of the strong links between

230

material content and abstract perception that characterised empiricist works. But Steuart did have a concept of 'real value', which he associated with the performance of *generalised* labour (that he called 'industry'), and distinguished from use value produced by particular forms of labour (*CCPE*,58).

It was Adam Smith who finally generalised labour as the sole source of exchange value and wealth and founded his analysis of capitalism on this premise. In Marx's view, though, Smith failed to realise the potential of this insight and confused 'the determination of the value of commodities by the labour time contained in them with the determination of their value by the value of labour' (*CCPE*,59). Ricardo tackled this problem and endeavoured to establish firmly the *bona fides* of the embodied-labour explanation of exchange value even in the presence of capital (*CCPE*,60). The crucial issue that Ricardo did not consider was the essential origin of exchange value as a category entailed by the particularities of the capitalist mode of production and its relations of production. Marx considered that Ricardo had no sense of history, although he did have the ability to perceive important aspects of capitalism that were not apparent through immediate observation (*CCPE*,60–1).

Ricardo's contemporary, Sismondi, added a further dimension to the total insights of political economy by going so far as critically to question the viability of large-scale capitalist production. Marx summarised his admiration for these two writers, who provided the most advanced developments of 'classical' political economy, as follows: 'Whereas Ricardo's political economy ruthlessly draws its final conclusion and therewith ends, Sismondi supplements this ending by expressing doubt in political economy itself' (*CCPE*,61). The pity is that while Marx later pursued his critical exposition of Ricardo's 'ruthless' logic of capitalism further, he afforded Sismondi only the briefest mention as a figure in the critical history of political economy.

As perceived by Ricardo's critics, several crucial analytical problems remained for political economy to solve. And: 'If this polemic is stripped of its mainly trivial form' (*CCPE*,61), Marx found it to have four main components which he argued confidently that he could transcend.

Firstly, the labour theory of exchange value appeared to be circular in its reasoning. This problem resulted from the difficulty of valuing the labour itself, but Marx felt that an adequate 'theory

231

of wage labour' would provide a solution. He probably had in mind here the key role played by his concept of labour power. Secondly, and integrally related to the first issue, was the problem of explaining how with a labour theory of exchange value, the exchange value of the commodity exceeds the exchange value of the labour utilised to produce it. This differential would be explained by a proper 'analysis of capital' which, no doubt, included the theory of surplus Value. Thirdly, Marx recalled that commodities did not actually sell as their embodied-labour exchange values. There exists a 'market price' which, he argued, reflects supply and demand determinants and is thus capricious. The link between value and 'market price' would be provided by 'the theory of competition'. However, Marx had really only partially solved this issue so far. The effects of competition which needed to be considered did not only concern supply and demand, but also competition between capitals and the generation of a uniform general rate of profits. At the level of circulation, supply and demand *per se* determine the short-run *market* price to which Marx referred here. Between this price and Value, there exists the *price of production* which he had not yet formally analysed. This latter price *varies systematically* from Value. Overall, Marx's statement of this third issue was quite superficial and did not even embody the, albeit limited, advances made in the *Grundrisse*. Fourthly, an explanation of the exchange value of commodities produced in part by *natural* agents of production was required. Such an explanation would be provided by the 'theory of rent', a theory to which Marx had so far given little attention.

These four key analytical limitations were carried forward by Marx into his critico-historical writings of 1862–3. There he provided some details of his solutions in the context of a lengthy critique of the antecedent political economy which exhibited such problems.

MONEY OR SIMPLE CIRCULATION

Chapter 2 of the *Contribution* contained Marx's presentation of the process of simple circulation of commodities as it is facilitated by the various operational functions of money. He included in these functions money as a measure of exchange value, as a medium of exchange, as the medium for hoarding wealth and as the means of payment in settlement of debts. There were also brief considerations of the precious metals as money, the history of money in political economy and money in the world market setting in the chapter. This present section emphasises those parts of Marx's critical analysis which relate more or less directly to the involvement of money in circulation and to the potential for crises that emerges as a consequence of this process.

Commodity circulation was interpreted by Marx to comprise two notionally separate views of the circuit of capital. The symbols C for commodity and M for money can be combined in the expression C–M–C. This implies that post-production, the embodied exchange value of the commodity expressed initially as an *ideal* price is converted into the universal expression of exchange value, money, and that subsequently this money is converted back into the commodity capital form in order to renew production. Thus Marx emphasised here the role of money as the mediation in a commodity conversion involving a change of use value. The other view of *the same circuit of capital* was expressed as M–C–M. Here, the conversion process focuses upon money as the object rather than the commodity as in the previous view. For the holder of money, the mediation is the commodity in the sense that it provides the means through which additions to the money held can be achieved. In effect, this expression of the circuit involves capital in the production phase and the character of bourgeois production emerges in the symbols M–C–M', where M' exceeds M (*CCPE*,123).

In the C–M–C view, the act of selling, C–M, is followed by the act of purchasing, M–C. Both these acts are simultaneously purchase and sale, but there is an important sense in which they form a sequence in time for a particular capitalist. In this sequence, he acts in turn as seller and buyer, with the significant thing being, in Marx's view, that the *motivations* for these two acts are different. In the first stage, the capitalist acts to realise exchange value including a surplus, while in the second stage he acts to satisfy some physical need, either personal or industrial (*CCPE*,126). The completion of the sequence requires a coincidence of actions by capitalists in their roles as sellers and buyers.

The circulation process as a whole comprises a mass of such sequences in an interdependent relationship. Marx summarised his interpretation of this when he wrote that the circulation of the world of commodities – since every individual commodity goes through the circuit C–M–C – constitutes an infinitely intricate network of such series of movements, which constantly end and constantly begin afresh at an infinite number of different points. But each individual sale or purchase stands as an independent isolated transaction, whose complementary transaction, which constitutes its continuation, does not need to follow immediately, but may be separated from it temporally and spatially. (*CCPE*,93;cf.86–7)

It is the mediation of money which isolates these transactions in spite of their complementarity. Money acts as suspended purchasing power in this sequence: 'A golden chrysalis state [which] forms an independent phase in the life of the commodity, in which it can remain for a shorter or longer period' (*CCPE*,91;cf.126). Marx found in this potential suspension of the circulation sequence the roots of commercial crises. And it is the mediation of money which renders the impediment possible, for while: 'circulation of money can occur . . . without crises, crises cannot occur without circula-tion of money' (*CCPE*,96).

Capitalist circulation, C–M–C, is more than just barter, C–C, with money 'added in' for convenience.

If, because the process of circulation of commodities ends in C–C and therefore appears as barter merely mediated by money, or because C–M–C in general does not only fall apart into two isolated cycles but is simultaneously their dynamic unity, the conclusion were to be drawn that only the unity and not the separation of purchase and sale exists, this would display a manner of thinking the criticism of which belongs to the sphere of logic and not of economics. (*CCPE*,96)

This barter view of the circulation process was ascribed by Marx to the idea espoused by James Mill and Say that supply and demand are effectively identified in that they are opposite views of a single process. Marx quoted Mill to this effect and concluded that such an argument implied a 'metaphysical equilibrium' that ignored the observable realities of capitalism (*CCPE*,96–7 and 97n.).

Marx went on to consider some additional aspects of the role of money in the C–M–C sequence. He identified two distinct motives

234

for holding money. The money balance acquired as an immediate consequence of C–M is initially a store of exchange value. In order to elaborate upon this idea, Marx adopted the distinction between 'coin' that is money in active circulation and 'money' that is money in temporary suspension from circulation (*CCPE*,125). There is in the process of circulation a continual movement between the 'coin' and 'money' status for money. The suspended 'money' balances can be considered as taking either of two forms. One is a reserve fund of 'coin' held to facilitate exchange transactions and the other is as a 'hoard' of exchange value as an asset and not taking part in the circulation process (*CCPE*,126–7,137–8).

'Hoards' were significant in Marx's view because they represent the initial, *potential* form of capital. They are, though, once removed from capital in that the motivation for hoarding *per se* is purely avarice rather than a desire to generate additional exchange value (*CCPE*,128–9). In hoarding, 'money' itself is *the* object of 'the passion for enrichment' (*CCPE*,132,133). However, Marx argued, the hoarding of 'money' has two preconditions which are in contradiction. *Parsimony* is its *negative* precondition while *industry* is its *positive* precondition (*CCPE*,128). That is, hoarding depends simultaneously upon the *desire* to hoard and upon the need *not* to hoard in order to obtain through production the wherewithall to do the hoarding. Thus in a more complete analysis of capitalism which goes beyond simple circulation, hoarding really has no role to play in explaining the processes involved. The contradiction of hoarding disappears when what is hoarded becomes capital in the commodity forms of means of production and advances for labour (purchase of labour power).

In considering the idea of money as a means of payment in the settlement of debts, Marx added a further dimension to the need for the reserve fund of 'coin' designed to facilitate transactions. The point is that money as a means of payment acts to mediate in exchange without any immediate transfer of 'coin'. It thus enters circulation without being a means of exchange in the usual sense. Payment is deferred and money as a means of payment is the measure of a future liability for payment. In this case, then, the act of selling comprises only the nominal realisation of exchange value with the actual realisation coming later on. Thus, 'The buyer buys as the representative of future money, whereas the seller sells as the owner of a commodity available here and now' (*CCPE*,139;

235

cf.148). The consequence of this is that payment ultimately involves the transfer of 'coin' and the reserve fund of 'coin', active balances, needs to be built up to ensure that the debts contracted can be settled when due.

> Payments in their turn necessitate reserve funds, accumulations of money as means of payment. The formation of reserve funds, unlike hoarding, no longer seems an activity extraneous to circulation, or, as in the case of coin reserves, a purely technical stagnation of coin; on the contrary money has to be gradually accumulated so as to be available at definite dates in the future when payments become due. (*CCPE*,147)

The real significance of this aspect of the role of money in circulation for the 'law of motion' of capitalism is that it further exacerbates the potential for crises, even though it also further expedites the circulation process: 'The difference between means of purchase and means of payment becomes very conspicuous, and unpleasantly so, at times of commercial crises' (*CCPE*,141). The disruptive potential of the separation of the acts of sale and purchase is accentuated by the chain of debt liabilities that circulation based on trade credit involves. With the need for these debts to be met in 'coin', there emerges the possibility that the forced realisation of commodities at reproductively inappropriate prices may ensue. Marx referred explicitly to the phenomenon of falling prices as the 'most common and conspicuous phenomenon *accompanying* commercial crises' (*CCPE*,182, emphasis added). The *cause* of this periodic decline was not explained in the present context and Marx did not link it directly to the failure of the circulation process. Overall, the discussion of commercial crises in the *Contribution* remained impressionistic and the evident analytical potential of Marx's critique was not realised.

THE *CONTRIBUTION* AND AFTER

The publication of the *Contribution* was not a success and Marx was very disappointed at the lack of interest shown in the work. It was the case, though, that the book lacked any coherent critico-theoretical message because of his failure to include the vital third chapter dealing with capital. In retrospect, modern readers can appreciate the significance of the *Contribution* as a vital stage in the evolution of Marx's critique of political economy. For his contemporaries, who held the promise of a revolutionary theoretical work, it must have been a disappointing first effort.

Marx himself ascribed the failure of the *Contribution* to the book's form of presentation. It was too 'scientific', too abstract, to serve any popular purpose. While *he* saw the analyses as presenting the beginnings of the complete theoretical foundation for the revolutionary transition out of capitalism (Marx to Lassalle, 6 November 1859, *MEW*,29,618), this was evidently not the impression conveyed to his readers. As Marx's subsequent correspondence reveals, from this point onwards he became very sensitive to the problems associated with the *presentation* of the critique of political economy (see, for example, the letter to Kugelmann, 28 December 1862, *MEW*,30,640). It is not unreasonable to suggest that this sensitivity was one of the significant factors that contributed to Marx's future failure to get on with the publication of his work.

Once the manuscript for the *Contribution* was with the publisher, Marx set about redrafting the investigations of capital for publication as the third chapter of the work. He reviewed the materials from the *Grundrisse* that had not been used so far (*G(EV)*,951ff.) and drew up a plan for the new chapter. The three main sections of the chapter were to be as follows (*G(EV)*,969ff.):

   I Production process of capital
  II Circulation process of capital
 III Capital and profit

In addition, the critico-historical pieces from the *Grundrisse* were listed under the heading 'Miscellaneous' indicating that their placement remained uncertain at this stage. Marx had set the precedent in the *Contribution* of including such analyses in the main text of his critique. This approach was initially to be followed in subsequent work as his later plans suggested (see, for example, those drawn up early in 1863, *TSV*,I,414ff.). However, the idea of presenting the critical history as a separate, but still integrated, book was eventually formulated as part of the plans for *Capital* (see Marx to Engels, 31 July 1865, *MEW*,31,132).

There is no extant evidence that Marx wrote anything for the third chapter beyond the plan during 1859. It was not until the middle of 1861 that he finally returned to the preparation of his work on capital in the massive manuscript he entitled 'Critique of political economy'. This manuscript is the object of discussion in the next volume of the present study.

Notes

INTRODUCTION

1 The idea of a *telos* is that there exists a particular set of
  objectives and purposes towards which a reasoned and
  systematic programme of analysis is directed.
2 This interpretation of Marx's thought does not enjoy universal
  acceptance amongst scholars. Some interpreters have found an
  intellectual rupture, an absolute discontinuity, in the evolution
  of Marx's critical theory. Such a reading dichotomises his work
  into two stages: firstly, the phase of the 'young Marx' whose
  writings expressed a humanist and ethically based critique of
  capitalism; and secondly, the phase of the 'mature Marx' who
  had developed an 'objective science' of capitalism in which the
  exposed contradictions had an objective rather than an ethical
  basis. For an exposition of this reading see especially Louis
  Althusser, *For Marx*, Penguin Books, Harmondsworth, 1969,
  but compare the opposite views argued by Robert Tucker in
  Philosophy and Myth in Karl Marx, second edition, Cambridge
  University Press, London, 1972. A summary of the debate is
  provided by John Maguire in the Preface to *Marx's Paris
  Writings: An Analysis*, Gill & Macmillan, Dublin, 1972.
3 By a 'problematic' I mean a set of statements and hypotheses
  about some reality which provides the theoretical and/or
  ideological structure in which to situate the categories of an
  analytical explanation of the existence of such a reality.
4 On the issue of the bibliographical and substantive status of
  Capital in Marx's writings, see my *The Making of Marx's
  Critical Theory: A Bibliographical Analysis*, Routledge &

Kegan Paul, London, 1983, especially Chapters 5 and 6.

5 The term *Aufhebung* has a multi-dimensional meaning. It conveys the idea that in the process of dialectical change, some elements of an earlier stage are preserved in an enhanced form while other elements are annulled through the working out of contradictions. In the context of discussing revolutionary change, it implies, *inter alia*, the abolition of private property, the preservation of the material means of production to which private property rights previously adhered, and the enhancement of the form of and total rewards from human labour. The word *transcendence* is most generally used to convey the meaning of *Aufhebung* in English. Cf. István Meszáros, *Marx's Theory of Alienation*, Merlin Press, London, 1970, p.12, and Abraham Rotstein, 'Lordship and bondage in Luther and Marx', *Interpretation: A Journal of Political Philosophy*, 8:1, January 1979, p.93.

6 Marx's early intellectual development has been subjected to much analysis. It is not my intention here to emulate any of the detailed and erudite studies that exist. My objective is to give the reader a generalised feeling for Marx's intellectual background as it impinges more or less directly upon my theme. In preparing my discussion I found the following works helpful: Roger Garaudy, *Karl Marx: The Evolution of His Thought*, International Publishers, New York, 1967; Dick Howard, *The Development of the Marxian Dialectic*, Southern Illinois University Press, Carbondale, 1972; David McLellan, *Marx Before Marxism*, Macmillan, London, 1970; and Joseph O'Malley, 'Introduction' to *CHPR*.

7 For a splendid exposition of Hegel's thought see Charles Taylor, *Hegel*, Cambridge University Press, London, 1975.

8 Although Marx read for his doctoral thesis in Berlin University, he was awarded his degree by the University of Jena where the demands of examination were less rigorous.

9 See David McLellan, *The Young Hegelians and Karl Marx*, Macmillan, London, 1969.

10 Reprinted in *CW*,1,109ff., and see the commentary by Arthur McGovern, 'Karl Marx's first political writings: the *Rheinische Zeitung*, 1842–1843', in F.J. Adelmann (ed.), *Demythologising Marxism: A Series of Studies on Marxism*, Martinus Nijhoff, The Hague, 1969.

11 Three pieces are of significance here: the 'Critique of Hegel's Philosophy of Right' manuscript (in *CHPR*); 'On the Jewish question' (*CW*,3,146ff.); and 'Critique of Hegel's Philosophy of Right: introduction' (in *CHPR*).

12 See McLellan, *Marx Before Marxism*, pp.155ff., for a discussion of Marx's acquisition of the concept of the proletariat.

13 *Philosophy of Right*, translated with notes by T.M. Knox, Oxford University Press, London, 1967, pp.126–7. The role of political economy in Hegel's thought is a complex issue. In the early stages of his intellectual development, he studied works in political economy, especially those of Sir James Steuart and Adam Smith, but the exact course of these studies is not known because the associated manuscript notes are not extant. The influence of political economy is most evident in some of Hegel's early manuscript writings and lecture materials, although Marx did not have access to these. In the later works which Marx studied, especially the *Phenomenology of Mind* and the *Philosophy of Right*, economic ideas were important in the formulation of Hegel's system and methodology. Marx's critique of the *Phenomenology* in the *Paris Manuscripts* (*CW*,3,326ff.) indicated this (see Chapter 3 of this work). Hegel's direct reference to political economy in his discussion of the system of man's needs as a part of civil society in the *Philosophy of Right* (paragraph 189) was not commented upon directly by Marx. On this issue, see Georg Lukács's *The Young Hegel: Studies in the Relations between Dialectics and Economics*, (1954), Merlin Press, London, 1975, *passim*, but especially Part II, Chapter 5 and Part III, Chapters 5 and 7.

14 As we know it today, the term *philosophy* usually refers to an identifiable and more or less separable academic discipline. In Marx's day, the term was used more broadly to imply an organised body of principles that could be applied in the comprehension of religious, social, political and economic issues. It was a way of thinking about man in history and society. In reading Marx, a generous interpretation of the term is called for.

15 My present treatment of the bibliographical structure and development of Marx's critical theory is only intended to be a sketch. For a more complete analysis, see my *The Making of*

Marx's Critical Theory: A Bibliographical Analysis cited in
note 4 above.

16 It is to be noted that the version of 'Wage-labour and capital'
reprinted in *CW*,9 is taken directly from the *Neue Rheinische
Zeitung*. It differs from the pamphlet version published by
Engels in 1891 (*MESW*,1,142ff.). The latter piece contains
additional argument and updated terminology, including, most
importantly, the use of the category '*labour power*' which
Marx had not clearly defined in 1849.

17 See Maximilien Rubel and Margaret Manale, *Marx Without
Myth: A Chronological Study of His Life and Work*, Blackwell,
Oxford, 1975, pp.97–8. Unfortunately, no source is given for
this information.

18 References to these two pieces in the Marxological literature
are not very helpful. Martin Nicolaus ('Foreword' to *G*,12)
assumes that the first piece was written *in toto* during 1851
when this is not evident from the editorial comment in *G(EV)*.
Maximilien Rubel's comment on this first piece associates it
with a notebook from 1854–5 on monetary problems but he is
not specific about the date of composition of the piece itself.
Then, to cloud the situation even further, while Nicolaus dates
the second piece from 1854–5 (*G*,12), which accords with
Rubel's notebook on monetary problems, Rubel goes on to cite
another notebook which he asserts carried the exact title of the
second piece. But, he suggests that this was written in April
1857! – see *Rubel on Karl Marx: Five Essays*, edited by J.
O'Malley and K. Algozin, Cambridge University Press,
London, 1981, p.144 and p.145n.

19 Cited in *Rubel on Karl Marx*, p.134.

20 Marx referred to the stimulus he received from the apparent
economic downturn in his letters of 1857. See especially those
to Engels, 8 December 1857, and to Lassalle, 21 December
1857 (*MEW*,29,225 and 548 respectively).

CHAPTER 1

1 On the significance of writing Value with a capital letter see
note 3 to this chapter below.

2 According to István Meszáros (*Marx's Theory of Alienation*,

p.14 n.3), Marx used three terms which may be rendered as 'alienation' or 'estrangement'. The two most frequently used are *Entäusserung* and *Entfremdung*, and the third is *Veräusserung*. *Veräusserung* is the 'action' form of *Entäusserung* and relates to the disposal, separation, externalisation or objectification of something. The concept of *Entfremdung* is the opposition, hostility, separation or isolation which a man feels as a result of the externalisation or objectification of something. From these meanings can be drawn the core conception that man's actions of externalising and objectifying *under capitalism* create things which stand in a hostile relationship to him in spite of their being his own creations. The terms '*estrangement*' and '*alienation*' both convey the existence of this *situation* or the *process* of its formation. Cf. Dick Howard, *The Development of the Marxian Dialectic*, p.152, n.30; and Abraham Rotstein, 'Lordship and bondage in Luther and Marx', pp.90ff.

3 Throughout this study, Marx's concept of Value will be referred to with the first letter of the term in upper case. The point of this is to emphasise that he conceived of Value as an immediate and essential characteristic of commodities produced under capitalism. For Marx, the category Value could be defined independently of its apparent, phenomenal form as exchange value, even though the latter was usually simply referred to as 'value' by political economists. Cf. Anwar Shaikh's view in 'Marx's theory of Value and the transformation problem', in J. Schwartz (ed.), *The Subtle Anatomy of Capitalism*, Goodyear, Santa Monica, California, 1977, p.113.

CHAPTER 2

1 The *Paris Manuscripts* are extremely complex. In my discussion, I do not attempt to emulate the specialist studies of this work. My reading is confined to tracing the theme of my study. Cf., for example, István Meszáros, *Marx's Theory of Alienation*; and John Maguire, *Marx's Paris Writings*, especially Chapters 3–5.

2 Cf. Howard, *The Development of the Marxian Dialectic*, pp.52,56–7.

3 This is a generalised and ambiguous concept in any strictly quantitative sense. The important point, though, is that there exists some wage value generally accepted as a necessary minimum and fixed by tacit or other agreement amongst the capitalists for some, however short, period of time. Its relation to the *concept of 'subsistence'* more generally considered is then not really important and labour market pressures just modify this basic wage value. In principle at least, there will always exist a general wage which may be considered to express the Value of labour power and to which surplus Value may be related as the remaining item in the Value of net output.

4 Marx cited and quoted the following works of these writers: Schulz-Bodmer, *Die Bewegung der Production etc.*, Zurich and Winterthur, 1843; Pecqueur, *Théorie nouvelle d'économie sociale et politique etc.*, Paris, 1842; Buret, *De la misère des classes laborieuses en Angleterre et en France etc.*, vol.1, Paris, 1840.

5 Although it needs to be remembered that the *Paris Manuscripts* were rough-drafted only and how Marx would have *presented* these ideas in any published version is unknown.

6 Marx's quotations from the *Wealth of Nations* are often not verbatim, but no distortion of meaning occurs. I have used Marx's own version of the quoted passages and given the relevant page number(s) in the following edition of the work: *An Inquiry into the Nature and Causes of the Wealth of Nations*, edited by Edwin Cannan, Methuen, London, 1961, vol. 1. This edition is cited hereafter as *WN* and any emphases in quotations are Marx's.

7 But recall the *caveat* in note 5 to this chapter above.

8 See Thomas Sowell's work on Sismondi in *Say's Law: An Historical Analysis*, Princeton University Press, Princeton, New Jersey, 1972, Chapter 2, and 'Sismondi: a neglected pioneer', *History of Political Economy*, 4:1, Spring 1972.

CHAPTER 3

1 Although as David McLellan emphasises, neither Feuerbach

nor Marx was consistent and precise in his treatment of the materialism–humanism nexus. See *The Young Hegelians and Karl Marx*, pp.100–1,112.

2　It can be argued that Marx's interpretation of Hegel's account of the role of man's labour activity in the context of real historical events is distorted to emphasise his objections to idealism. In this respect, it is important to note that in the *Phenomenology of Mind*, Hegel's objective was to trace the development of man's consciousness and reason and their role in comprehending the world that man faced. It was not intended to embrace fully a philosophy of man. The *Philosophy of History* and the *Philosophy of Right*, on the other hand, do reveal Hegel's concern to consider human and social history in terms of events and institutions. On this issue see Maguire, *Marx's Paris Writings*, p.97 and Louis Dupré, *The Philosophical Foundations of Marxism*, Harcourt, Brace & World, New York, 1966, pp.135–6.

3　I have based my comparative framework on that suggested by John Maguire in *Marx's Paris Writings*, pp.87ff.

4　Cf. Maguire, *Marx's Paris Writings*, pp.92,108.

5　In preparing this section, I have drawn some guidance from Dupré, *The Philosophical Foundations of Marxism*, Chapter 6; and Maguire, *Marx's Paris Writings*, Chapter 6.

6　In this section, these works are cited as *HF*, *TF* and *GI* respectively.

7　The 'Young Hegelians' included Bruno and Edgar Bauer, August von Cieszkowski, Friedrich Engels, Ludwig Feuerbach, Moses Hess, Karl Marx, Arnold Ruge and Max Stirner (a pseudonym for Johann Schmidt). Most had academic backgrounds in theology and philosophy, but were generally excluded from university teaching because of their radical views. The centre of their activities was Berlin where Hegel had dominated the teaching of philosophy at the university from 1818 until his death in 1831. For a detailed account of the lives and works of this group, see McLellan, *The Young Hegelians and Karl Marx*.

8　Feuerbach's main works were *Das Wesen des Christentums (The Essence of Christianity)*, 1841; 'Vorläufige Thesen zur Reform der Philosophie' ('Provisional theses for the reform of philosophy'), published in the journal *Anekdota*, February

1843; and *Grundsätze der Philosophie der Zukunft (Principles of the Philosophy of the Future)*, 1843. Of these works, the last two had the most impact on Marx's thought. See McLellan, *The Young Hegelians and Karl Marx*, pp.85ff. on Feuerbach.

9 Quoted in McLellan, *The Young Hegelians and Karl Marx*, p.107.

10 On the development of the idea of the unity of theory and practice in philosophy, and of the concept of *praxis*, first used by von Cieszkowski in 1838, see McLellan, *The Young Hegelians and Karl Marx*, pp.9ff. and Maguire, *Marx's Paris Writings*, pp.109ff.

CHAPTER 4

1 In *CW*,6,ed.n.219 (pp.692–3), it is argued that the 'Wages' manuscript represents a 'draft outline of the concluding lectures which Marx had no time to prepare for the press'. My reading of the manuscript suggests that it is more like a set of notes prepared *during* the period in which the lectures were given. Marx referred at the beginning to what had been 'explained already' (*CW*,6,415), and this can only refer to the *lectures* already given, for so much of the manuscript material was treated again in 'Wage-labour and capital'. Comparisons between the manuscript and 'Wage-labour and capital' cannot definitely establish the relationship between the two pieces as there is no record extant of the format of the *lectures* themselves.

2 The material in the 'Wages' manuscript is mostly developed more fully in 'Wage-labour and capital' except for one or two points which are made more explicit in the former work. The 'Wages' manuscript also includes some topics not covered in 'Wage-labour and capital', especially the effects of worker combinations. See also note 16 to the Introduction above.

CHAPTER 5

1 The difficulties of interpreting the meaning and significance of the 'Introduction' have been discussed many times in writings

about Marx. In preparing this chapter, I found the following contributions of great assistance in formulating my ideas about the piece: Martin Nicolaus, 'Foreword' to *G*,24ff.; Terrel Carver, *Karl Marx: Texts on Method*, Blackwell, Oxford, 1975, Part I; Erwin Marquit, 'Nicolaus and Marx's method of scientific theory in the *Grundrisse*', *Science and Society*, 41: 4, Winter 1977–8; and Derek Sayer's two especially insightful studies, *Marx's Method: Ideology, Science and Critique in Capital*, Harvester Press, Sussex, 1979 and 'Science as critique: Marx vs Althusser' in J. Mepham and D.-H. Ruben (eds), *Issues in Marxist Philosophy*, vol. III, Harvester Press, Sussex, 1979. My appreciation of Hegel's work has been much enhanced by Charles Taylor's study, *Hegel*.

2 Donald Winch (ed.), *James Mill: Selected Economic Writings*, Oliver & Boyd, Edinburgh, 1966, p.211, emphasis added. Edwin Cannan, *A History of the Theories of Production and Distribution in English Political Economy from 1776 to 1848*, 3rd edn, Staples Press, London, 1917, Chapter 2 contains an informative discussion of the emergence of 'the idea of production' in classical political economy. Cannan notes that prior to Mill, and certainly to Say, the production, distribution, exchange, and consumption *organisation* of analysis was not used in political economy.

3 Cited in Cannan, *History of the Theories of Production and Distribution*, p.28.

4 Cf., for example, William Baumol, 'Say's (at least) eight laws, or what Say and James Mill may really have meant', *Economica*, 44, May 1977, the title of which is indicative of the point!

5 *The Works and Correspondence of David Ricardo*, edited by Piero Sraffa with the collaboration of M.H. Dobb, Cambridge University Press, London, 1970, vol. I, *On the Principles of Political Economy and Taxation*, 3rd edn, p.5.

6 In this section, my analysis draws heavily upon the work of Derek Sayer cited in note 1 to this chapter above. I believe that Sayer's particular emphasis on the distinction between Marx's method of investigation and method of presentation, and Sayer's adaptation of the work of Norwood Hanson on *retroduction* in the philosophy of science, are of tremendous importance in comprehending the evolution of Marx's critique

of political economy. Marx actually had access to this method in the works of Aristotle that he studied while at university. In these works, it appeared as a third alternative to induction and deduction. Retroduction may be summarised as follows:

1 identify a set of phenomena that require explanation – the *explananda*;
2 by *a posteriori* reasoning, devise a set of hypothetical arguments which would wholly account for the appearance of the phenomena – the *explanans*;
3 the reasonable inference is then that these arguments are an adequate explanation for the phenomena, *provided* they meet the criteria of exhaustively accounting for them, of being internally consistent and of being independent of the terms of the phenomena themselves.

The resulting explanation of the phenomena does not claim to be *true, per se*. Indeed, 'truth' is not at issue. Rather, the method claims to generate logically coherent conjectures, although it must be conceded that Marx probably envisaged that his critical theory involved more definite conclusions.

7 Quoted in Carver, *Karl Marx: Texts on Method*, p.131.
8 In the *CCPE* reprint of the 'Introduction', the translation of this passage is in error, at least in a literal sense. The piece there opens with, 'The concrete concept is concrete because . . .' (*CCPE*,206), whereas the word 'concept' does not appear in and is not inferred by the German text itself. The text reads, 'Das Konkrete ist konkret, weil . . .' (*MEW*,13,362). Cf. also the translation in David McLellan, *Marx's Grundrisse*, Paladin, St. Albans, 1971, p.45 and in Carver, *Karl Marx: Texts on Method*, p.72. However, the *message* of the *CCPE* translation is correct. Marx was discussing the intellectual process of grasping the meaning of real phenomena in thought through the formulation and organisation of *concepts*.
9 My discussion here is based on that in Taylor, *Hegel*, pp.158ff.
10 Quoted in Taylor, *Hegel*, p.274.
11 Quoted in Taylor, *Hegel*, p.275, I have added the emphasis.
12 The details of the process of formation of the components of this plan have been dealt with in my *The Making of Marx's Critical Theory: A Bibliographical Analysis*, Chapters 4 and 5.
13 See the detailed argument in my *The Making of Marx's Critical Theory: A Bibliographical Analysis*, Chapters 5 and 6.

14 A more subtle, linguistic point is that the German text indicates that the words *einzelnen* (individual) and *allgemeinen* (general) are used as adjectives with an inferred singular masculine or neuter noun. The noun *Kategorie* is feminine so this is probably not the noun involved. The context suggests that *Resultat* (result) may have been meant and this is appropriately a neuter noun. The argument then implied is that the reader should follow the path from the individual result to the general result via the synthetic method.

CHAPTER 6

1 Cf. Keith Tribe, 'Remarks on the theoretical significance of Marx's *Grundrisse*', *Economy and Society*, 3:2, May 1974, pp.181–2.

2 Roman Rosdolsky, *The Making of Marx's 'Capital'*, Pluto Press, London, 1977, Chapters 6 to 8, provides a much more detailed analysis of the treatment of money in the *Grundrisse* than is attempted here.

3 Marx's continued use of the fixed–circulating dichotomy of capital did not represent a confusion as Keith Tribe has suggested; cf. 'Remarks on the theoretical significance of Marx's *Grundrisse*', pp.191ff.

4 In translating *Verwertung*, Nicolaus has used *realisation*. This is perhaps too narrow in its meaning and can be confused with *Realisierung*. I have therefore followed Pete Burgess, the translator of Rodolsky's *The Making of Marx's 'Capital'*, and used *valorisation* and *realisation* respectively.

5 It must be recognised that Marx's critique of his antecedents was relatively superficial at this time because he had only partially worked out his own critical paradigm of capitalism. His treatment of their work in the 'Theories of surplus value' manuscript of 1862–3 (see *TSV*) was much more detailed and by that time his critical insights were based upon a stronger theoretical basis. This applied especially to the critique of Adam Smith and Ricardo, whose works were here treated rather loosely. The 'Theories' manuscript is the object of my analytical exposition in Volume II of this study.

6 This basis for calculating the uniform rate of profit in Marx's

analysis of the Value–price of production–distribution articulation has been pointed to as its fatal flaw by Ian Steedman, *Marx After Sraffa*, New Left Books, London, 1977, especially Chapter 2.

7 In the 'Theories of surplus value' manuscript, Notebook X written during 1862 (*TSV*,II,25ff.). The details of this emergence are considered in Volume II of this study.

CHAPTER 7

1 See G.A. Cohen, *Karl Marx's Theory of History: A Defence*, Princeton University Press, Princeton, New Jersey, 1978, Chapter I.

2 Maximilien Rubel refers to two 'notebooks' in which Marx recorded his observations of the crisis: 'Book of the crisis 1857' from December 1857 and 'Book of the commercial crisis' from January 1858. The former contained statistics on bankruptcies, rates of exchange, commodity markets, *inter alia* along with clippings from the *Economist* and other newspapers. The latter contained statistics on fluctuations in financial markets, commodity market, and industrial market, *inter alia*. Unfortunately, Rubel gives no further information about these notebooks and they do not appear to have been published. See *Rubel on Karl Marx*, p.147, n.137.

3 My interpretation of Marx's analyses of the crisis have been particularly influenced by the work of three Marx scholars: Michael Lebowitz, 'Marx's falling rate of profit: a dialectical view', *Canadian Journal of Economics*,9:2, May 1976; Anwar Shaikh, 'Political economy and capitalism: notes on Dobb's theory of crisis', *Cambridge Journal of Economics*, 2, June 1978; and 'Marxian competition versus perfect competition: further comments on the so-called choice of technique', *Cambridge Journal of Economics*, 4, March 1980; John Elliott, 'Marx's *Grundrisse* vision of capitalism's creative destruction', *Journal of Post Keynesian Economics*,1:2, Winter 1978–9.

4 The algebraic analysis runs as follows:

Let:

$$\begin{aligned}
\text{particular period of analysis} &= \text{T days} \\
\text{production period} &= \text{p days} \\
\text{circulation period} &= \text{c days} \\
\text{surplus labour time per} & \\
\text{production period} &= \text{S days}
\end{aligned}$$

The surplus Value generated in period T is:

$$(1) \quad S' = S . \frac{T}{(p+c)}$$

on the assumption that the production period equals the labour time, i.e. that there are no interruptions within the production process itself.

The actual effect of having a positive period of circulation, $c > o$, is given by:

$$(2) \quad \frac{ST}{p} - \frac{ST}{(p+c)} = \frac{STc}{p(p+c)}$$

and from this S' may be re-expressed as:

$$(3) \quad S' = \frac{ST}{p} \left(1 - \frac{c}{p+c} \right)$$

In this expression, $\%p+c$ is the fraction of the total production–circulation time which is occupied by the circulation process. It is possible to demonstrate Marx's point that an increase in production and/or circulation time will reduce the aggregate surplus Value generated by applying some simple calculus to equation (1):

$$\frac{\delta S'}{\delta p} = \frac{\delta S'}{\delta c} = - \frac{ST}{(p+c)^2}$$

This expression is always negative, given positive values for S and T.

5 The analysis which Marx began in algebraic terms may be developed along the following lines in order to demonstrate the

points that he made. Let:

$$\text{particular period of analysis} = \text{T years}$$
$$\text{total capital employed} = \text{K money units}$$
$$\text{fixed capital proportion} = \text{K/x}$$
$$\text{circulating capital proportion} = \text{K/y}$$
$$\text{where: } (\frac{1}{x} + \frac{1}{y}) = 1$$
$$\text{fixed capital durability} = \text{d years } (\geqslant 1)$$
$$\text{circulating capital turnover} = \text{t years } (< 1)$$

Then, in period T:

$$\frac{K}{x} \text{ capital turns over } \frac{T}{d} \text{ times}$$

$$\frac{K}{y} \text{ capital turns over } \frac{T}{t} \text{ times}$$

The total capital turnover in period T is given by:

$$(\frac{K}{x} \cdot \frac{T}{d} + \frac{K}{y} \cdot \frac{T}{t})$$

If the surplus Value generated each time capital turns over in period T is given by S, then the aggregate surplus Value generated is:

$$(1) \quad S' = S(\frac{K}{x} \cdot \frac{T}{d} + \frac{K}{y} \cdot \frac{T}{t})$$

$$= SKT(\frac{1}{xd} + \frac{1}{yt})$$

From $\quad (\frac{1}{x} + \frac{1}{y}) = 1$, this becomes:

$$(2) \quad S' = SKT(\frac{1}{xd} + \frac{1}{t} - \frac{1}{tx})$$

This formulation is consistent with an arithmetical example given by Marx in the course of his analysis (G,684).

$$\text{total capital } K = 100 \text{ thalers}$$
$$\text{analysis period } T = 1 \text{ year}$$

Case (a): no fixed capital, with t = ½ year.

$$\frac{1}{x} = 0, \ \frac{1}{y} = 1$$

let S = 0.05 and substitute in equation (5)

S′ = 10 thalers.

Case (b): introduce fixed capital, with d = 1 year

$$\frac{1}{x} = \frac{1}{2}, \ \frac{1}{y} = \frac{1}{2}$$

S′ = 7.5 thalers.

The effect of increasing the fixed capital proportion of total capital is to reduce the surplus Value generated in the period because of reduced capital turnover. This result can be generalised by applying calculus to equation (2):

$$(3) \quad \frac{\partial S'}{\partial x} = \frac{SKT}{x^2}(\frac{1}{t} - \frac{1}{d})$$

With $^1/t > {}^1/d$ by definition, this expression is always positive for positive values of S, K and T. Thus, as x decreases and the proportion of fixed capital in total capital rises, the surplus Value generated decreases also.

$$(4) \quad \frac{\partial S'}{\partial d} = \frac{-SKT}{x.d^2}$$

This expression is always negative for positive values of S, K, T and x implying that an increase in the durability of the fixed capital employed reduces surplus Value generated.

$$(5) \quad \frac{\partial S'}{\partial t} = \frac{SKT}{t^2}(\frac{1}{x} - 1)$$

This expression is always negative for positive values of S, K and T because $^1/x < 1$ by definition implying than an increase in the circulation period of circulating capital reduces the surplus Value generated.

6 I owe this point to Peter Groenewegen.
7 My comprehension of this part of the *Grundrisse* has been improved by reading Rosdolsky's treatment in *The Making of Marx's 'Capital'*, pp.329ff.
8 Cf. Marx's more detailed and insightful critique of Ricardo's theory of rent in *TSV*,II,236ff. This critique is analysed in Volume II of the present study.
9 See Paul Sweezy, 'Karl Marx and the Industrial Revolution', in R.V. Eagly (ed.), *Events, Ideology and Economic Theory*, Wayne State University Press, Detroit, 1968.
10 Marx developed the ideas summarised here more fully in the context of his critique of Ricardo's *Principles* in *TSV*,II. On these developments see Volume II of the present study.

CHAPTER 8

1 In the 'Theories of surplus value' manuscript of 1862–3.

Bibliography

1 Karl Marx

Critique of Hegel's Philosophy of Right, edited with an Introduction and Notes by Joseph O'Malley, Cambridge University Press, London, 1972.

The Poverty of Philosophy: Answer to the 'Philosophy of Poverty' by M. Proudhon, Progress Publishers, Moscow, 1975.

Grundrisse der Kritik der politischen Ökonomie, Europäische Verlagsanstalt, Frankfurt, n.d.

Grundrisse: Foundations of the Critique of Political Economy (Rough Draft), edited and translated with a Foreword by M. Nicolaus, Allen Lane, London, 1973.

A Contribution to the Critique of Political Economy, edited by M. Dobb, translated by S. Ryazanskaya, Lawrence & Wishart, London, 1971.

Theories of Surplus Value, three Parts, edited by S. Ryazanskaya, translated by E. Burns, Progress Publishers, Moscow, 1963–71.

Capital: A Critique of Political Economy, Volume I, introduced by E. Mandel, translated by B. Fowkes, Penguin Books, Harmondsworth, 1976.

2 Karl Marx and Friedrich Engels

Historische-kritische Gesamtausgabe, Section I and II, Verlag
Detlev Auvermann and Dietz Verlag, Berlin, 1970–80.

Werke, 42 volumes, Dietz Verlag, Berlin, 1961–71.

Selected Works, three Parts, Progress Publishers, Moscow,
1969–70.

Collected Works, 50 volumes forthcoming, Lawrence &
Wishart, London, 1975–.

3 Other writers

Althusser, L., *For Marx*, Penguin Books, Harmondsworth, 1969.

Baumol, W., 'Say's (at least) eight laws, or what Say and James
Mill may really have meant', *Economica*, 44, May 1977.

Brewster, B., 'Introduction to Marx's "Notes on machines" ',
Economy and Society,1:3, August 1972.

Cannan, E., *A History of the Theories of Production and
Distribution in English Political Economy from 1776 to 1848*,
3rd edn, Staples Press, London, 1917.

Carver, T., *Karl Marx: Texts on Method*, Blackwell, Oxford,
1975.

Cleaver, H., *Reading Capital Politically*, University of Texas
Press, Austin, 1979.

Cohen, G.A., *Karl Marx's Theory of History: A Defence*,
Princeton University Press, Princeton, New Jersey, 1978.

Dupré, L., *The Philosophical Foundations of Marxism*,
Harcourt, Brace & World, New York, 1966.

Elliott, J.E., 'Marx's *Grundrisse* vision of capitalism's creative
destruction', *Journal of Post Keynesian Economics*, 1:2,
Winter 1978–9.

Elliott, J.E., 'Continuity and change in the evolution of Marx's
theory of alienation: from *Manuscripts* through the
Grundrisse to *Capital*', *History of Political Economy*, 11:3,
Fall 1979.

Garaudy, R., *Karl Marx: The Evolution of His Thought*, International Publishers, New York, 1967.

Gould, C.C., *Marx's Social Ontology: Individuality and Community in Marx's Theory of Social Reality*, Massachusetts Institute of Technology Press, Cambridge, Massachusetts, 1978.

Hegel, G.W.F., *Philosophy of Right*, translated with notes by T.M. Knox, Oxford University Press, London, 1967.

Howard, D., *The Development of the Marxian Dialectic*, Southern Illinois University Press, Carbondale, 1972.

Lebowitz, M., 'Marx's falling rate of profit: a dialectical view', *Canadian Journal of Economics*, 9:2, May 1976.

Lukács, G., *The Young Hegel: Studies in the Relations Between Dialectics and Economics*, translated by R. Livingstone, Merlin Press, London, 1975.

McGovern, A.F., 'Karl Marx's first political writings: The *Rheinische Zeitung*, 1842–43', in F.J. Adelmann (ed.), *Demythologising Marxism: A Series of Studies on Marxism*, Martinus Nijhoff, The Hague, 1969.

McLellan, D., *The Young Hegelians and Karl Marx*, Macmillan, London, 1969.

McLellan, D., *Marx Before Marxism*, Macmillan, London, 1970.

McLellan, D., *Marx's Grundrisse*, Paladin, St. Albans, 1971.

McLellan, D., *Karl Marx: His Life and Thought*, Macmillan, London, 1973.

Maguire, J., *Marx's Paris Writings: An Analysis*, Gill & Macmillan, Dublin, 1972.

Mandel, E., *The Formation of the Economic Thought of Karl Marx 1843 to Capital*, New Left Books, London, 1971.

Marquit, E., 'Nicolaus on Marx's method of scientific theory in the *Grundrisse*', *Science and Society*, 41:4, Winter 1977–8.

Meszáros, I., *Marx's Theory of Alienation*, Merlin Press, London, 1970.

Mill, James, *Selected Economic Writings*, edited by Donald Winch, Oliver & Boyd, Edinburgh, 1966.

Oakley, A., 'Two notes on Marx and the transformation problem', *Economica*,43, November 1976.

Oakley, A., 'Aspects of Marx's *Grundrisse* as intellectual foundations for a major theme of *Capital*', *History of Political Economy*,11:2, Summer 1979.

Oakley, A., *The Making of Marx's Critical Theory: A Bibliographical Analysis*, Routledge & Kegan Paul, London, 1983.

Parsons, H.L., *Humanism and Marx's Thought*, C.C. Thomas, Springfield, Illinois, 1971.

Ricardo, D., *The Works and Correspondence of David Ricardo,* edited by P. Sraffa with the collaboration of M.H. Dobb, Cambridge University Press, London, 1970, vol. 1, *On the Principles of Political Economy and Taxation*, 3rd edn (1821).

Rosdolsky, R., *The Making of Marx's 'Capital'*, translated by P. Burgess, Pluto Press, London, 1977.

Rotstein, A., 'Lordship and bondage in Luther and Marx', *Interpretation: A Journal of Political Philosophy*,8:1, January 1979.

Rubel, M., *Rubel on Karl Marx: Five Essays*, edited by J. O'Malley and K.Algozin, Cambridge University Press, London, 1981.

Rubel, M. and Manale, M., *Marx Without Myth: A Chronological Study of His Life and Work*, Blackwell, Oxford, 1975.

Sayer, D., *Marx's Method: Ideology, Science and Critique in Capital*, Harvester Press, Sussex, 1979.

Sayer, D., 'Science as critique: Marx vs Althusser', in J. Mepham and D.-H. Ruben (eds), *Issues in Marxist*

Philosophy, Volume III, Harvester Press, Sussex, 1979.

Shaikh, A., 'Marx's theory of value and the transformation problem', in J. Schwartz (ed.), *The Subtle Anatomy of Capitalism*, Goodyear, Santa Monica, California, 1977.

Shaikh, A., 'Political economy and capitalism: notes on Dobb's theory of crisis', *Cambridge Journal of Economics*, 2, June 1978.

Shaikh, A., 'Marxian competition versus perfect competition: further comments on the so-called choice of technique', *Cambridge Journal of Economics*, 4, March 1980.

Shoul, B., 'Karl Marx's solutions to some theoretical problems of classical economics', *Science and Society*, 31:4, 1967.

Smith, Adam, *An Inquiry into the Nature and Causes of the Wealth of Nations*, two volumes, edited by E. Cannan, Methuen, London, 1961.

Sowell, T., *Say's Law: An Historical Analysis*, Princeton University Press, Princeton, New Jersey, 1972.

Sowell, T., 'Sismondi: a neglected pioneer', *History of Political Economy*, 4:1, Spring 1972.

Steedman, I., *Marx After Sraffa*, New Left Books, London, 1977.

Sweezy, P., 'Karl Marx and the Industrial Revolution', in R.V. Eagly (ed.), *Events, Ideology and Economic Theory*, Wayne State University Press, Detroit, 1968.

Taylor, C., *Hegel*, Cambridge University Press, London, 1975.

Tribe, K., 'Remarks on the theoretical significance of Marx's *Grundrisse*', *Economy and Society*, 3:2, 1974.

Tucker, R., *Philosophy and Myth in Karl Marx*, 2nd edn, Cambridge University Press, London, 1972.

Vygodski, V., *The Story of a Great Discovery: How Karl Marx Wrote 'Capital'*, Abacus Press, Tunbridge Wells, Kent, 1974.

Woodcock, G., *Pierre-Joseph Proudhon: His Life and Work*, Schocken Books, New York, 1972.

Index